Mountain Bike ™

AMERICA

WASHINGTON

Contact

Dear Readers:

Every effort was made to make this the most accurate, informative, and easy-to-use guidebook on the planet. Any comments, suggestions, and/or corrections regarding this guide are welcome and should be sent to:

Outside America™
c/o Editorial Dept.
300 West Main St., Ste. A
Charlottesville, VA 22903
editorial@outside-america.com
www.outside-america.com

We'd love to hear from you so we can make future editions and future guides even better.

Thanks and happy trails!

Mountain Bike AMERICA™

WASHINGTON

SECOND EDITION

An Atlas of Washington State's Greatest
Off-Road Bicycle Rides

by Amy & Mark Poffenbarger

Updated by Rob McNair-Huff

The
Globe
Pequot
Press

Guilford, Connecticut

Published by
The Globe Pequot Press
P. O. Box 480
Guilford, CT 06437
www.globe-pequot.com

Produced by
Beachway Press Publishing, Inc.
300 West Main St., Ste A
Charlottesville, VA 22903
www.beachway.com

Editorial Assistance given by Lacey Pipkin, Catherine Collins

Production Assistance given by Dana Coons

Cover Design Beachway Press

Photographers Amy Poffenbarger, Mark Poffenbarger, Rob
McNair-Huff

Maps designed and produced by Beachway Press

Find Outside America™ at **www.outside-america.com**

Library of Congress Cataloging-in-Publication Data
is available

ISBN: 0-7627-0925-1

Printed in the United States of America
Second Edition/First Printing

Acknowledgments

For Jonathan

To all those in pursuit of a dream, a challenge, a goal: Keep pedaling.
Many thanks to our friends who ventured with us upon our first edition adventure and to Scott Adams and Ryan Croxton at Beachway Press for bringing both editions to life. Special thanks to Rob McNair-Huff for his invaluable assistance in this second edition.
The road ahead may be bumpy, but the downhill makes the hard climb worthwhile.

Amy and Mark Poffenbarger

owledgme

Table of

Contents

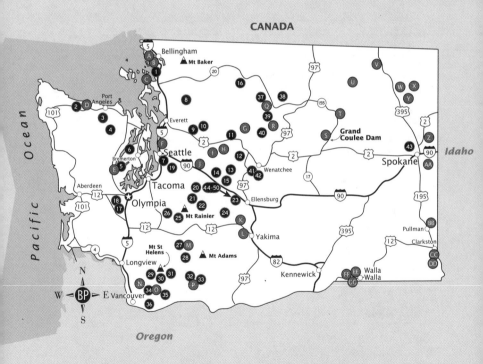

RIDES AT A GLANCE

1. Lily/Lizard Lakes Loop

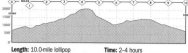

Length: 10.0-mile lollipop
Difficulty Rating: Moderate to Difficult
Time: 2–4 hours
Nearby: Bellingham, WA

2. Spruce Railroad Trail

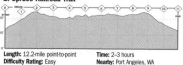

Length: 12.2-mile point-to-point
Difficulty Rating: Easy
Time: 2–3 hours
Nearby: Port Angeles, WA

3. Foothills Trail

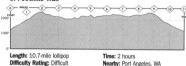

Length: 10.7-mile lollipop
Difficulty Rating: Difficult
Time: 2 hours
Nearby: Port Angeles, WA

4. Gold Creek

Length: 19.5-mile loop
Difficulty Rating: Moderate to Difficult
Time: 3 hours
Nearby: Swquim, WA

5. Tahuya Ramble

Length: 14.3-mile loop
Difficulty Rating: Intermediate
Time: 3–4 hours
Nearby: Belfair, WA

6. Wildcat Trail and Beyond

Length: 13.5-mile out-and-back
Difficulty Rating: Moderate
Time: 2–4 hours
Nearby: Bremerton, WA

7. Tapeworm

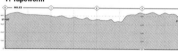

Length: 3.8-mile circuit
Difficulty Rating: Moderate to Difficult
Time: 1–2 hours
Nearby: Renton, WA

8. Walker Valley/Cavanaugh Loop

Length: 10.0-mile circuit
Difficulty Rating: Moderate to Difficult
Time: 2–3 hours
Nearby: Mount Vernon, WA

9. Wallace Falls Loop

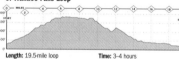

Length: 19.5-mile loop
Difficulty Rating: Difficult
Time: 3–4 hours
Nearby: Goldbar, WA

10. Silver Creek

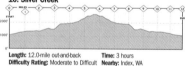

Length: 12.0-mile out-and-back
Difficulty Rating: Moderate to Difficult
Time: 3 hours
Nearby: Index, WA

11. Nason Ridge

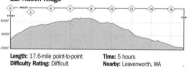

Length: 17.6-mile point-to-point
Difficulty Rating: Difficult
Time: 5 hours
Nearby: Leavenworth, WA

12. Mountain Home Loops

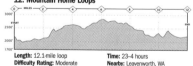

Length: 12.1-mile loop
Difficulty Rating: Moderate
Time: 23–4 hours
Nearby: Leavenworth, WA

13. Jolly Mountain

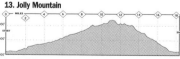

Length: 18.2-mile loop
Difficulty Rating: Difficult
Time: 4–5 hours
Nearby: Roslyn, WA

14. West Fork of the Teanaway

Length: 23.5-mile shuttle
Difficulty Rating: Difficult
Time: 5–7 hours
Nearby: Roslyn, WA

15. Kachess Ridge

Length: 19.7-mile loop
Difficulty Rating: Moderate to Difficult
Time: 3–4 hours
Nearby: Easton, WA

16. Cedar Creek Out-and-Back

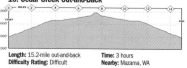

Length: 15.2-mile out-and-back
Difficulty Rating: Difficult
Time: 3 hours
Nearby: Mazama, WA

17. Capitol Forest–Lost Valley Loop

Length: 21.2-mile loop
Difficulty Rating: Moderate
Time: 3–4 hours
Nearby: Tumwater, WA

18. Capitol Forest–Larch Mountain Loop

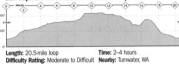

Length: 20.5-mile loop
Difficulty Rating: Moderate to Difficult
Time: 2–4 hours
Nearby: Tumwater, WA

19. Tiger Mountain

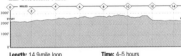

Preston/NW Loop

Length: 11.5-mile loop
Difficulty Rating: Moderate
Time: 2 hours
Nearby: Issaquah, WA

20. Ranger Creek

Length: 23.0-mile loop
Difficulty Rating: Difficult
Time: 4–5 hours
Nearby: Greenwater, WA

21. Skookum Flats

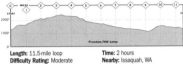

Length: 14.9-mile loop
Difficulty Rating: Moderate
Time: 4–5 hours
Nearby: Greenwater, WA

22. Crystal Mountain Loop

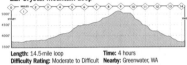

Length: 14.5-mile loop
Difficulty Rating: Moderate to Difficult
Time: 4 hours
Nearby: Greenwater, WA

23. Taneum Creek Loop

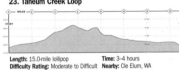

Length: 15.0-mile lollipop
Difficulty Rating: Moderate to Difficult
Time: 3–4 hours
Nearby: Cle Elum, WA

24. Fifes Ridge

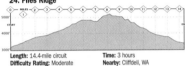

Length: 14.4-mile circuit
Difficulty Rating: Moderate
Time: 3 hours
Nearby: Cliffdell, WA

25. Osborne Mountain

Length: 24.4-mile loop
Difficulty Rating: Difficult
Time: 6 hours
Nearby: Ashford, WA

26. Elbe Hills

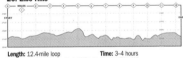

Length: 12.4-mile loop
Difficulty Rating: Moderate to Difficult
Time: 3–4 hours
Nearby: Elbe, WA

27. Tongue Mountain

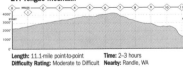

Length: 11.1-mile point-to-point
Difficulty Rating: Moderate to Difficult
Time: 2–3 hours
Nearby: Randle, WA

28. Chain of Lakes/Figure Eight

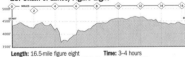

Length: 16.5-mile figure eight
Difficulty Rating: Moderate to Difficult
Time: 3–4 hours
Nearby: Eandle, WA

29. Mount St. Helens: McBride/Kalama Loop

Length: 12.0-mile loop
Difficulty Rating: Easy to Moderate
Time: 1 hours
Nearby: Cougar, WA

30. Mount St. Helens: Blue Lake Ride

Length: 12.8 mile out-and-back
Difficulty Rating: Moderate
Time: 3–4 hours
Nearby: Cougar, WA

31. Mount St. Helens: Plains of Abraham

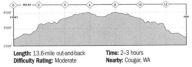

Length: 13.6-mile out-and-back
Difficulty Rating: Moderate
Time: 2–3 hours
Nearby: Cougar, WA

32. Service Trail/Surprise Lakes

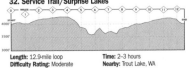

Length: 12.9-mile loop
Difficulty Rating: Moderate
Time: 2–3 hours
Nearby: Trout Lake, WA

RIDES AT A GLANCE

33. Gotchen Creek Loop

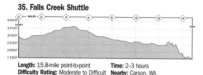

Length: 15.7-mile loop **Time:** 4 hours
Difficulty Rating: Moderate to Difficult **Nearby:** Trout Lake, WA

35. Falls Creek Shuttle

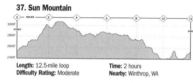

Length: 15.8-mile point-to-point **Time:** 2–3 hours
Difficulty Rating: Moderate to Difficult **Nearby:** Carson, WA

37. Sun Mountain

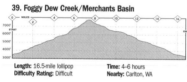

Length: 12.5-mile loop **Time:** 2 hours
Difficulty Rating: Moderate **Nearby:** Winthrop, WA

39. Foggy Dew Creek/Merchants Basin

Length: 16.5-mile lollipop **Time:** 4–6 hours
Difficulty Rating: Difficult **Nearby:** Carlton, WA

41. Mission Ridge

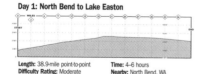

Length: 26.4-mile loop **Time:** 3–5 hours
Difficulty Rating: Moderate to Difficult **Nearby:** Cashmere, WA

34. Siouxon Creek Out-and-Back

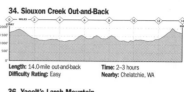

Length: 14.0-mile out-and-back **Time:** 2–3 hours
Difficulty Rating: Easy **Nearby:** Chelatchie, WA

36. Yacolt's Larch Mountain

Length: 13.4-mile out-and-back **Time:** 3–4 hours
Difficulty Rating: Difficult **Nearby:** Cougar, WA

38. Lightning Creek to Starvation Mountain

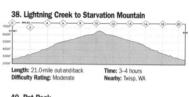

Length: 21.0-mile out-and-back **Time:** 3–4 hours
Difficulty Rating: Moderate **Nearby:** Twisp, WA

40. Pot Peak

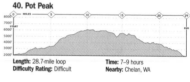

Length: 28.7-mile loop **Time:** 7–9 hours
Difficulty Rating: Difficult **Nearby:** Chelan, WA

42. Devils Gulch

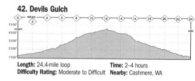

Length: 24.4-mile loop **Time:** 2–4 hours
Difficulty Rating: Moderate to Difficult **Nearby:** Cashmere, WA

43. Centennial Trail to Riverside Park

Multiple Route Options

Length: 10.0-mile lollipop **Time:** 2–4 hours
Difficulty Rating: Moderate to Difficult **Nearby:** Bellingham, WA

The Great Escape
John Wayne Pioneer Trail

Day 1: North Bend to Lake Easton

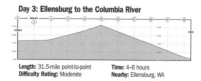

Length: 38.9-mile point-to-point **Time:** 4–6 hours
Difficulty Rating: Moderate **Nearby:** North Bend, WA

Day 2: Lake Easton to Ellensburg

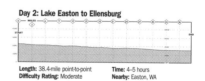

Length: 38.4-mile point-to-point **Time:** 4–5 hours
Difficulty Rating: Moderate **Nearby:** Easton, WA

Day 3: Ellensburg to the Columbia River

Length: 31.5-mile point-to-point **Time:** 4–6 hours
Difficulty Rating: Moderate **Nearby:** Ellensburg, WA

Day 4: Columbia River to Warden

Length: 60.3-mile point-to-point **Time:** 5–6 hours
Difficulty Rating: Moderate **Nearby:** Beverly, WA

Day 5: Warden to Lind

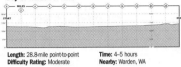

Length: 28.8-mile point-to-point
Difficulty Rating: Moderate
Time: 4–5 hours
Nearby: Warden, WA

Day 6: Lind to Ewan

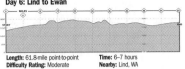

Length: 61.8-mile point-to-point
Difficulty Rating: Moderate
Time: 6–7 hours
Nearby: Lind, WA

Day 7: Ewan to Tekoa

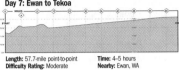

Length: 57.7-mile point-to-point
Difficulty Rating: Moderate
Time: 4–5 hours
Nearby: Ewan, WA

RIDES AT A GLANCE

This guidebook is designed to show you the many faces of Washington State. But there are so many places to go that we thought we'd make it easier for you to choose by categorizing the favorite rides by special interest. Have a great ride!

Rides for families and new mountain bikers

Ride 2: Spruce Railroad Grade
Ride 5: Tahuya Ramble
Ride 6: Wildcat Trail and Beyond
Ride 9: Wallace Falls Loop
Ride 19: Tiger Mountain
Ride 29: Mount St. Helens: McBride/ Kalama Loop
Ride 30: Mount St. Helens: Blue Lake
Ride 31: Mount St. Helens: Plains of Abraham
Ride 32: Service Trail/Surprise Lakes
Ride 34: Siouxson Creek Out-and-Back
Ride 37: Sun Mountain
Ride 43: Centennial Trail to Riverside Park
Ride 44: North Bend to Lake Easton
Ride 45: Lake Easton to Ellensburg
Ride 46: Ellensburg to Columbia River
Ride 47: Columbia River to Warden
Honorable Mention: Lake Padden Park
Honorable Mention: Bellingham's Interurban Trail
Honorable Mention: Tolt Pipeline Trail
Honorable Mention: Echo Valley
Honorable Mention: Steamboat Rock State Park
Honorable Mention: Down River Trail

Rides that lead to water, but bring a filter before you drink

Ride 2: Spruce Railroad Grade
Ride 4: Gold Creek

Ride 5: Tahuya Ramble
Ride 9: Wallace Falls Loop
Ride 10: Silver Creek
Ride 14: West Fork of the Teanaway
Ride 16: Cedar Creek Out-and-Back
Ride 17: Capitol Forest-Lost Valley
Ride 18: Capitol Forest-Larch Mountain Loop
Ride 21: Skookum Flats
Ride 22: Crystal Mountain Loop
Ride 25: Osborne Mountain
Ride 26: Taneum Creek Loop
Ride 28: Chain of Lakes Figure Eight
Ride 29: Mount St. Helens: McBride/Kalama Loop
Ride 30: Mount St. Helens: Blue Lake
Ride 32: Service Trail/Surprise Lakes
Ride 33: Gotchen Creek Loop
Ride 34: Siouxson Creek Out-and-
Ride 35: Falls Creek Shuttle
Ride 38: Lightning Creek to Starvation Mtn
Ride 42: Devils Gulch
Ride 44: North Bend to Lake Easton
Ride 45: Lake Easton to Ellensburg
Ride 46: Ellensburg to Columbia River

Rides for geology lovers

Ride 10: Silver Creek
Ride 14: West Fork of the Teanaway
Ride 22: Crystal Mountain Loop
Ride 24: Fifes Ridge
Ride 25: Osborne Mountain
Ride 27: Tongue Mountain
Ride 28: Chain of Lakes Figure Eight
Ride 29: Mount St. Helens: McBride/ Kalama Loop

Ride 30: Mount St. Helens: Blue Lake
Ride 31: Mount St. Helens: Plains of Abraham
Ride 36: Yacolt's Larch Mountain
Ride 39: Foggy Dew Creek/ Merchants Basin
Ride 40: Pot Peak
Ride 48: Warden to Lind
Ride 49: Lind to Ewan
Ride 50: Ewan to Tekoa

Rides with incredible views

Ride 1: Lily/Lizard Lakes Loop
Ride 6: Wildcat Trail and Beyond
Ride 11: Nason Ridge
Ride 13: Jolly Mountain
Ride 20: Ranger Creek
Ride 22: Crystal Mountain Loop
Ride 24: Fifes Ridge
Ride 25: Osborne Mountain
Ride 27: Tongue Mountain
Ride 28: Chain of Lakes Figure Eight
Ride 30: Mount St. Helens: Blue Lake
Ride 31: Mount St. Helens: Plains of Abraham
Ride 36: Yacolt's Larch Mountain
Ride 38: Lightning Creek to Starvation Mountain
Ride 39: Foggy Dew Creek/Merchants Basin
Ride 40: Pot Peak
Ride 41: Mission Ridge

Rides with incredible mud

Ride 8: Walker Valley/Cavanaugh Loop
Ride 17: Capitol Forest-Lost Valley Loop
Ride 18: Capitol Forest-Larch Mountain Loop
Ride 19: Tiger Mountain
Ride 23: Elbe Hills

Rides with technical trails and/or gonzo descents

Ride 3: Foothills Trail
Ride 4: Gold Creek
Ride 7: Tapeworm
Ride 11: Nason Ridge
Ride 13: Jolly Mountain
Ride 14: West Fork of the Teanaway
Ride 15: Kachess Ridge
Ride 16: Cedar Creek Out-and-Back
Ride 19: Tiger Mountain
Ride 20: Ranger Creek
Ride 21: Skookum Flats
Ride 22: Crystal Mountain Loop
Ride 23: Elbe Hills
Ride 24: Fifes Ridge
Ride 25: Osborne Mountain
Ride 26: Taneum Creek Loop
Ride 27: Tongue Mountain
Ride 36: Yacolt's Larch Mountain
Ride 39: Foggy Dew Creek/Merchants Basin
Ride 40: Pot Peak
Ride 41: Mission Ridge
Honorable Mention: Sadie Creek
Honorable Mention: Mad Lake
Honorable Mention: Sawtooth Backcountry

Rides that will wipe you out

Ride 11: Nason Ridge
Ride 13: Jolly Mountain
Ride 14: West Fork of the Teanaway
Ride 20: Ranger Creek
Ride 21: Skookum Flats
Ride 25: Osborne Mountain
Ride 39: Foggy Dew Creek/Merchants Basin
Ride 40: Pot Peak

HOW TO USE THIS BOOK

Take a close enough look and you'll find that this little guide contains just about everything you'll ever need to choose, plan for, enjoy, and survive a ride in the state of Washington. We've done everything but load your pack and tie up your bootlaces. Stuffed with 363 pages of useful Washington-specific information, *Mountain Bike America: Washington* ™ features 50 mapped and cued rides and 39 honorable mentions, as well as everything from advice on getting into shape to tips on getting the most out of hiking with your children or your dog. And as you'd expect with any Outside America™ guide, you get the best maps man and technology can render. With so much information, the only question you may have is: How do I sift through it all? Well, we answer that, too.

We've designed our Mountain Bike America™ series to be highly visual, for quick reference and ease-of-use. What this means is that the most pertinent information rises quickly to the top, so you don't have to waste time poring through bulky ride descriptions to get mileage cues or elevation stats. They're set aside for you. And yet, an Outside America™ guide doesn't read like a laundry list. Take the time to dive into a ride description and you'll realize that this guide is not just a good source of information; it's a good read. And so, in the end, you get the best of both worlds: a quick-reference guide and an engaging look at a region. Here's an outline of the guide's major components.

WHAT YOU'LL FIND IN A MOUNTAIN BIKE AMERICA™ GUIDE.
Let's start with the individual chapter. To aid in quick decision-making, we start each chapter with a **Ride Summary**. This short overview gives you a taste of the hiking adventure at hand. You'll learn about the trail terrain and what surprises the route has to offer. If your interest is peaked, you can read more. If not, skip to the next Ride Summary. The **Ride Specs** are fairly self-explanatory. Here you'll find the quick, nitty-gritty details of the ride: where the trailhead is located, the nearest town, ride length, approximate riding time, difficulty rating, type of trail terrain, and what other trail users you may encounter. Our **Getting There** section gives you dependable directions from a nearby city right down to where you'll want to park. The **Ride Description** is the meat of the chapter. Detailed and honest, it's the author's carefully researched impression of the trail. While it's impossible to cover everything, you can rest assured that we won't miss what's important. In our **Miles/Directions** section we provide mileage cues to identify all turns and trail name changes, as well as points of interest. Between this and our Route Map, you simply can't get lost. The **Ride Information** box is a hodgepodge of information. In it you'll find trail hotlines (for updates on trail conditions), park schedules and fees, local outdoor retailers (for emergency trail supplies), and a list of maps available to the area. We'll also tell you where to stay, what to eat, and what else to see while you're hiking in the area. Lastly, the **Honorable Mentions** section details all of the rides that didn't make the cut, for whatever reason—in many cases it's not because they aren't great rides, instead it's because they're over-crowded or environmentally sensitive to heavy traffic. Be sure to read through these. A jewel might be lurking among them.

Map Legend

We don't want anyone, by any means, to feel restricted to just the routes and trails that are mapped here. We hope you will have an adventurous spirit and use this guide as a platform to dive into Washington's backcountry and discover new routes for yourself. One of the simplest ways to begin this is to just turn the map upside down and ride the course in reverse. The change in perspective is fantastic and the ride should feel quite different. With this in mind, it will be like getting two distinctly different rides on each map.

For your own purposes, you may wish to copy the directions for the course onto a small sheet to help you while riding, or photocopy the map and cue sheet to take with you. Otherwise, just slip the whole book in your fannypack and take it all with you. Enjoy your time in the outdoors and remember to pack out what you pack in.

Interstate Highway
U.S. Highway
State Road
County Road
Township Road
Forest Road
Paved Road
Paved Bike Lane
Maintained Dirt Road
Unmaintained Jeep Trail
Singletrack Trail
Highlighted Route
Ntl Forest/County Boundaries
State Boundaries
Railroad Tracks
Power Lines
Special Trail
Rivers or Streams
Water and Lakes
Marsh

Symbol	Name	Symbol	Name
✝	Airfield	⛳	Golf Course
✈	Airport	🏃	Hiking Trail
🚲	Bike Trail		Mine
🚳	No Bikes		Overlook
	Boat Launch		Picnic
)(	Bridge	P	Parking
🚌	Bus Stop	✕	Quarry
▲	Campground	((A))	Radio Tower
	Campsite		Rock Climbing
	Canoe Access		School
	Cattle Guard		Shelter
†	Cemetery		Spring
	Church		Swimming
	Covered Bridge		Train Station
	Direction Arrows		Wildlife Refuge
	Downhill Skiing		Vineyard
	Fire Tower	♦♦	Most Difficult
	Forest HQ	♦	Difficult
	4WD Trail	☐	Moderate
	Gate	●	Easy

HOW TO USE THESE MAPS Map Descriptions

1 Area Locator Map

This thumbnail relief map at the beginning of each ride shows you where the ride is within the state. The ride area is indicated with a star.

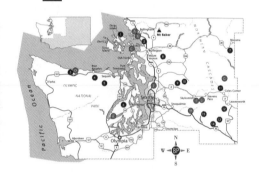

2 Regional Location Map

This map helps you find your way to the start of each ride from the nearest sizeable town or city. Coupled with the detailed directions at the beginning of the cue, this map should visually lead you to where you need to be for each ride.

3 Profile Map

This helpful profile gives you a cross-sectional look at the ride's ups and downs. Elevation is labeled on the left, mileage is indicated on the top. Road and trail names are shown along the route with towns and points of interest labeled in bold.

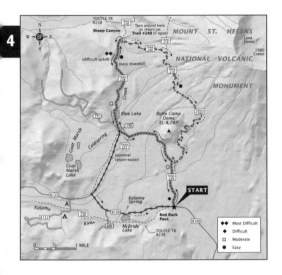

4 Route Map

This is your primary guide to each ride. It shows all of the accessible roads and trails, points of interest, water, towns, landmarks, and geographical features. It also distinguishes trails from roads, and paved roads from unpaved roads. The selected route is highlighted, and directional arrows point the way. Shaded topographic relief in the background gives you an accurate representation of the terrain and landscape in the ride area.

Ride Information *(Included in each ride section)*

Trail Contacts:
This is the direct number for the local land managers in charge of all the trails within the selected ride. Use this hotline to call ahead for trail access information, or after your visit if you see problems with trail erosion, damage, or misuse.

Schedule:
This tells you at what times trails open and close, if on private or park land.

Fees/Permits:
What money, if any, you may need to carry with you for park entrance fees or tolls.

Maps:
This is a list of other maps to supplement the maps in this book. They are listed in order from most detailed to most general.

Any other important or useful information will also be listed here such as local attractions, bike shops, nearby accommodations, etc.

A note from the folks behind this endeavour...

We at Outside America look at guidebook publishing a little different-ly. There's just no reason that a guidebook has to look like it was published out of your Uncle Ernie's woodshed. We feel that guidebooks need to be both easy to use and nice to look at, and that takes an innovative approach to design. You see, we want you to spend less time fumbling through your guidebook and more time enjoying the adventure at hand. We hope you like what you see here and enjoy the places we lead you. And most of all, we'd like to thank you for taking an adventure with us.

Introdu

Introduction

Welcome to mountain biking in Washington! There is no better way to get into the heart of the woods quickly or to experience the exhilaration of a winding downhill trail than on the back of a mountain bike.

This guidebook is designed to expose you to some of the best mountain biking available in the state. Each of the 50 rides in this edition includes a detailed map and instructions on how to get to the trail, where to go once you are on the trail, and information about the area the trail covers. The rides range from easy jaunts accessible to first-time mountain bikers and families, to hard-core rides that'll lead you up and over some of the most extreme biking terrain the state has to offer. Check the information at the beginning of each chapter to be sure that the ride you choose fits your ability level. And since many of these rides venture into the backcountry, make sure you're prepared to be self-sufficient once you leave the trailhead. Many of the rides in this guide are also dog friendly.

While a huge part of mountain biking fun lies in the speed of the decent, once you choose a destination and set out, take time to notice and enjoy the scenery along the way. Washington is a beautiful state that has much to offer outdoor enthusiasts. Please be aware that other people use these trails, too. Access to these trails is a privilege, and with that privilege comes the responsibility to be courteous to others and to maintain the good standing of mountain bikers on each and every route.

Washington's Weather

Washington is divided into two halves by the Cascade Mountain Range, giving the state two distinct weather faces. Marine air dominates the western half of the state while drier air occupies that of the east.

Marine air brings mild temperatures, overcast skies, and frequently rain from October through May west of the Cascades. Outside of these months the weather becomes absolutely gorgeous. It's rarely too hot to ride in western Washington—summer highs commonly top out below 90°F. Natives to the area know that July 4th marks the beginning of a four-month dry season here.

Winter conditions in the west are mild as well. Snow seldom slicks trails at low elevations, however, late fall to late spring riding on mountain trails with elevation can be dicey. Regardless of the season, it's a good idea to pay attention to weather forecasts to be prepared.

East of the Cascade Range, rain is less common due to the rain shadow effect. Prevailing winds push marine air from the Pacific Ocean eastward forming clouds, heavy with moisture, along the western approach to the mountains. As these clouds attempt to pass over the mountain peaks they frequently get *stuck* and drop their wet loads of rain on the western face of the range, frequently leaving the eastern side high and dry.

Drier air means more extreme weather conditions in eastern Washington. Summer temps frequently crest 100°F and abrupt weather changes can bring high winds and thunderstorms. Winter white-outs are also common, as are single-digit temperatures. If you're venturing to the east side of the state, again, pay attention to weather forecasts.

Flora and Fauna

Washington's *split personality* between the lush western side and the arid eastern side provides for a wide range of ecosystems and wildlife. Stands of Douglas fir are neighbors to Western hemlock, cedar, oak, and maple trees throughout western Washington's forests. Below tree cover—at least in areas that haven't been clearcut—live native mosses, ferns, salmonberries, salal, rhododendron, vine maple, prickly devil's club, and nettles. Wetland areas offer other plants, such as the odiferous skunk cabbage, fragile trillium, and bleeding hearts.

Western Washington's wildlife includes a host of song birds and slithery reptiles. Although rarely encountered along the trail, there's always the chance of seeing deer, black bear, or cougar, but mountain bikers are more likely to see smaller mammals such as rabbit and squirrel.

Douglas fir and ponderosa and lodgepole pine stand tall in aastern Washington's forests. East of the Cascade Mountains, plant life becomes rather sparse. Beyond the heavily irrigated farmlands, much of the Columbia Basin is dominated by sagebrush, paintbrush, and other drought-resistant plants. Trees are less common across the vast areas between Cle Elum and Wenatchee and around Spokane.

Mule deer and black-tailed deer graze the high plains of eastern Washington as raptors, such as turkey vultures, red-tailed hawks, and golden and bald eagles, circle upon thermal currents searching for prey. Mountain bike trails here are usually dusty, rock-strewn paths, also home to rattlesnakes, so beware.

Wilderness Restrictions and Regulations

In the year 2000, Washington and Oregon national forests and scenic areas teamed up in an effort to make trailhead passes easier to obtain. Trailhead fees are now $5 per day. Alternatively, you can buy an annual Northwest Forest Pass for $30—good at all participating national forests and scenic areas in Washington and Oregon. Trail park passes can be purchased at local ranger stations, at participating outdoor retail outlets, and at some trailheads. More information about participating national forests and locations for purchasing a Northwest Forest Pass can be found at *www.fs.fed.us/r6/feedemo* or by calling 1–800–270–7504.

Before you head into the backcountry, find out what type of permit you'll need and what restrictions are in place for the area you're going to visit. If you're planning an overnight trip into a wilderness area, call ahead to the local ranger station to see if a permit is required.

Thanks for choosing the second edition of *Mountain Bike America: Washington* and enjoy.

Getting around Washington

◐ Area Codes

Washington currently has five area codes. The Seattle area uses **206**; Tacoma and south Seattle suburbs (including Auburn) use **253**; north Seattle suburbs including Everett use **425**; western Washington (except Seattle and surrounding areas) uses **360**; and Spokane and eastern Washington use **509**.

● Roads

To contact the **Washington Department of Transportation**, call 1–800–695–7623 or visit *www.wsdot.wa.gov*. For mountain pass reports, visit *www.traffic.wsdot.wa.gov/sno-info*.

✈ By Air

Two major airports service the state of Washington: **Sea-Tac International Airport** (SEA) in the Seattle-Tacoma area and **Spokane International Airport** (GEG) in Spokane. A travel agent can best advise you on the least expensive and/or most direct way to connect from wherever you're departing. They can also arrange transportation from the airport to your destination.

To book reservations on-line, visit your favorite airline's website or search one of the following travel sites for the best price: *www.cheaptickets.com*, *www.expedia.com*, *www.previewtravel.com*, *www.priceline.com*, *http://travel.yahoo.com*, *www.travelocity.com*, *www.trip.com*—just to name a few. Many of these sites can connect you with a shuttle or rental service to get you from the airport to your destination.

⊜ By Bus

Washington is well covered by bus service; however, intercity bus services often require that you box your bicycle. The major carriers are **Greyhound** and **Northwestern Trailways**. Schedules and fares for Greyhound are available online at *www.greyhound.com* or by phone at 1–800–231–2222. Greyhound charges $15 to carry a boxed bicycle. **Olympic Bus Lines** runs between the Olympic Peninsula and Seattle. Contact them through their website at *www.tourtheolympics.com* or by phone at (360) 452–3858. Nearly all local buses in Washington are equipped with bicycle racks.

⊕ By Train

Amtrak's Cascade Corridor trains serve Seattle, Tacoma, and Olympia four times a day from Portland, OR. From the north there are two trips a day between Seattle and Vancouver, BC. These trains have onboard bicycle racks that can be reserved for a $5 fee. The **Empire Builder** runs daily to Seattle, Wenatchee, and Spokane from Chicago, IL, and Minneapolis, MN. The **Coast Starlight** services Seattle every day from Los Angeles, San Francisco, and Sacramento, CA. Long distance trains carry only boxed bicycles as checked baggage to select stations for $12. Amtrak information and reservations are available online at *www.amtrak.com* or by calling 1–800–872–7245. Brand new **Sounder** commuter rail service runs weekday trains between Seattle and Tacoma, and will carry your bike at no charge. Schedules, fares, and bike rules are online at *www.sounder.org*.

❷ BY FERRY

The **Victoria Clipper** is a high-speed ferry service between Seattle and Victoria, BC. For more information and schedules, visit *www.victoriaclipper.com* or call (206) 448–5000 (in Seattle), (250) 382–8100 (in Victoria, BC), or 1–800–888–2535 (outside of Seattle & Victoria only). **Washington State Ferries** has many routes that cross Puget Sound. Most connect Seattle with the islands and the Olympic Peninsula. Visit their website at *www.wsdot.wa.gov/Ferries* or call 1–888–808–7977 (in Washington). The **Coho Ferry** runs between Port Angeles and Victoria. For fare and schedule information call (360) 457–4491 or visit their website at *www.northolympic.com/coho.* (Most ferries accommodate bikes.)

❷ VISITOR INFORMATION

For visitor information or a travel brochure, call the **Washington State Tourism Division** at 1–800–544–1800 ext. 800 or visit their website at *www.tourism.wa.gov.* The state's official site is *www.access.wa.gov.*

The Rides

Northwest
WASHINGTON

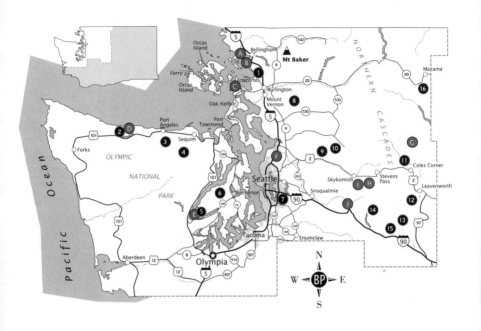

The Rides

Lily/Lizard Lakes Loop **1.**
Spruce Railroad Trail **2.**
Foothills Trail **3.**
Gold Creek **4.**
Tahuya Ramble **5.**
Wildcat Trail & Beyond **6.**
Tapeworm **7.**
Walker Valley/Cavanaugh Loop **8.**
Wallace Falls Loop **9.**
Silver Creek **10.**
Nason Ridge **11.**
Mountain Home Loops **12.**
Jolly Mountain **13.**
West Fork of the Teanaway **14.**
Kachess Ridge **15.**
Cedar Creek Out & Back **16.**

Honorable Mentions

A. Lake Padden Park
B. Bellingham's Interurban Trail
C. Cranberry Lake in Anacortes
D. Sadie Creek
E. Tahuya River Ride
F. Tolt Pipeline Trail
G. Mad Lake
H. The Summit at Snoqualmie/Ski Acres Trails
I. Money Creek Road #6420
J. Mill Creek Valley

Northwest Washington

From the foothills of the Cascade Range, in the direction of the setting sun, lies the Puget Sound and the ancient, evergreen arm of the Olympic Peninsula. A perfect place for adventure and observations, the Puget Sound region is home to big trees, big fish, and only a few venomous spiders (but no poisonous snakes). Northwest Washington enjoys fairly mild temperatures year round, allowing for especially long mountain bike seasons. The rides here may get muddy from time to time—the blustering force of the Pacific winds accounts for that—but it's also what makes Washington the Evergreen State. From the San Juans to Tacoma to the Olympics, the elevation gains can range from gentle to intense, but the beauty of this region is in this diversity. There are more than enough trails to choose from for a sensational singletrack experience.

Lily/Lizard Lakes Loop

Ride Summary

Located on Chuckanut Mountain, one of the most popular recreational areas in Bellingham, the trails in and around Lily and Lizard lakes are fun and semi-technical (this particular loop has a descent that even Hans Rey might have trouble negotiating). But the views of the water, the San Juan Islands, the hang gliders, and the trail itself make that one small, annoyingly steep section not so bad after all. This loop can be completed in just a couple of hours, leaving plenty of time to explore the mountain's other trails.

Ride Specs

Start: From the Blanchard Hill Road (B-1000) parking lot

Other Starting Locations: From the second gravel parking lot around the bend on Blanchard Hill Road (B-1000)

Length: 10.0-mile loop

Approximate Riding Time: 2–4 hours

Difficulty Rating: Moderate to Difficult due to technical trail

Terrain: Singletrack through rolling hills of second-growth forest, with a few steep sections

Land Status: Department of Natural Resources

Nearest Town: Bellingham, WA

Other Trail Users: Hikers and equestrians

Canine Compatibility:
Dogs not permitted

Wheels: Front suspension recommended

Getting There

From Bellingham: Take I-5 South to Exit 240, Alger Road. Turn left and head west over the freeway. Take the first left on Barrel Springs Road toward the Blanchard Hill Trail System. Pass Shaw Road. Turn right in 0.75 miles on Blanchard Hill Road (B-1000). Park at the Blanchard Hill Trails parking area. *DeLorme: Washington Atlas & Gazetteer:* Page 109 C5

The impressive Chuckanut Scenic Drive—the state's first designated scenic highway—travels north and south along an 11-mile stretch of Washington 11, passing the Samish, Chuckanut, and Bellingham bays. To the south, the by-way stretches across the bulb-growing flatlands of the Skagit Valley and then travels north along the bay side of the Chuckanut Mountain Range. Hugging the foothills of the mountains, the drive brushes the 2,500-acre Larrabee State Park—Washington's first—and then skirts along Chuckanut Bay until the mountains give way to the city of Bellingham, the last major town before the Canadian border.

Bellingham is just 18 miles south of the Canadian border and is home to Western Washington University. A city with *four* histories, present-day

Bellingham began as four independent and distinct communities: Fairhaven, Sehome, Whatcom, and Bellingham. Bellingham was the smallest of these communities, but when it came time to choose a name for the consolidated city, the other towns fought so hard that the only acceptable compromise was the less significant *Bellingham*. If you have time, you'll want to visit some of the area's points of interest such as Fairhaven, where you can take a self-guided tour of some of the more interesting historic sites (just follow the granite plaques). One such site is where an entire freight wagon was engulfed in quicksand.

This ride takes place a few miles south of Bellingham in the Blanchard Hill area, sandwiched between Interstate 5 and the Samish Bay in the southern portion of the Chuckanut Mountain Range. You'll likely share the mountain with hang gliders launching from the Samish Overlook, llama-trekkers out for a stroll, equestrians, hikers, and of course, mountain bikers.

The Lily/Lizard Lakes Loop comes recommended by local riders. It's appealing because you can go at your own pace, for as long or as far as you want, without ever being too far from your car. There's even a popular spot along the trail for those interested in learning a little bit about the geologic

Hang glider off the Samish Overlook.

make-up of the Chuckanut Mountains. The attraction is an enormous boulder—which happens to tell its own story. A sign on the rock reads:

> *Grooved striations atop this particular matrix of Chuckanut sandstone were made by regolith slowly rumbling along about 18,000 years ago under the pressure of glaciers one mile high. Ice extended westward over Vancouver Island and worldwide freezing lowered the sea level 100 meters.*

Regolith is just a fancy name for the layer of loose rock that rests on the earth's mantle. It's not an easy climb up the boulder, but the view on top is worth it.

The ride starts from the B-1000 parking lot and begins ascending rather quickly—it's a great climb that will leave you gasping for air within half a mile. The trail switches back and forth through a clearcut area into a gravel parking lot on B-1000 (which could easily substitute as a starting point). Once across B-1000, the well-groomed trail makes for an enjoyable ride. The trail wanders by a couple of openings in the trees that offer spectacular views of the salty waters of Samish Bay speckled with islands: Samish, Vendovi, Guemes, Sinclair, and Cypress. Along the horizon you can see the turtle-like hump of Orcas Island's Mount Constitution.

Continuing toward the lakes, the climb intensifies. Tree roots pose the most difficulty for non-technical climbers. After passing the lakes, there is an intersection for Max's Shortcut. Horses use this shortcut frequently, so depending on the weather, the conditions may be challenging. On wet days, it'll likely be slippery and bumpy, on dry days, just bumpy. Max's Shortcut empties on to the Larry Reed Trail and heads back on the Lily Lake Trail for some fun descents.

The Pacific Northwest Trail (PNT)

After nearly 30 years of creative assembling and trail blazing, the Pacific Northwest Trail (PNT) now stretches some 1,200 miles, from Glacier National Park in Montana to the northwestmost point of the Olympic Peninsula—from the Continental Divide to the sea. You'll have no problem following the PNT through the Lily and Lizard lakes area as it shares its path with some of the trails featured in this ride, but if you're interested in exploring it further, be sure to pick up the PNT guidebook, written by Pacific Northwest Trail Association founder Ronald Strickland and available from Sasquatch Books. And don't forget your map and compass; parts of this trail can get sketchy. A lot of the trail is open to mountain bikes, but not all of it, so check beforehand. If you're curious, a thru-hike generally takes roughly 100 days, and it's best to start in the east in late June.

For more information, visit the Pacific Northwest Trail Association at www.pnt.org.

Our directions take a slightly longer route that involves some hiking. Passing Max's Shortcut, the descending trail gets pretty difficult at times. You can ride some of it, but after passing the Talus Trail to the Bat Caves, forget it. There is an incredible hike down that covers some amazingly beautiful (though absolutely non-rideable) trail. But it is worth the effort. The forest here is textured with boulders and rocks of all kinds, deep green plant life, huge fallen trees, and colored mushrooms. The Rosario Strait catches your eye from time to time as the nastiness of the trail gives way to incredible singletrack riding again. The trail then leads to the hang gliding overlook, which is definitely worth a stopover before riding back to B-1000 on fabulous singletrack.

Ride Information

ⓒ Trail Contacts:
Department of Natural Resources, Chehalis, WA (360) 748–2383 or 1–800–527–3305

ⓞ Schedule:
Open year round

ⓢ Fees/Permits:
No fees or permits required

ⓠ Local Information:
Bellingham and Whatcom County Convention and Visitors Bureau, Bellingham, WA (360) 671–3990 or 1–800–487–2032

ⓠ Local Events/Attractions:
Chalk Art Festival, in late August, Bellingham, WA (360) 676–8548

ⓖ Local Bike Shops:
Fairhaven Bicycle & Ski, Bellingham, WA (360) 733–4433 • **Kulshan Cycles,** Bellingham, WA (360) 733–6440 or 1–888–733–6440

ⓝ Maps:
USGS maps: Bellingham South, WA; Bow, WA

MilesDirections

0.0 START at the B-1000 parking area and take B-1000 to where it meets the Lower Link Trail.

0.1 Take the Lower Link Trail (marked Lily Lake/Lizard Lake Trails).

0.7 *[FYI. Reach a small opening for a view. You've just climbed 740 feet.]*

0.9 Reach B-1000 again. Turn left to pick up trail on the right.

1.0 Begin the ascent up the Lily Lake Trail.

1.3 *[FYI. Notice the spectacular view of the San Juan Islands, Samish Bay, and Rosario Strait. The long island to the right is Lummi Island. The large land-mass out in front is the east side of Orcas Island.]*

2.3 Reach an intersection with the Larry Reed/Samish Overlook Trail. Continue straight. Watch for the waterfall.

2.9 Run into a swamp area and follow the trail to the right.

3.0 Cross a log bridge and follow the trail left.

3.3 Cross another wooden bridge and start climbing again.

3.6 Reach the intersection of the Lily Lake and Lizard Lake trails. Turn left toward Lily Lake.

3.7 Cross a wooden bridge.

3.9 Arrive at the intersection of Max's Shortcut. Stay straight.

4.0 Cross a creek. Continue straight ahead for the Samish Bay Connection.

4.1 Cross the river again.

4.4 Reach the intersection of Rock Trail and a view of Oyster Dome. Follow the trail left toward the Bat Caves. Prepare to descend some incredibly steep trail.

4.5 Arrive at the intersection of the Talus Trail. Continue down.

4.6 Riding once again! Arrive at the great boulder. *[FYI. Stop and climb over for a look.]*

4.8 Cross the river.

5.0 Arrive at the intersection of Oyster Bay Trail and the Samish Bay Connection. Stay on the Samish Bay Connection.

5.4 Descend man-made steps in the trail.

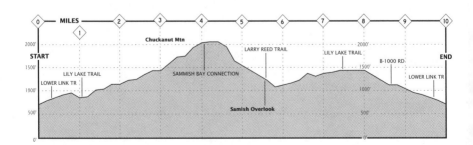

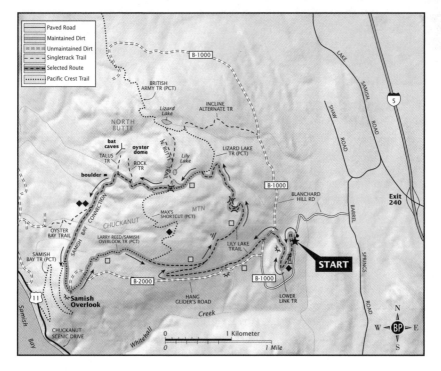

5.5 Come to a fork and go left and up. *[**Option.** The right trail is the Samish Bay Trail, which not surprisingly leads down to Samish Bay.]*

5.9 Arrive at a parking lot for the Samish Overlook. *[**FYI.** This is where hang gliders launch. Hang out and drink in the views.]*

6.2 Reach B-2000 and follow the Larry Reed/Samish Overlook Trail.

6.9 Reach the intersection with Max's Shortcut. Continue straight.

7.5 Arrive at an intersection—a reversed fork—with the Lily Lake Trail. Follow the trail sharply to the right.

8.9 Arrive at B-1000. Turn left and then immediately right for the last mile of singletrack. *[**Option.** Turn right down the road and arrive at the parking lot in a little more than the same distance.]*

9.0 Arrive at the small parking area and catch the trail on the right.

9.9 Arrive at the base of the singletrack. Turn left.

10.0 Back at the parking lot.

Spruce Railroad Trail

Ride Summary

A perfect trail for the whole family, this old railroad grade runs right next to Lake Crescent and is wide enough for even a bike trailer! Everyone can enjoy riding on the dirt road, then advancing to its mountain trail. If there are two cars to shuttle you, you may choose to continue all the way to the beach along a paved road, or you can turn around and enjoy the trail in the other direction. This is a very pretty ride along the water as the trail goes in and out of the trees. It's also very popular, especially in the summer.

Ride Specs

Start: From North Shore Road
Length: 12.2-mile point-to-point
Approximate Riding Time: 2–3 hours
Difficulty Rating: Easy, a good family ride
Terrain: Singletrack, dirt and paved road. A nearly flat roll on a converted railroad bed along the tree-covered shores of Lake Crescent.
Land Status: National park
Nearest Town: Port Angeles, WA
Other Trail Users: Hikers
Canine Compatibility: Dogs not permitted
Wheels: Can be done with or without suspension

Getting There

From Port Angeles: Take U.S. 101 West to Lake Crescent. Just past the west end of the lake, turn right on Camp David Junior Road (a.k.a. North Shore Road), just past the Fairholm Store and Campground. Park here or at the boat launch area. Parking is also available at the trailhead (4.6 miles ahead) for a shorter ride. *DeLorme: Washington Atlas & Gazetteer:* Page 92 D1

The Olympic Mountains are relatively young (as mountains go) and contain some of the largest and *healthiest* glaciers in the Lower 48, despite their being all less than 8,000 feet tall and right next to the ocean. Olympic National Park is considered an International Biosphere Reserve because within its boundaries there exists everything from glaciated peaks to sea level shores. The forest was first set aside as a reserve in 1897 and was later enlarged and dedicated as Mount Olympus National Monument in 1906. In 1938, at the urging of President Franklin D. Roosevelt and Congressman Monrad Wallgren, Congress gave the area its national park status—creating what is today the largest coniferous forest in the Lower 48. Congress enlarged the park in 1953 to include a 57-mile coastal strip. Of the

remaining 15 percent of old-growth in the Pacific Northwest, nearly half lies within the Olympic and Mount Rainier National Parks.

Nestled in the foothills of the Olympic Mountains is the 10-mile-long Lake Crescent, sitting at 620 feet above sea level—and interestingly enough, with a depth of 620 feet. Wrapped along its northern edge is the scenic Spruce Railroad Trail. The actual railroad (which lent the trail both its path and its name) hasn't been in operation since 1918. Built to transport spruce from the Olympic forest to Port Angeles, the railroad never saw

MilesDirections

0.0 START riding east on Camp David Junior Road.

1.5 Pass Eagle View Lane and head down to the lake. Stay on the road.

2.5 Come to a wooden car bridge. Cross with care.

3.0 Pass the Pyramid Creek Trail to the left. *[Note. This trail is open to hikers only.]*

4.6 Reach the Spruce Railroad trailhead. *[Optional Start. Parking is available here.]*

4.7 Super nice singletrack, wide and mellow. *[FYI. There is a restroom at the trailhead, in the woods, away from the lake.]*

5.7 Cross a small rocky section.

6.0 Cross another rockslide area.

7.4 Cross the bridge and a great swimming hole. Hike up a little here.

7.9 Cross a footbridge.

8.0 Cross a substantial ascent.

8.5 Pass an abandoned trail on the left, head downhill, and then cross a wooden bridge. *[Note. Deer like to hang out here; keep an eye out for them.]*

8.6 Arrive at the end of the singletrack. The trailhead from the east end of Lake Crescent is below.

8.7 Turn left onto the improved gravel road.

8.8 Cross the bridge of the lake drainage. Now you're on paved road.

8.9 Head downhill.

9.5 Turn right at the intersection. *[Note. Watch for oncoming traffic.]*

9.6 Pass the Log Cabin Resort on the right.

12.2 Hit the East Beach Picnic Area on the right and connect with your shuttle. *[Option. You always have the option of turning around at any point and retracing your tracks back to the starting point.]*

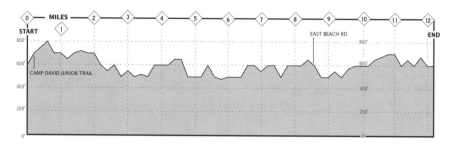

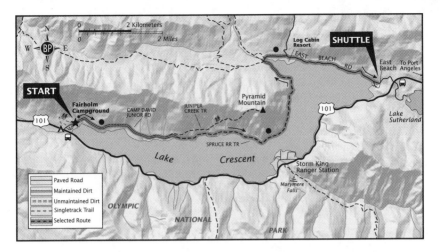

completion—nor did the Port Angeles sawmill (which, even shy of completion, ranked among the world's largest). The U.S. military was responsible for the great and sudden demand for timber; with the birth of aerial warfare during World War I, spruce was needed for airplane production. But in November of 1918 the war ended and so did the need for spruce. The logging was discontinued, and the sawmill closed.

The Spruce Railroad Grade was converted specifically for bicycle use as an alternative to riding on U.S. Route 101. The trail's wide paths (trailer-width in some parts) make it ideal for beginners or families. Generally smooth, the trail has a few rough sections that are easily negotiated on foot. Because this trail is flat, the natural tendency is to pedal fast. Out of common courtesy, avoid the impulse. After all, this is a family trail.

The ride begins on the northwestern edge of the lake by the boathouse on Camp David Jr. Road. Camp David Jr. is a county youth camp where once a naturopathic doctor named Louis Dechmann built and operated a lakeside resort called Qui Si Sana (Latin for "Here Get Well"). Hot baths, vinegar wraps, open-air cabins, and the promise of good health through diet and exercise were his techniques. He lost his spa in a battle over water rights in the early 1900s. Many groups tried to reopen the business, but none could make it a profitable venture. In the 1970s, due to vandalism and deterioration, the buildings were torn down and rebuilt to replicate the resort. Camp David Jr. moved in soon after the new buildings were dedicated in 1981. Today, the camp is open for retreats and reunions whenever the youth camp is not in session.

Two and a half miles west along Lake Crescent is the Olympic National Park Information Station. This station is housed in an historic cabin, built in 1905 by Chris Morgenroth, an early forest ranger. Morgenroth is best known for advocating the preservation of old-growth forests and for planting trees after the 1907 Soleduck fire. His reseeding efforts are considered to be the Forest Service's first motion toward official reforestation.

The Spruce Railroad Trail is one of only two trails open to bicycles inside the national park. The other trail is the relatively easy route to Olympic Hot Springs. To get there, take U.S. Route 101 west from Port Angeles. Turn left on Olympic Hot Springs Road. Drive to the Elwa Ranger Station to park your car. From there, ride your bike up the road by Lake Mills for about six miles to the trail (actually an old beat-up paved road). This ride can be fun, but it's a popular area because of the free hot springs, and most of the ride is on a paved road shared with vehicles. The mere 2.2-mile stretch that's closed to traffic is frequently bustling with a traffic of its own—other cyclists and hikers. There is a trailhead for the final hike up to the hot springs. No bicycle access is permitted beyond this point (you may walk your bike), and dogs aren't allowed beyond the trailhead, either—even on a leash.

Lake Crescent.

Ride Information

Trail Contacts:
Storm King Ranger Station: (360) 928–3380 – *during summer months* • Olympic National Park Visitor Center, Port Angeles, WA (360) 452–0330

Schedule:
Open year round, but best April through November

Fees/Permits:
No fees or permits required

Local Information:
Port Angeles Chamber of Commerce Visitors Center, Port Angeles, WA (360) 452–2363 • Olympic National Park Visitor Center, Port Angeles, WA (360) 452–0330

Local Events/Attractions:
Juan De Fuca Festival of the Arts, in May, Port Angeles, WA (360) 457–5411 or 1–800–942–4042

Local Bike Shops:
Sound Bike and Kayak, Port Angeles, WA (360) 457–1240 • D & G Cyclery, Sequim, WA (360) 681–3868

Maps:
USGS maps: Mount Muller, WA; Lake Crescent, WA; Lake Sutherland, WA

Foothills Trail

Ride Summary

Rising above the Straight of Juan de Fuca, these moderate trails are popular among the locals. Within the Foothills there are several loop combinations that can keep you riding all day. You can complete the main course in a couple of hours, enjoying keen views of the Straight before the trail heads into the forest. Most of the intersections are very well marked, so if you choose to create your own loops, you'll have a tough time getting lost. The singletrack is in good condition, and most of the climbs are only moderately tough.

Ride Specs

Start: From the parking lot off FS 6804 and Mount Angeles Road
Length: 10.7-mile lollipop
Approximate Riding Time: 2 hours
Difficulty Rating: Difficult due to some climbs and some technical singletrack
Terrain: Double wide, singletrack, and a little pavement, all rolling through second- and third-growth forest hills in the foreground of the Olympic Mountains
Land Status: Department of Natural Resources land
Nearest Town: Port Angeles, WA
Other Trail Users: Hikers, equestrians, and motorcyclists
Canine Compatibility: Dogs not permitted
Wheels: Front suspension recommended

Getting There

From Port Angeles: (The *locals'* way) Take U.S. 101, following the signs, to the Heart of the Hills Parkway and drive toward Hurricane Ridge. Just before entering the park boundary, turn left onto Mount Angeles Road. Follow this 2.5 miles to FS 6804. It's easy to miss this little turn-off, so look for the almost 90-degree turn to the left, and FS 6804 is right there on the right. This is where you'll park to start the ride. • **Alternate Start:** (The *official* way) From 8th and Pine streets in Port Angeles, head south on Pine Street (Old Black Diamond Road) for almost five miles. Turn left on Little River Road. Travel 1.1 miles and then turn left onto Foothills Trailhead Road and travel 0.2 miles to the trailhead on the right. ***DeLorme: Washington Atlas & Gazetteer:*** Page 93 D5

M ountain biking on the northern tip of the Olympic Peninsula can be a challenge. It's not that the terrain is especially difficult—there's a fair sampling of both easy and difficult rides—it's that the Olympic National Park covers so many acres! And, of course, mountain biking is prohibited in the national park, with the exception of the Spruce Railroad Trail and the Olympic Hot Springs Trail, both farther west. So locals look to the Foothills to stretch their mountain biking legs.

View of Port Angeles.

The Foothills are barely five miles from Port Angeles and convenient to some spectacular natural landmarks that should not be overlooked. Among these landmarks are Hurricane Ridge, the Dungeness Spit, and Ediz Hook.

Hurricane Ridge is one mile above sea level and a mere 18 miles from Port Angeles. From the top of Hurricane Ridge (6,000 feet), visitors can see

MilesDirections

0.0 START at the locals parking area. Ride around the gate and up the semi-dirt, semi-paved FS 6804.

0.1 Cross the overpass of the Heart of the Hills Parkway.

0.3 Pass an overgrown spur on the right. *[**Note.** The trail has deep erosion ruts—be careful not to fall in.]*

0.4 Pass another overgrown spur.

0.6 Big ol' switchback left... up, up, up. Wide doubletrack now.

1.0 At the fork, turn left. The trail is overgrown to the right.

1.6 Take a half turn and head straight up the mountain without a switchback.

1.7 The trail levels out a little here. Pass a spur trail on the right. Ahead is the singletrack trail for the loop of this ride. It's marked with a sign and a map.

1.8 At the trail intersection, turn left and continue up.

1.9 Pass the top of the trail spur you passed on the road just a bit ago.

2.2 Cross over a loosely boarded bridge.

2.4 At the intersection, turn left heading down.

3.3 Turn left at the fork. The right is a short cut back.

4.0 Come upon a new logging road, turn right and hook up with the trail in 0.5 mile.

4.1 Hit the trail on the right next to a huge berm. Climb up a quick, steep section.

4.4 At the fork, turn right.

5.6 Reach a parking area. Follow along the right to meet the trailhead again.

6.1 Pass an overgrown trail on the right. Follow the bend left.

7.5 At the intersection, turn left.

8.5 You're now back at the original intersection where you started the loop. Head straight.

8.9 Take the spur to the left.

9.0 Hit the road. Turn left and head down.

10.7 Arrive at the parking area.

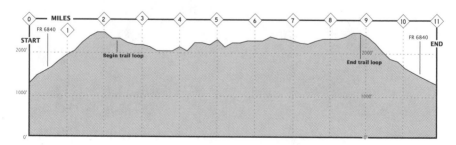

the interior of the Olympic Range, its peaks and valleys created by glacial change. Some of the lowest glaciers in the Lower 48 can be seen here, too, while wispy clouds waft up and out of the valley making the lush hillsides appear and disappear like phantoms. A visitor center at the top offers an outstanding observation deck, with indoor and outdoor viewing, an information center, snack bar, gift shop, and rest rooms. To ride your bike up the road to the top of Hurricane Ridge is to experience the cleansing power of fresh air and unadulterated sweat. The ride down is pedal-free, just make sure you apply alternating brake pressure so you don't heat your rims up too much—it makes for nasty blowouts.

Located about 14 miles east of Port Angeles is the Dungeness Spit, a 5.5-mile long protrusion that frames the Dungeness Bay. A "spit" is simply a narrow point of land (or reef) that extends into a body of water. Said to be the longest natural spit in the world, the Dungeness Spit was designated a national wildlife refuge in 1915 and makes for a relaxing place to stroll during warm summer days. The Dungeness Spit's sandy soil, scattered with

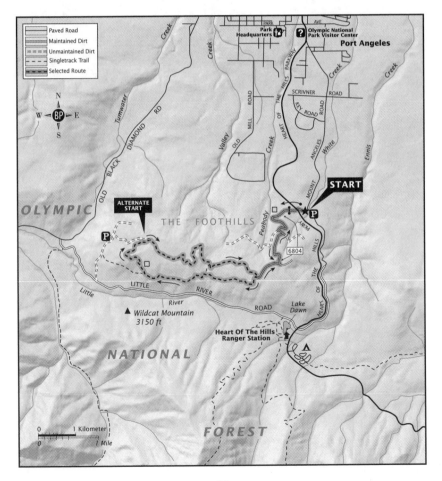

driftwood and eelgrass, is home to a variety of wild birds like loons, Canadian geese, and the black brant, as well as seals.

The Ediz Hook is a three and a half-mile long spit reaching into the Strait of Juan de Fuca to guard the Port Angeles harbor. It has provided many a sailor safe haven, including Francisco de Eliza who named the harbor Puerto de Nuestra Senora de los Angeles—Port of Our Lady of the Angels. It was under President Abraham Lincoln's administration that the spit was officially reserved for military purposes. A lighthouse and U.S. Coast Guard station sit at its tip and a navy and military reservation at its base.

This area of Washington is said to be in a *rain shadow*—sheltered from the Pacific Ocean by the Olympic Mountains. Storms rising from the ocean hit the Olympics first and are wrung, like a sponge, of the majority of their rain. The Hoh Rainforest, for instance, snags an average 150 inches of rain

a year, leaving only 24 inches for Port Angeles and merely 12 inches for Sequim. So enjoy this pocket of heavenly weather while you're there. The trail in the Foothills is a great place to start.

Steep, lush, and fun are just a few of the things that can be said about the Foothills trail. Incredibly convenient to Port Angeles, and incredibly popular, these trails are extremely well maintained considering the amount of use they get. There are all sorts of loops you can make. This particular loop was designed for shorter climbs and lots of descents.

The climb starts out on an old paved road no longer open to cars. It crosses over the Heart of the Hills Road to Hurricane Ridge and then turns into a dirt road with deep ruts that can be annoying to some and out-of-control fun for others. The road climbs a fair distance and in some places is pretty steep. As the view opens up to the Straight of Juan de Fuca, the switchbacks become more intense. Once you reach the trails you head deeper into the woods. With the exception of one short chewed-up section, these trails are divine. There are great map markers at almost every intersection. Beware, however, that frequent logging in the area can cause trails in our directions to unexpectedly reroute briefly.

Ride Information

◉ Trail Contacts:
Department of Natural Resources, Sedro Woolley, WA 1-800-527-3305

◔ Schedule:
Open year round

⑤ Fees/Permits:
No fees or permits required

❓ Local Information:
Port Angeles Chamber of Commerce Visitors Center, Port Angeles, WA (360) 452-2363 • Sequim-Dungeness Valley Chamber of Commerce Visitor Information, Sequim, WA (360) 683-6197 or 1-800-737-8462 • Port Townsend Chamber of Commerce Tourist Information Center, Port Townsend, WA (360) 385-2722

◉ Local Events/Attractions:
Juan De Fuca Festival of the Arts, in May, Port Angeles, WA (360) 457-5411 or 1-800-942-4042 • Classic Mariners Regatta, in June, Port Townsend, WA (360) 385-3628 • Premiere Jazz Festival, in July, Port Townsend, WA 1-800-733-3608 • Salmon Bake, in August, Sequim, WA (360) 683-7988 • Hurricane Ridge Visitor Center, Port Angeles, WA (360) 452-0329 • Dungeness National Wildlife Refuge, Port Angeles, WA (360) 457-8451 or (360) 683-5847

◉ Local Bike Shops:
Sound Bike and Kayak, Port Angeles, WA (360) 457-1240 • D & G Cyclery, Sequim, WA (360) 681-3868

◉ Maps:
USGS maps: Port Angeles, WA • Custom Correct Map: Hurricane Ridge, WA

4

Gold Creek

Ride Summary

This sensational ride weaves around the base of Dirty Face Ridge within the Olympic Range, just outside the boundaries of the national forest and the Buckhorn Wilderness Area. Wide switchbacks in the forest road take you up the west side of the Dungeness River to some adventuresome singletrack on the eastern side of the river below Dirty Face Ridge. The trail is steep and narrow and has several drop-offs. It's a ripping good ride that will take you by surprise.

Ride Specs

Start: From the Gold Creek trailhead
Other Starting Locations: Anywhere along FS 2860
Length: 19.6-mile loop
Approximate Riding Time: 3 hours
Difficulty Rating: Moderate to Advanced, due to steep drop-offs and extreme downhill sections
Terrain: Singletrack and forest roads under the cover of second-growth forests through the rolling foothills of the Olympic Mountains
Land Status: Department of Natural Resources land and national forest
Nearest Town: Sequim (pronounced "skwim"), WA
Other Trail Users: Hikers
Canine Compatibility: Dogs permitted
Wheels: Front suspension recommended

Getting There

From Sequim: Head east on U.S. 101. (This ride is approximately 55 miles from the Bainbridge Ferry landing.) After passing through the tiny town of Jamestown, turn right onto Louella Road toward the Dungeness Trail. In about one mile, turn left at the T-intersection onto Palo Alto Road, again following signs toward the Dungeness and Tubal Cain trails. Follow the paved road. After 6.2 miles, the road forks. Take the left fork toward the Dungeness Trail where the pavement ends. (Don't confuse this with Dungeness Forks.) After 7.1 miles, turn right onto FS 28 (which turns into FS 2860). At mile 9.2, see the campground on the right. At mile 11.0, you're at the trailhead. Park on either side of the bridge. You'll begin the ride up FS 2860, across the bridge from the trailhead.
DeLorme: Washington Atlas & Gazetteer: Page 77 A8

H ave you ever imagined yourself as a link in the food chain? Well, it's unlikely you'll have to consider it, but this is cougar country. It's more of an academic issue than a real concern, but should you come across a cougar (which, again, is unlikely), don't stop to chat. We have run across cubs on trails before, and yes, they are cute to look at, but you definitely do not want to meet the parents. In the inter-

The Olympic foothills.

est of excessive preparedness, since forewarned is forearmed, you should know what to do in case you're cornered or jumped.

Chances are the noise you'll be making will keep the wildlife away, but should you have an encounter, don't run. Maintain eye contact and back off slowly. Don't cower or look scared. The more imposing you look, the less inviting you look—you could try raising your arms or spreading your jacket

MilesDirections

0.0 START at the Gold Creek trailhead, climbing up the fire road FS 2860 away from the river and the trailhead.

0.4 Pass a parking lot pullout on left for the Lower Dungeness Trail (Trail 833).

1.9 Follow the main road left. The sign says the Dungeness Trail is in seven miles and the Tubal Cane Trail is in 11 miles. Gold Creek Trail is just across the road from the Tubal Cane Trail, so 11 miles to go!

2.9 Continue up. Pass a spur road on the right.

3.8 Pass a nice view of the valley.

4.1 The climb levels out a little.

4.4 Start the descent.

7.0 Turn left on FS 2860. The sign reads: "Dungeness Trail: 2 miles; Tubal Cane Trail: 6 miles."

8.6 Cross a bridge over Mueller Creek and Lower Dungeness Trail. *[FYI. This trail enters Buckhorn Wilderness Area, so it's closed to bikes.]*

8.8 Cross the creek and the climb begins again.

11.3 Cross a small paved section and a bridge. Continue the climb.

11.8 Pass two short spurs on the left. Keep right, riding around the pyramid-shaped mountain and continue climbing.

12.8 Turn left onto the Gold Creek Trail (Trail 830) at the parking lot. The sign reads: "Shelter 6.1 miles; FS 2860 6.3 miles." *[**Note.** There is 20 percent maximum grade on the downhill from here, losing 2,050 feet.]* Head into the Quilcene District of Olympic National Forest.

16.6 Stay left at the fork and head downhill.

19.5 Pass the remains of an old shelter. Go over the one-log bridge.

19.6 Come to the end of the trail and FS 2860.

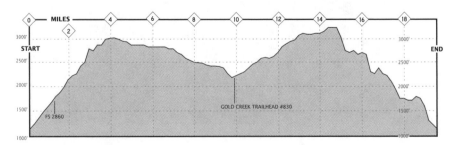

to appear larger than you actually are (a common defense tactic among animals). Like most cats (as the saying goes), cougars are simply curious. They're less likely to have dinner on their mind than play—and humans aren't exactly a delicacy. Their idea of play, however, doesn't necessarily jibe with ours. So in the worst-case scenario, if you are jumped, try to protect your head and stomach area, but by all means fight back. The majority of experts say that a forceful defense sends the message that you don't want to play. Otherwise, to the cougar, you're just a big ball of yarn.

White-tailed deer and Roosevelt elk populations in the Olympic Range have been a topic of debate lately. At the center of this discussion is overpopulation. With a lack of natural predators (like the cougar), there's an increase in the number of wildlife crossing paths with people. This has urged some to consider allowing limited hunting in the national park. As of yet, no decision has been made. Along this ride you'll most likely see footprints and scat (animal excrement)—and maybe, if you're lucky, you'll catch a glimpse of a deer along the riverbank.

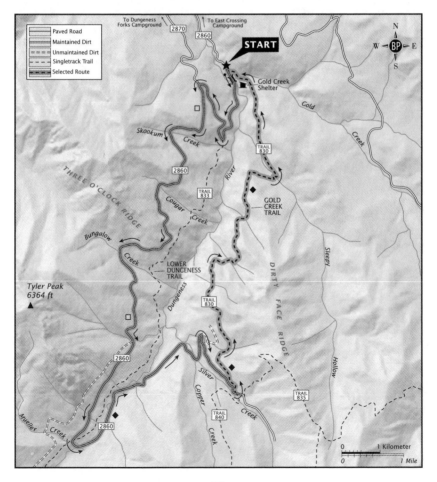

In the early part of summer you may run across a far safer encounter: berries. Just some of the varieties you may see are saskatoon, wild blueberry, huckleberry, raspberry, blackberry, gooseberry, currants, and even a bunch-berry or two. In late fall, the salal berry arrives along with the blue elder-berry and cranberry or rosehip. Though typically smaller than our cultivat-ed varieties, wild berries have an intensely sweet flavor.

Err on the side of caution when berry picking. You don't want to eat a berry that you cannot identify; however, with over 200 varieties in Washington, identification can be difficult. Aside from making a proper identification, there's no sure-fire sign that a berry is safe to eat, so get a good field guide or travel with someone who knows berries well.

This ride is fun, though a little short. It's probably not the best ride for beginners or intermediates since there are drop-offs and some rather steep sections. Be sure to concentrate on the trail ahead. Consider taking the Three O'clock Ridge Trail to add a little more singletrack to the ride's downhill. The real challenge comes with the descent. Roots and rocks won't present too much of a problem. The downhill is sweet, steep, and nar-row. Although water is scarce along this trail, the Dungeness Creek is down in the valley to the left. Watch out for blind corners, and enjoy the few short, grunting climbs.

Ride Information

🕐 Trail Contacts:
Ranger District, Quilcene, WA (360) 765-2200 – also for cougar sightings

🕐 Schedule:
Open year round

💲 Fees/Permits:
$5 per car, per day ($30 for an annual pass). For ferry rates, call 1-800-84-FERRY (WA only) or visit *www.wsdot.wa.gov/ferries.*

❓ Local Information:
Sequim-Dungeness Valley Chamber of Commerce Visitor Information Center, Sequim, WA (360) 683-6197 • **Port Townsend Chamber of Commerce Tourist Information Center,** Port Townsend, WA (360) 385-2722 • **Port Angeles Chamber of Commerce Visitor Center,** Port Angeles, WA (360) 452-2363

💡 Local Events/Attractions:
Sequim Salmon Bake, in August, Sequim, WA (360) 683-7988 • **Port Townsend Classic Mariners Regatta,** in June, Port Townsend, WA (360) 385-3628 • **Port Townsend Premiere Jazz Festival,** in July, Port Townsend, WA 1-800-733-3608 • **Juan De Fuca Festival of the Arts,** in May, Port Angeles, WA (360) 457-5411 or 1-800-942-4042 • **Kingston Bluegrass Festival,** in September, Kingston, WA (360) 297-7866

🚲 Local Bike Shops:
D & G Cyclery, Sequim, WA (360) 681-3868 • **Sound Bike and Kayak,** Port Angeles, WA (360) 457-1240

🅝 Maps:
USGS maps: Tyler Peak, WA; Mount Zion, WA

Tahuya Ramble

Ride Summary

The perfect course for beginner and intermediate riders, the Tahuya Ramble offers a maze of singletrack with plenty of options to lengthen or shorten the ride. Come prepared to get wet, especially in the spring, fall, and winter when puddles occasionally cover the entire trail. Also beware of the sand, because combined with the watery nature of this ride, you can end up with grit in and on everything by the end of the ride.

Ride Specs

Start: From the Mission Creek Trail trailhead

Length: 14.3-mile loop

Approximate Riding Time: 3–4 hours

Difficulty Rating: Beginner to intermediate

Terrain: Singletrack with puddles and sandy soils over relatively flat land with a few rolling hills in recovering clearcuts and second-growth forest

Land Status: State forest

Nearest Town: Belfair, WA

Other Trail Users: Motorcycles, ATVs, and equestrians

Canine Compatibility: Dogs permitted

Wheels: Front suspension recommended, but hardtails are okay

Getting There

From Tacoma: Take the WA 16 exit from I-5 and proceed over the Narrows Bridge and westward until WA 16 intersects with WA 3 in Gorst. Before Bremerton, exit left to head south on WA 3 to Belfair. Turn right on NE Clifton Lane and follow it until it becomes WA 300 and then North Shore Road. Go 3.6 miles before turning right onto NE Belfair-Tahuya Road. Drive one mile up a hill to find the Mission Creek Trail trailhead on the right.

Public Transportation: From the West Bremerton Transit Center (connections from Seattle), take Mason Transit Authority bus No. 3 to Belfair (Intersection of WA 3 and Clifton Lane). Now on your bike, turn right on NE Clifton Lane and follow it until it becomes WA 300 and then North Shore Road. Go 3.6 miles before turning right onto NE Belfair-Tahuya Road. Ride one mile up a hill to find the Mission Creek Trail trailhead on the right. *DeLorme: Washington Atlas & Gazetteer:* Page 62 A1

L ocated on the southern tip of the Kitsap Peninsula, nestled in the bend of Hood Canal, the Tahuya State Forest is a playground for mountain bikers. You can't go wrong exploring the miles of trails in this forest managed by the Washington Department of Natural Resources, but you definitely can get lost. The myriad of crisscrossing trails, roads, and off-road vehicle tracks that make up more than 200 miles of possible riding can confuse cyclists familiar with the area, let alone visitors. Unless you are prepared to find your way out of the maze, the best bet is to stick to marked routes.

Unlike many mountain biking destinations in western Washington, Tahuya is rideable nearly year round. It's relatively flat and offers sandy soil—decent tires will shed the dirt rather than clogging. But beware riding after recent storms. Trailside creeks and dips in the trail can fill with water quickly and turn a ramble through the maze of trails into an unexpected swim. Ice adds a whole new dimension to the ride if you venture to Tahuya in the dead of winter.

The Tahuya State Forest offers some great close-up views of the nearby Olympic Mountains all year long. The Olympic Mountains—the range at the heart of the popular Olympic National Park and surrounded by the Olympic National Forest—rise abruptly from sea level to elevations of nearly 8,000 feet. Several of the largest glaciers in the contigu-

MilesDirections

0.0 START from the Mission Creek Trail trailhead, and take the trail to the right of the parking area, following the blue and gray diamonds tacked to trailside trees.

1.4 The trail heads right and intersects with a road. *[Note. Watch for a quick right-hand turn back onto the trail.]*

2.1 Come to a fork and take the trail to the right.

2.2 Cross a bridge over a small creek and begin a steep climb.

2.4 The trail levels out and turns right.

2.9 Turn left onto a road and continue about 50 yards before turning right back onto the trail.

5.0 Take a left at an intersection. A number of trails spur off the main trail in this area, so be sure to stick to the trail marked by the blue and gray diamonds.

7.0 Continue down the main trail, which is the right fork at this point.

7.6 Cross Goat Ranch Road and link up with the trail on the opposite side.

8.5 Stay straight on the Mission Creek Trail, following signs to the staging area.

10.6 Take a hard left at a four-way intersection onto the Tahuya River Trail.

11.8 Cross Elphendal Pass Road and continue on the Tahuya River Trail on the opposite side.

11.9 Ride over a bridge at an unmarked intersection. Then follow the trail marked with blue and gray diamonds back to the trailhead.

14.3 Arrive back at the trailhead.

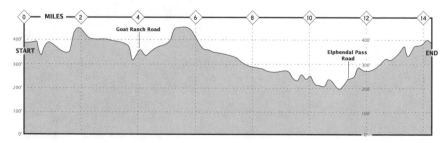

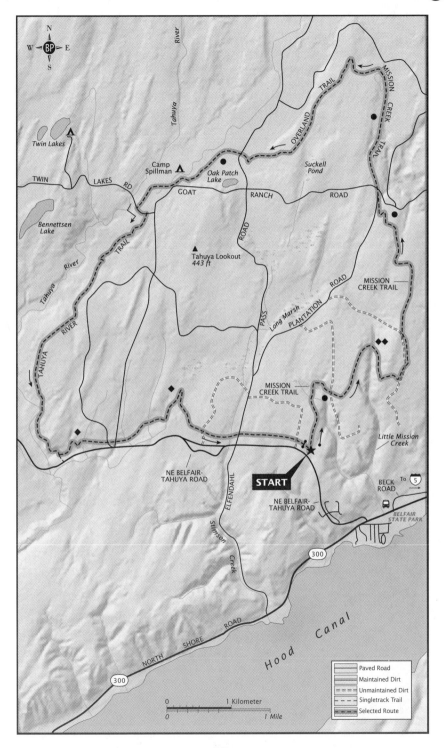

ous states lie within the range, despite the proximity to the temperate coast and the Pacific Ocean.

With the combination of views, rideability, and easy access, Tahuya is also a popular destination for motorcyclists and other off-road vehicle users, so the weekends from late spring through early fall can frustrate the mountain biker with intermittent forced pull-offs to make way for motorized trail users. Weekdays are much more forgiving and offer little to no competition for trail use.

Thankfully, riders don't have to pedal through the lake.

This ride starts at the Mission Creek Trail trailhead. Find the trail to the right of the parking area. The first few miles are marked by a speedy descent toward Little Mission Creek and then a long climb back to the hilltop on the other side. Be prepared for a series of short, steep downhills. Some riders may want to dismount. The trail crosses a number of paved roads, but you simply pick the trail up on the opposite side. Just be sure to follow the blue-and-gray-diamond-marked trail along the route and it will wind back to the starting point after 14.3 miles of rolling riding.

Ride Information

📞 Trail Contacts:
Department of Natural Resources: 1–800–527–3305 or *www.wa.gov/dnr*

🕐 Schedule:
Open year round

💲 Fees/Permits:
No fees or permits required

❓ Local Information:
North Mason Chamber of Commerce: (360) 275-5548 or *www.nmcoc.com* • **Mason County Transit:** (360) 426-9434 or *www.olympicpeninsula. com/travel/gettingAbout/busMason. html*

📍 Local Events/Attractions:
Belfair State Park: 1–800–233–0231 or *www.parks.wa.gov/belfair.htm* • **Kitsap County Fair,** third weekend in August (360) 692-3655

🚲 Local Bike Shops:
Kitsap Key & Bike Shop, Bremerton, WA (360) 373–6133 • **Mount Constance Mountain Shop,** Bremerton, WA (360) 377-0668

🅝 Maps:
USGS maps: Lake Wooten, WA

6

Wildcat Trail and Beyond

Ride Summary

A mere ferry ride away for mountain bikers in the Seattle/Tacoma area, the Wildcat Trail makes a great afternoon getaway. Entirely on singletrack, except for a few road crossings here and there, the trails on Green Mountain are a blast, only occasionally technical, and offer a great workout. Local groups keep these trails in excellent condition. Beginners may have a hard time with some of the climbs, but more experienced riders will definitely enjoy the ride.

Ride Specs

Start: From the Wildcat Trailhead

Other Starting Locations: Green Mountain Camp and Picnic Area—an especially good idea if you're camping

Length: 13.5-mile out-and-back

Approximate Riding Time: 2–4 hours

Difficulty Rating: Beginner to Moderate

Terrain: Singletrack through rolling hills under the cover of second-growth forests

Land Status: Department of Natural Resources land

Nearest Town: Bremerton, WA

Other Trail Users: Motorcyclists, hikers, and equestrians

Canine Compatibility: Dogs permitted (better to bring dogs on weekdays)

Wheels: Front suspension recommended

Getting There

From Seattle: Take the Bremerton Ferry from Seattle. *[**Note.** Sunday nights during the summer months are heavy traffic times for ferries. This ride will be less crowded during the week and very early on weekends.]* After disembarking the ferry, follow 11ᵗʰ Street through town. After two miles, turn right onto Kitsap Way (WA 310). Follow the Bike Route signs toward Silverdale (see large purple dinosaur). Take WA 3 north toward the Hood Canal Bridge and Silverdale. After five or six miles, exit onto Chico Way. Follow the exit left under the bridge heading toward Seabeck. Turn right on Northlake Way NW, after Suburban Propane. Turn right at the first intersection up a sharp and steep hill onto Seabeck Highway, toward Luther Haven Park. At the stop sign, keep right, continuing up the hill. Pass the Mountaineers Forest Theater. Turn left onto NW Holly Road at the flashing yellow light. Turn left into the Wildcat Lake Trailhead parking lot. This trailhead has outdoor facilities.

From Tacoma: Take I-5 to WA 16 North. Follow WA 16 to Bremerton. Take WA 3 North toward Silverdale and follow the directions above. ***DeLorme: Washington Atlas & Gazetteer:*** Page 78 D2

The Wildcat Trail sits within a few miles of Bremerton. Like many northwestern towns, Bremerton began as a logging community. In 1891 U.S. Navy Lieutenant A.B. Wycoff purchased 190 acres of waterfront property—now home to the oldest naval installation on Puget Sound. In that same year, William Bremer laid out the town of Bremerton, and in no time the local industry shifted to shipping.

Bremerton (now home to some 37,000 people) has experienced a few hard times since its shipbuilding heyday, particularly with recent military downsizing. But the city is currently experiencing a period of revitalization—the Sinclair Landing Waterfront Redevelopment Project is just one

MilesDirections

0.0 START at the Wildcat Trail trailhead.

1.0 Cross GM 41, following the trail straight ahead.

1.3 Climb a steep section, the worst of the ride.

1.5 [*FYI. Come to a fabulous viewpoint of Seattle.*]

1.7 Turn left onto GM 41, catching the trail immediately on the right that's marked "Wildcat Trail."

2.0 Cross GM 41. Switchback, following the trail straight-ahead.

2.7 Cross GM 3 at a three-way intersection. Turn right up the steep trail to the Trail Vista. [*FYI. To the left is the Green Mountain Camp and Picnic Area. The trail to Beaver Pond is on the right.*]

2.8 Pass a river wash on the right; stay to the trail on the left. Cross the forest road again, turn right, and continue on the Wildcat Trail on the left.

3.5 Come to GM 1. At the fork, follow the trail left by the gate and the road. It's marked so you can't miss it.

4.0 Cross GM 41 and head back into woods.

4.3 Reach the junction of the Gold Creek/Beaver Pond Trail and the Vista Trail. Take a hard left up the Vista Trail. Reach the Green Mountain Lookout parking lot. [*FYI. There's a picnic area and an outdoor toilet here.*] Follow the trail around the gate, continuing up to the vista (0.2 miles). To continue the ride, return to the Green Mountain Lookout parking lot and back down the Vista Trail.

4.5 Back at the bottom of the Vista Trail, take a left following the sign directing you to the Gold Creek/Beaver Pond Trail.

6.1 Arrive at the junction of the Gold Creek Trail and Beaver Pond Trail. Stay left on Gold Creek Trail.

6.4 Pass a short loop trail, staying to the right. Pass a small trail on the right, listening for Gold Creek below.

7.1 Arrive at the base of the Gold Creek Trail and a parking lot. Turn around here and head back up the trail.

8.1 Arrive back at the Gold Creek Trail and Beaver Pond Trail intersection. Take a right, going back the way you came. [*Option. You can go left on Beaver Pond Trail, which will lead you back to a junction with Wildcat Trail at the Green Mountain Campground*]

8.4 Continue up, passing the Vista Trail to the viewpoint. Stay straight on Beaver Pond Trail.

9.0 Arrive at the Wildcat Trail (4.3 milemarker). Come to GM 1, cross, and turn right on the trail heading down.

9.6 Cross GM 3 again and head up the trail to the left.

11.0 At the junction, follow the trail downhill. The Green Mountain Campground and picnic area is off to the right. A brief trail offshoot provides a downhill jaunt and avoids an uphill section. Follow the gravel road less than a mile to the Wildcat Trail, on the right.

11.9 Take the Wildcat Trail into the woods, over the wooden bridges, across the forest roads, and then back up the steep soft, scree section.

12.5 Cross the road and continue downhill.

13.5 Arrive at the Wildcat Trail trailhead and parking lot.

sign of that. *Money Magazine* recognized as much by citing Bremerton as the most livable city in America in 1990. Narrated boat tours are available of the Navy shipyard and the mothballed fleet of battleships. The USS *Turner Joy*, a Forest Sherman-Class destroyer, has been turned over to a private group and is open to the public as a floating museum on the Bremerton boardwalk. The Bremerton Naval Museum has an interesting collection of naval artifacts as well—and it's free. The Naval Undersea Museum, located

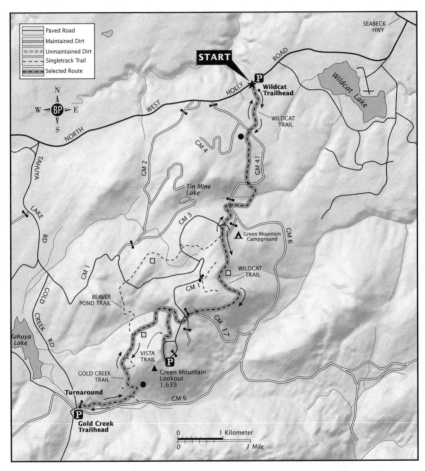

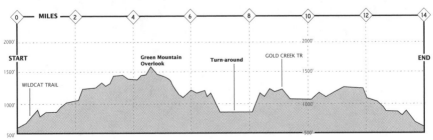

a few miles north of Bremerton in Keyport, contains the largest collection of naval undersea artifact exhibits in the United States—and it's free, too!

Aside from shipyards, the Bremerton area is able to tout both seaside and mountain recreation: from swimming at Miami Beach near Seabeck to mountain-lake fishing at Kitsap and Wildcat Lakes. And of course there's always mountain biking. The Wildcat Trail itself is located within a 6,000-acre state forest, operated by the Department of Natural Resources (DNR) and set amidst the sprawling hillsides of Green Mountain. Since 1970, the harvest of timber, rock, and brush in this area has brought Washington State over $4 billion. These monies go to building new schools, as well as to stocking the Kitsap County general fund, designed to ensure the protection of fish and wildlife habitats, as well as recreational sites used by hikers and mountain bikers.

In 1993, the DNR had to close down Green Mountain area and the Wildcat trailhead because of vandalism. The concerted efforts of supportive citizens allowed the area to reopen. Today, with the help of volunteers who take care of the trails, host campgrounds, open and close the gates, as well as make sure visitors don't get locked inside, the Wildcat Trail is again a clean place to play. Local groups keep the trail well marked and in excellent condition. They have work parties on alternate Saturdays. Feel free to join in or call the DNR office number listed below to volunteer.

Don't be surprised if the parking lot at Green Mountain has a few cars in it on the weekend. Because of its accessibility to some major urban centers and because it's simply a great ride, this park gets a lot of attention. From

the parking lot, the singletrack heads directly into the woods. The dense forest canopy serves as the perfect bumbershoot—shading the trail on warm days and keeping it dry on rainy days. The surface of the trail is smooth, with the occasional forest rock or root. The climbs are gradual; the descents are fast. This trail offers simple pleasures and good views.

Traversing the hillsides, the Wildcat Trail meanders through groves of rhododendrons and crosses a couple of logging roads. Logged hillsides are soft in places and negotiating your way down them may seem more like skiing or skidding than actually riding—but these sections are brief. From there, the trail leads up to a scenic vista—a panoramic picnic spot. From the vantage of 1,690 feet, the Puget Sound weaves its way around its evergreen banks like a silky blue ribbon. Heading down from the vista, the singletrack is narrow and steep. Because this is an out-and-back, when the trail ends on the opposite side of Green Mountain, it's time to turn around and ride back up and over. The entire ride is less than 15 miles, making this an ideal afternoon get-away, with many trails left to explore.

Ride Information

❶ Trail Contacts:
Department of Natural Resources, South Puget Sound Region: (360) 825–1631 or 1–800–527–3305 • **To report vandalism:** 1–800–527–3305 • **To report wildfires:** 1–800–562–6010

❶ Schedule:
Open daily, year round. Vehicle access is limited—the road to the Vista and the Green Mountain Campground is open from 9 A.M. to 6 P.M. on Saturday and Sunday, June through September.

❶ Fees/Permits:
No fees or permits required. For ferry rates, call 1–888–808–7977 (WA only) or visit *www.wsdot.wa.gov/ferries*

❶ Local Information:
Bremerton/Kitsap Peninsula Visitor and Convention Bureau, Bremerton, WA (360) 297–8200 or 1–800–416–5615

❶ Local Events/Attractions:
Blackberry Festival, in August/September, Bremerton, WA (360) 377–3041 • **Armed Forces Festival and Parade,** in May, Bremerton, WA (360) 479–3579 • **Bremerton Naval Museum,** Bremerton, WA (360) 479–7447 • **Kitsap Harbor Tours,** Bremerton, WA (360) 377–8924 • **USS Turner Joy Tours,** Bremerton, WA (360) 792–1008 • **The Naval Undersea Museum,** Keyport, WA (360) 396–4148

❶ Local Bike Shops:
Northwest Bike & Lock, Bremerton, WA (360) 479–4833 • **Kitsap Key & Bike,** Bremerton, WA (360) 373–6133 • **Mount Constance Mountain Shop,** Bremerton, WA (360) 377–0668

❶ Maps:
USGS maps: Wildcat Lake, WA

Tapeworm

Ride Summary

Don't let the distance deceive you. This nearly four-mile trail will twist you, turn you, and quite likely humble you—all within a distance short enough to be considered a warm-up on some mountain bike rides. A popular quick, in-city ride near Renton, Tapeworm and its cousin trail DNA offer hills, obstacles, tree roots, and descents all within relatively tiny Philip Arnold Park.

Ride Specs

Start: From the parking lot at Philip Arnold Park
Length: 3.8-mile circuit
Approximate Riding Time: 1–2 hours
Difficulty Rating: Intermediate to Advanced, due too extreme turns and technical trail conditions
Trail Surface: Singletrack and gravel road. Wind through a thicket while making constant short climbs and descents, as well as almost unimaginable turns.
Land Status: City park
Nearest Town: Renton, WA
Other Trail Users: Walkers
Canine Compatibility: Dogs permitted
Wheels: Front suspension recommended

Getting There

From Renton: Take the Bronson Way exit off I-405 North. Merge with Sunset Boulevard North, and then turn right onto Bronson Way North. After a stoplight, turn left onto Mill Avenue South. At the stoplight, continue straight and take an immediate left onto Renton Avenue South and go up the hill, over an overpass. Continue on Renton Avenue South up a steep hill before turning left on South Seventh Street. Turn right onto Beacon Way South and find a parking spot at Philip Arnold Park. *DeLorme: Washington Atlas & Gazetteer:* Page 63 A7

Tapeworm is an oddity in Pacific Northwest mountain biking. It offers the technical challenge of a ride three or four times longer, but the challenge is set within a small park on serpentine trails that flank a hillside. Winding underneath power lines, with views of the city of Renton and the huge Boeing Aerospace complex in the valley below, the trail could be considered scenic by many standards. But don't give in to the temptation to gaze on the scenery if you want to stay on your bike. The technical, root-strewn riding on the Tapeworm Trail demands complete attention to negotiate hairpin right and left turns.

Tapeworm winds downhill on the first loop and then makes the first of a series of cuts across a doubletrack road. The trail that was built to challenge

the best mountain bike riders lives up to its billing when it doubles back uphill and makes a sharp right and continues downhill over the first of a series of obstacles on the course. The obstacles on Tapeworm include the railroad tracks—a snake-like series of tracks made of two-by-fours laid like tracks along underlying lumber—as well as the *octopus*, which is a stump with roots covered by old bike tires. There are also a number of tough-to-negotiate roots to hop over and a couple of passages between trees set so close to each other that a bike and rider can barely squeeze through them.

There is no one key to making it through Tapeworm without major problems. I learned from two rides on the trail that handle bar ends are a bad idea on this trail, and that unlike on so many mountain bike trails, speed is not the key to rolling over and through the obstacles on this ride. Beware of tight turns and watch your shoulders. My shoulders bore proof of my passage through the trees after each of my rides on Tapeworm. Another factor to consider on such a technical ride is the weather. In wet conditions, making

MilesDirections

0.0 START from the parking lot at Philip Arnold Park.

0.3 Turn right between concrete barriers under the power lines and continue straight down this unnamed trail en-route to the start of Tapeworm.

0.5 Turn left onto a connecting trail and then take the second right to lead the last few yards up to the sign marking the start of Tapeworm. Once you enter the trail, there is no way to get lost. Just follow the tracks.

2.6 Reach the exit of Tapeworm and take the short connecting trail out to a T-intersection. Turn right and continue up a short hill.

2.8 Cross a small doubletrack road and take a left to start the DNA Trail. Once on DNA, much like Tapeworm, there is no way to get lost. Just follow the trail in front of you.

3.5 Reach the end of the DNA Trail. Turn right and follow the power line trail back to the concrete barriers where you entered the trail system and then go left back toward the parking lot.

3.8 Arrive at the parking lot.

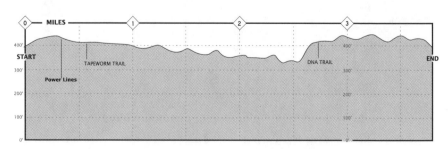

the turns on Tapeworm can be treacherous. And the same can be said of cold and icy weather. On one ride, I started out in the cold with hard, frozen ground and by the time I finished the ride the temperature had risen and the trail turned slick.

After making one last long climb, the ride breaks from the undergrowth and trees that characterize Tapeworm and into the open ground. After a short hill, the DNA Trail starts across a small doubletrack road. The DNA Trail is also snakelike and winding, but it's even narrower than Tapeworm.

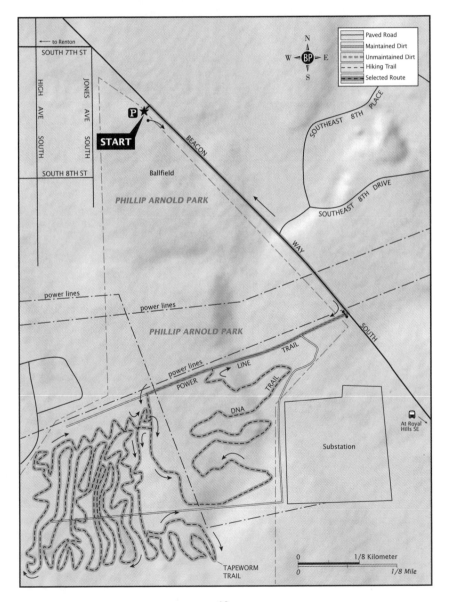

Prepare for a series of sharp right and left turns through tight singletrack lined by brush and blackberries. Although there are no major obstacles on DNA, it still offers a few tight turns through spindly trees.

Tapeworm and DNA are pretty straightforward trails, but there are other trails in Philip Arnold Park that can offer similar challenges. Although not included in the map for this ride, an even more technical trail named Parasite offers nearly insurmountable obstacles such as downed logs and turns through tight sections with trees forming upside-down V's over the trail. Feel free to explore the rest of the park or to combine the trails in alternative ways to create other challenging rides.

Plenty of trail obstacles along the way.

Enough said.

Ride Information

🕿 Trail Contacts:
Send a self-addressed stamped envelope to CycoActive Products, 701 34th Ave., Seattle, 98122

🕒 Schedule:
Open year round

💲 Fees/Permits:
No fees or permits required

❓ Local Information:
City of Renton, Renton, WA (425) 430–6400 or *www.ci.renton.wa.us* • **Seattle/King County Convention and Visitors Bureau:** (206) 461–5840

♀ Local Events/Attractions:
Seattle International Film Festival, in mid May to early June, Seattle, WA (206) 324–9996 • **University District**

Street Fair, in May, Seattle, WA (206) 547–4417 • **Northwest Folklife Festival,** over Memorial Day weekend, Seattle, WA (206) 684–7300 • **Bite of Seattle,** in mid July, Seattle, WA (206) 684–7200 • **Seafair,** from mid July to mid August, Seattle, WA (206) 728–0123 • **Bumbershoot,** over Labor Day weekend, Seattle, WA (206) 684–7200

🚲 Local Bike Shops:
The Bicycle Center of Issaquah, Issaquah, WA (425) 392–4588

Ⓝ Maps:
USGS maps: Renton, WA

🚌 Local Bus Service:
Metro Renton Transit Center, *transit.metrokc.gov* (206) 553–3000

Mountain Biking with Your Dog

Many people love to bring their canine companion along on mountain bike trails. Our furry friends make great trail partners because they're always good company and they never complain. If you take your dog mountain biking with you, or you're considering it, remember that there are a number of important items to keep in mind before hitting the trails.

Getting in Shape

It would be no better for your dog than it would you to tackle running a marathon without first getting into good physical condition. And if your pet has been a foot warmer much of his life, you will need to train him into reasonable shape before taking him along on those long weekend bike rides.

You can start your dog's training regimen by running or walking him around the neighborhood or, better yet, a local park. Frisbees and balls are also great tools to help get your dog physically fit for those upcoming mountain bike rides. Always remember that on a trail your dog probably runs twice as far as you ride. Build your dog's exercise regimen based on the mileage you plan to ride each time you head out. If you're going on a five-mile trail, assume your dog needs to be in shape for a 10-mile trail. Gradually build up your dog's stamina over a two to three month period before committing him to arduous afternoons of trying to keep up with you as you pedal along on your bike.

Training

Teaching your dog simple commands of obedience may help keep both you and your dog out of a heap of trouble while out there on public trails. The most important lesson is to train your dog to come when called. This will ensure he doesn't stray too far from the trail and possibly get lost. It may also protect him from troublesome situations, such as other trail users or perhaps coming in contact with local wildlife. Also teach your dog the "get behind" command. This comes in especially handy when you're on a singletrack trail and you run into other bikers. Teaching your dog to stay behind you and your bike and to follow your lead until the trail is clear can be a valuable and important lesson. Remember also to always carry a long leash with you in case, after all your prior training, you still have to tie your dog up to a tree at a campsite or succumb to local leash laws on crowded trails.

There are a number of good dog training books on the market that should help train you and your dog how to stay out of trouble with other trail users. Also, look to your local SPCA or kennel club for qualified dog trainers in the area.

Nutrition

Nutrition is important for all dogs. Never exercise a dog right after eating for the same reasons people shouldn't exercise right after eating. Feed your pet a high quality diet such as Hills Science Diet™ or Iams™. These products have higher quality ingredients and are more nutritionally balanced than generic grocery store dog foods. They may be more expensive than some generic brands, but your dog also doesn't need to eat as much of it to get the same nutrition and calories. If you insist on feeding your dog a grocery store diet, stick with the Purina™ brand, as it is still better for your dog than most others in this class.

Trail Tips

Try to pick your riding trails near lakes or streams. The biggest threat to your dog when biking is the heat, and water is essential to keep him cool. If the trail doesn't have water nearby then you need to bring as much liquid for him as you would drink yourself. A small lightweight plastic bowl can be used to give your dog water, or you can purchase a collapsible water bowl made from waterproof nylon (Call Ruff Wear™; (541) 388–1821). Also, you can use a waterbottle to squirt water into your dog's mouth.

- Try not to take your dog riding with you on a really hot day—hotter than 80°F. To avoid these temperatures, take your dog riding in the early morning or evening when the air is cooler and safer for your pet.
- Watch for signs of heat stroke. Dogs with heat stroke will: pant excessively, lie down and refuse to get up, become lethargic and disoriented. If your dog shows any of these signs, immediately hose him down with cool water and let him rest. If you're on the trail and nowhere near a hose, find a cool stream and lay your dog in the water to help bring his body temperature back to normal.
- Avoid the common foot pad injuries. Don't run your dog on hot pavement or along long stretches of gravel road. Always bring a first aid kit that includes disinfectant, cotton wrap, and stretchy foot bandage tape so you can treat and wrap your dog's paw if it becomes injured. You might also want to look into purchasing dog booties, useful for protecting your dog's pads and feet during long runs outdoors.
- Be sure to keep your dog's nails trimmed. If your dog's nails are too long, they might catch on an object along the trail and lead to soft tissue or joint injuries.
- Don't take your dog on crowded trails and always carry a leash with you. Remember, just because you love your dog doesn't mean other people will.

Walker Valley/ Cavanaugh Loop

Ride Summary

If you can't find singletrack to ride in Walker Valley, you're just not looking! Miles of trails meander through more than 10,000 acres of this DNR land, an area also popular with the ORV crowd. The loop described below is a moderate ride consisting of a short road climb and a rolling attack on the forest; the trails are semi-technical and can be muddy and wet. There are a number of loop variations, and the trails are marked at most intersections. Some local mountain bikers call Walker Valley the Capitol Forest of northern Washington because its trails and the conditions are similar to those found farther south in Olympia.

Ride Specs

Start: From the Walker Valley ORV parking lot
Length: 10.0-mile circuit
Approximate Riding Time: 2–3 hours
Difficulty Rating: Moderate, with difficult singletrack in rainy conditions
Terrain: Roll through up-and-down terrain under the intermittent cover of second-growth fir trees on singletrack, double-track, and fire roads
Land Status: Department of Natural Resources land
Nearest Town: Mount Vernon, WA
Other Trail Users: Motorcyclists
Canine Compatibility: Dogs permitted
Wheels: Front suspension recommended. During the rainy season (especially fall, winter, and spring) bring tires that shed mud.

Getting There

From Seattle: Take I-5 North to Exit 221 (south of Mount Vernon) onto WA 534 toward Lake McMurray. Turn right at the stop sign, heading east on WA 534. Follow WA 534 until it ends—approximately five miles. Turn left on WA 9 and head north toward Sedro-Woolley. Follow the "S" turns—see Lake McMurray on your right. Continue north, passing Lake Cavanaugh Road. Pass Big Lake on the left. One mile ahead, turn right on Walker Valley Road (see the sign for the trailhead and Fire Mountain Scout Reservation) at Milepost 46. Go 2.2 miles farther and turn right at the ORV park on the gravel road. Stay on the main road. In about a mile, come to the Walker Valley ORV parking lot. The trail begins at the end of the parking lot. *DeLorme: Washington Atlas & Gazetteer:* Page 95 A7

Walker Valley is located just east of Washington 9, about 10 miles southeast of the town of Mount Vernon. The 30 miles of trail within Walker Valley's 10,518 acres are well known among the off-road vehicle crowd. The terrain, very similar to that of the Capitol Forest south of Olympia, is managed by the Department of Natural Resources (DNR) and is used as a *working* for-

est; logging continues to change the lay of the trails. New roads appear every so often and will occasionally take over a trail, or in some cases they may re-route a trail. Unfortunately, the fragmentation of forests, destruction of trails, and erosion problems caused by these logging roads have a pretty negative effect on the natural workings of things. The eroded soil, for example, ends up in streams and rivers, sometimes blocking the path of spawning fish (the Chinook salmon, for example, is on the endangered species list). Nothing excuses irresponsible practices, but it's still important to respect the fact that this is a working forest. Timber sales on government lands pay for a lot of things we tend to take for granted.

The trails in Walker Valley are challenging and always a lot of fun. This ride begins in a large parking area that fills up quickly in summer months. The best time to ride here (if you'd like to be free of motorized vehicle noise) is early in the day on weekends or during the week. The route we've charted here climbs gradually away from the creek near the parking area. A fun offshoot trail is the EZ-Grade Trail, a short section of singletrack offering about a mile of semi-technical riding. Take JW-1100 up to the heart of

the singletrack—the road is in great condition and provides an easy warm-up grade before hitting the trails. Once in the woods, the trails, like any in the damp northwest, vary from packed dirt to exposed rocks and roots. There will probably be a few large, muddy holes and waiting-to-suck-you-in ruts. It's a thick forest, so the shade will be especially nice in the summer.

To the north of this ride is the famous Skagit Valley, well known for its tulip and daffodil bounty. Situated along the same longitudinal lines as the Netherlands, the climate in this western region of Washington—warm summers and cool winters—is ideal for growing bulbs. Riding along the color-washed roads in springtime, it's as if you've rolled into the end of the rainbow. Every imaginable color of tulip, daffodil, and even iris can be found here.

Bulbs first came to Washington around the turn of the century. In 1889 George Gibbs leased land on Orcas Island (in the San Juan chain) and tried his hand at growing produce. In 1900 he took a turn and tried growing some bulbs he'd procured from the Netherlands. They did well for him, but Gibbs was determined to find the ideal location for bulb production. He tested land farther north and then land as far south as Puyallup. His search finally ended in one of the best bulb growing regions in the country, the Skagit Valley.

Skagit Valley's bulb fields cover some 1,500 acres. All but 300 of these acres belong to one grower, the Washington Bulb Company. The Roozen

Ride Information

● Trail Contacts:
Department of Natural Resources, Northwest Region, Sedro Woolley, WA (360) 856–3500 or 1–800–527–3305

● Schedule:
Open year round, but best in dry summer weather

● Fees/Permits:
No fees or permits required

● Local Information:
Sedro Woolley Chamber of Commerce, Sedro Woolley, WA (360) 855–1841 • Mount Vernon Chamber of Commerce, Mount Vernon, WA (360) 428–8547 • La Conner Chamber of Commerce, La Conner, WA (360) 466–4778

● Local Events/Attractions:
Skagit Valley Tulip Festival, in late March or early April, Mount Vernon, WA (360) 428–5959 or www.tulipfestival.org • Wildflower Festival, in June, Darrington, WA (360) 436–1794

● Local Bike Shops:
Art's Bike Shop, Mount Vernon, WA (360) 336–5277 • Anacortes Cyclery, Anacortes, WA (360) 293–6205

● Maps:
USGS maps: McMurray, WA; Sedro Woolley South, WA

MilesDirections

0.0 START the ride on the Jam Trail, just left of the outhouses. Immediately pass the EZ Grade Trail on the right. *[Option. You can take this for some immediate singletrack riding.]*

0.2 Intersect with a small turnaround area and the other end of the EZ Grade Trail. Follow the Jam Trail to the left.

0.6 Pass three trails.

0.9 The Jam Trail hits JW-1100. Turn right on the road and head up hill. Pass a couple of trails. Cross a bridge. Pass another couple of trails on the left. They all join with the Muddled Meanderings Trail. Keep to the road.

1.7 At the fork with SW-JW-1190, stay left. Catch the Walker Valley Trail on the left ahead.

2.6 Intersect with the Scratch N' Sniff Trail on the left. Continue right on the Walker Valley Trail.

2.9 Intersect with a spur road. Stay left on the Walker Valley Trail.

3.2 Come to a fork with the Old Toad Trail and Walker Valley Trail. Stay straight on the Walker Valley Trail.

3.3 Come to another fork and head left. (The right goes to the road.)

3.5 Pass a spur on the right. Stay straight.

3.8 The trail empties onto a new logging road—the trail used to be here. Turn left and head down the road.

4.3 See the trail on the left and head back into the woods. Lots of thorny berry bushes in here.

4.5 The trail opens up again onto a logging road. Follow it down to the left.

5.4 See two trails on the left. They are the same trail, so follow one of them up off the road.

6.4 Come to a rocky uphill and see spurs on the left. Keep to the main trail.

6.5 Come to the intersection of SW-B-1040 and B-1000. Turn left onto the road and pick up the Cavanaugh Trail on the right a little ways down.

6.7 On the Cavanaugh Trail now, cross a wooden bridge, ride through a clearcut, and hit a T-intersection at a logging road. Follow the road straight and see the trail again on the right.

7.4 Head back into the woods.

7.7 Reach a fork and turn right. (The left trail will take you back into the woods.)

7.9 Reach the fork of Muddled Meanderings Trail. To the right (east) the trail heads up. Stay left, going back to the parking lot.

8.1 Cross another bridge.

8.8 Muddled Meanderings Trail finishes its bumpy downhill. Take the little left to get to the road, or take the right trail for more singletrack and eventually hit the road ahead. Turn right on the road.

9.1 Take the Jam Trail left.

9.8 See the EZ Grade Trail on the left. Stay on the Jam Trail.

10.0 Arrive back at the parking lot.

family, who own and operate the company, have been growing bulbs for 250 years and actually trace their roots to Holland. Speaking to the rumor that Washington's bulb production has progressed to the point where the Netherlands is placing orders, Richard Roozen, Vice President of the Washington Bulb Company, denies the claim. "The Netherlands grow tons more than we do here," he says, and thus far, the Washington Bulb Company just serves the United States. Still, the Roozens' production is impressive and makes this ride unforgettable in the spring.

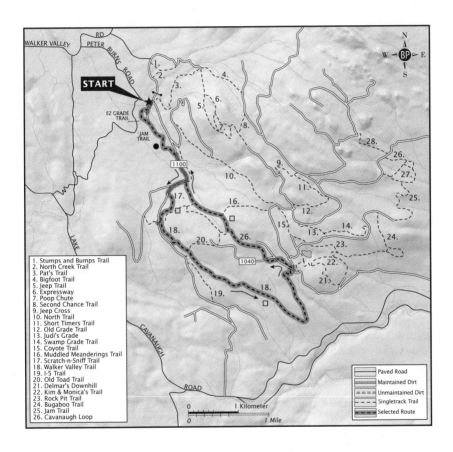

1. Stumps and Bumps Trail
2. North Creek Trail
3. Pat's Trail
4. Bigfoot Trail
5. Jeep Trail
6. Expressway
7. Poop Chute
8. Second Chance Trail
9. Jeep Cross
10. North Trail
11. Short Timers Trail
12. Old Grade Trail
13. Judi's Grade
14. Swamp Grade Trail
15. Coyote Trail
16. Muddled Meanderings Trail
17. Scratch-n-Sniff Trail
18. Walker Valley Trail
19. I-5 Trail
20. Old Toad Trail
21. Delmar's Downhill
22. Kim & Monica's Trail
23. Rock Pit Trail
24. Bugaboo Trail
25. Jam Trail
26. Cavanaugh Loop

Paved Road
Maintained Dirt
Unmaintained Dirt
Singletrack Trail
Selected Route

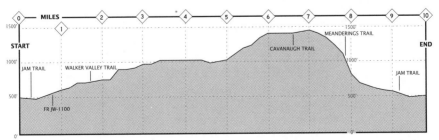

Wallace Falls Loop

Ride Summary

A very popular place to hike and mountain bike for many years, Wallace Falls can accommodate beginner, intermediate, and advanced mountain bikers. The climb to Wallace Lake advances gradually on singletrack, doubletrack, and minimal logging roads. Beginners will find a challenge in the climb, but will enjoy returning the same way once they reach Wallace Lake. For further adventuring, the route continues on the other side of Wallace River—crossing it is cold and difficult. The trails beyond the east side of the river are more technical, but travel mostly downhill; they're better suited for intermediate to advanced riders. The descent is sweet and ends up on a paved road, creating a loop that heads back to the state park trailhead.

Ride Specs

Start: From the Wallace Falls State Park trailhead
Length: 19.5-mile loop
Approximate Riding Time: 3–4 hours
Difficulty Rating: Difficult
Terrain: River and creek crossings, doubletrack, singletrack, dirt roads, and paved roads over both flat land and rolling hills
Land Status: State park
Nearest Town: Goldbar, WA
Other Trail Users: Hikers
Canine Compatibility: Dogs permitted
Wheels: Front suspension recommended, but not required

Getting There

From Seattle: Take I-405 North to WA 522 East, toward Monroe/Wenatchee. Turn left at the light onto U.S. 2 East. Follow U.S. 2 to Goldbar. Turn left on 1st Street. Go 0.3 miles to May Creek Road and turn right. Follow the signs for Wallace Falls State Park. Stay straight toward the dead-end. Continue to follow the signs for Wallace Falls. The entrance is on the left up the hill. The trail begins from the parking lot by the restrooms.
*DeLorme: **Washington Atlas & Gazetteer:** Page 80 A3*

Two miles northeast of the town of Goldbar (population 1,200), nestled in the beautiful Skykomish Valley (sky-KOH-mish or just *Sky Valley*), is Wallace Falls State Park. Established in 1977, the park's hallmark attraction—should its name not give it away—is a stunning 265-foot cataract. Visible from U.S. Route 2, the rushing falls are set in crisp relief against the deep green forest of Mount Stickney (5,367 feet), located in the Mount Baker Snoqualmie National Forest. Though obviously anglicized, the *wallace* in Wallace Falls is actually named after two Skykomish Indians who homesteaded the area, Sarah and Joe Kwayaylsh.

MilesDirections

0.0 START the ride on the trail below the power lines.

0.3 Head into the woods.

0.4 Intersect with the Woody Trail. *[FYI. This one-mile trail, open to hikers only, leads to views of Wallace Falls.]*

1.5 Turn left toward Wallace Lake.

2.5 The trail empties onto a logging road. Continue up the road.

4.5 Road divides. Stay straight.

6.3 Turn left onto the Wallace Lake Trail, following the sign for Wallace Lake.

6.8 Arrive at Wallace Lake. Ride over the wooden bridge to Wallace Falls (2.6 miles).

6.9 Pass a trail on the left heading back to the lake.

7.3 Pass an overgrown trail to the left for Stickney Ridge. Follow the signs to the falls.

7.5 Pass a trail on the right that connects with the logging road you saw a few miles ago.

9.1 Wallace Falls is to the right.

9.5 Arrive at the top of the falls. *[Option. This is the turning point for the out-and-back.]* Cross the river for the loop. Head upriver a bit to find an easy crossing.

9.6 Turn right at the intersection. You'll take right-hand turns all the way down.

10.6 Arrive at a steep embankment. Cross the creek and climb up the other side.

11.3 Cross another creek bed.

11.7 Keep straight at the intersection. *[Note. All the left-hand trail spurs are actually loops that go above the washouts on this trail.]* Stay straight at the switchback.

13.5 Pass a small spur. Stay straight.

13.6 Stay right at the intersection.

13.8 Follow the main dirt road, keeping straight.

14.3 At the fork, take the road under the power lines. *[Note. Don't follow the road running parallel to the power lines.]* Just cross underneath them, keeping to the right.

14.8 At Reiter Road, turn right.

16.0 At May Creek Road (paved), turn right.

18.9 Turn right on Ley Road up to Wallace Falls State Park.

19.3 Turn left up to the parking lot.

19.5 Arrive back at the trailhead and your car.

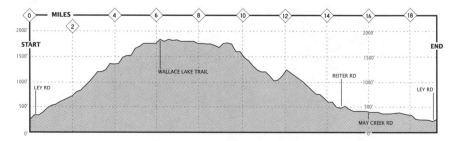

The best thing about Wallace Falls is its variety. In the beginning of the ride, the trail is wide and gravelly. Since it's covered in trees, you'll benefit from the shade in the summer months. Views of the waterfall can be seen from below by taking a one-mile, hiker-only trail. This ride climbs right to the top of the falls by winding up a mildly technical trail.

A few years ago logging returned to this area. About four miles of trail were replaced by gravel road. Though disappointing to those who've ridden Wallace Falls in the past, the road actually elevates you more quickly to Wallace Lake. Once at the lake, explore a little if you have time. This is a good turn-around point if you've had enough riding. If not, cross the bridge and follow the singletrack from here. Flying along on the padded forest floor, you'll arrive at the top of Wallace Falls in no time.

Crossing the river can be difficult—just getting down to the water is a chore. The embankments are steep and covered with wet rocks and slimy

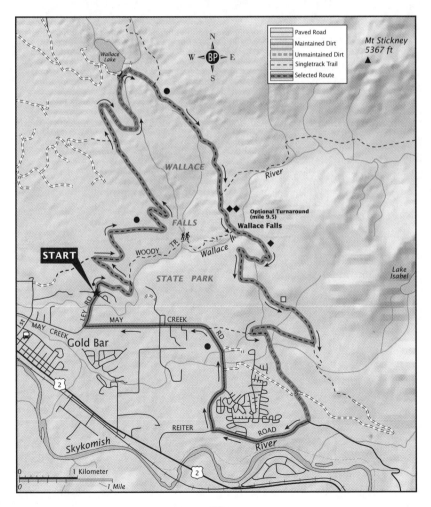

Splashing through May Creek.

green moss and algae. Find a spot where the water looks shallow and cross carefully. (Hope you remembered an extra pair of socks.) The river moves swiftly all year long, so the trick to crossing successfully is slow, steady movements. Don't look down at the water rushing over your feet; it will only make you dizzy. And remember to keep your bike on your downstream side, whether you walk it across or shoulder it. Cross as quickly as possible to avoid hypothermic conditions during inclement weather. If in doubt, TURN AROUND.

Once across, head along the bank down the river toward the falls. You'll have to bushwhack your way up, but once there, you'll feel exhilarated. On this side of the river, the trail is fast and more challenging. Your hands will be tired by the time you get back to the car—but you'll be too pumped to care.

There are full bathroom facilities and camping in the park. The ranger will sometimes provide a hose behind the restrooms for washing off your bike—and your body. The ranger works hard to keep this area open and safe for mountain biking.

If you hail from outside the area and want to explore the area a bit, you might consider stopping at one of the local wineries or microbreweries on your way home. The Columbia Winery and the Chateau Saint Michelle Winery, both in Woodinville, have beautiful gardens and are open daily for wine tasting. The Chateau Saint Michelle offers summer concerts on the lawn. If you prefer a bit of froth, try the Redhook Brewery, next to the Columbia Winery. They have a great restaurant and outdoor seating right along the Snohomish Bike Trail.

Ride Information

🍁 Trail Contacts:
Washington State Parks information line: 1–800–233–0321 • Wallace Falls State Park (360) 793–0420

🕐 Schedule:
Closed Mondays and Tuesdays from October to April. Open during daylight hours.

💲 Fees/Permits:
No fees or permits required

❓ Local Information:
Monroe Chamber of Commerce, Monroe, WA (360) 794–5488 • Sultan Chamber of Commerce (360) 793–0983

🌲 Local Events/Attractions:
Fair Days, Monroe, WA, (360) 805–6700 or (360) 794–5488 • Sultan Summer Shindig Logging Show, in mid July, Sultan, WA (360) 793–2565 • The Columbia Winery, Woodinville, WA (425) 488–2776 • Chateau Saint Michelle Winery, Woodinville, WA (425) 488–1133

🚲 Local Bike Shops:
Woodinville Ski & Bike, Woodinville, WA (425) 483–2453

Ⓝ Maps:
USGS maps: Wallace Lake, WA; Mount Stickney, WA; Goldbar, WA; Index, WA

10

Silver Creek

Ride Summary

This historical trail lures all kinds of people: mountain bikers, hikers, gold panners, miners, geologists, historians...you name it. The trail runs next to Silver Creek on doubletrack that used to be a forest road. Now overgrown and blocked by a huge avalanche field, this road makes a beautiful intermediate mountain biking trail. There are several waterfalls to photograph and a great river to cross, should you dare.

Ride Specs

Start: From the west side of the North Fork of the Skykomish River, across the bridge from Howard Creek and Index/Galena Road

Length: 12.0-mile out-and-back

Approximate Riding Time: 3 hours

Difficulty Rating: Moderate to difficult because of steep, technical ascents and the river crossing

Terrain: Forest roads, doubletrack, and singletrack cross terrain that includes a landslide area and thick brush. It's steep in sections with a few scrambles over rock slide area along the creek.

Land Status: National forest

Nearest Town: Index, WA

Other Trail Users: Hikers

Canine Compatibility: Dogs permitted

Wheels: Front suspension recommended

Getting There

From Seattle: Take I-405 North to the exit for WA 522. Drive east on WA 522 toward Monroe/Wenatchee. Once in Monroe, come to the intersection with U.S. 2 and turn left. Follow U.S. 2 East to Index. Once you see the Index Café, turn left and head north on Index/Galena Road. Follow the road nine miles to Howard Creek. Turn left after crossing Howard Creek onto a one-lane bridge over the North Fork of the Skykomish River. Drive up the dirt road and veer right at the intersection. Park anywhere in this area. You'll be biking up the dirt road, so drive up as far as you like; however, you might want to keep in mind that this one-mile section of logging road makes for a fun descent on your return. **DeLorme: Washington Atlas & Gazetteer:** Page 81 A5

The Silver Creek ride may not be very long, but it provides a very well-rounded workout within an extremely beautiful landscape. This doubletrack to singletrack route, once a working mining road, comes with short climbs, flat rolling sections, bike portages over landslides, and rock-jumping over Silver Creek itself. There are waterfalls all over the place, too, rushing to meet Silver Creek and eventually the Skykomish River below.

The climb begins on an average-grade forest road. This will provide an adequate warm-up for the ride ahead. Arriving at the trail in a little over a

Twin Falls.

mile, you may be surprised at the breadth of the avalanche area you have to cross. This rockslide happened after a flood in 1988. Before that, cars could still drive along what used to be County Road 6335. The trail, which is carved into the side of the slide, is a little daunting; walk your bike over this section.

MilesDirections

0.0 START climbing the gravel road to the right of the intersection (where you parked).

1.4 Pass a spur road on the left.

1.5 Come to a huge avalanche area that falls right into Silver Creek. *[Note. It's a good idea to walk and carry the bike across this.]*

1.7 Pass an old mine on the left. And then cross another small washout.

2.0 *[FYI. Nice waterfall on your right across the river.]*

2.2 Pass another mine on the left.

2.5 Pass a washout and a beautiful waterfall.

2.6 Another mine.

2.7 Cross the second wooden bridge.

2.9 Cross a small avalanche area. *[FYI. The right trail ahead is a camping area close to the creek.]* Take the trail up to the left.

3.7 Cross another nice wooden bridge marking a great waterfall on the left.

4.4 Wade across a tributary of Silver Creek to continue. *[Option. If you're not up to a lot of hike-a-bike sections, you might want to turn around here and enjoy a quick, fun downhill back to your car.]*

4.6 Cross Silver Creek on an old wooden bridge. *[FYI. This was once the location of Mineral City.]*

4.9 Head into the hills.

5.6 Bushwhacking your way up, continue on trail now to the falls. If the previous winter season has been especially tough, the trail will be in sad repair until late summer. Be prepared for a little hiking.

6.0 After checking out Twin Falls, turn around and head back for some screaming singletrack descents. *[Option. You can continue from here to the top of the pass, then hike down to the ghost town of Monte Cristo.]*

12.0 Arrive back at the parking lot and your car.

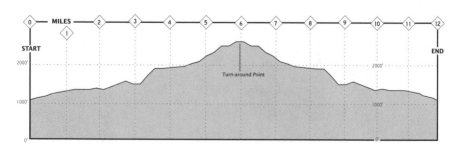

After the avalanche crossing, the trail is picture perfect for the next few miles. Wide because it used to carry wagons, and later cars, it's easy to ride side by side, admiring the waterfalls feeding Silver Creek and the mining tunnels along the way. The trail begins to wind up along Silver Creek before finally crossing one of its tributaries. There's no way to avoid getting wet here. There are great boulders along the creek bank for sunning yourself dry.

After you cross Silver Creek, the trail turns into singletrack and immediately begins to scale the hillside toward Hubbart Peak. Long before it reaches the peak, you'll find the trail huddling under thick brush. Most people don't cross the river, so it remains fairly overgrown here. Bushwhacking takes a little time, but getting past the brush is like being greeted by the sun after riding through a tunnel. Once on the other side, you find yourself sit-

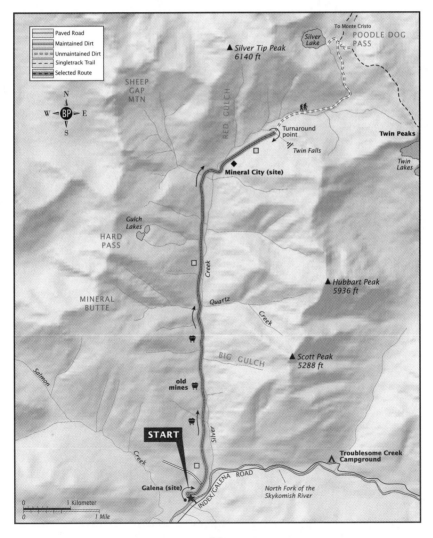

uated between two incredible peaks: Silvertip Peak (6,140 feet) and Hubbart Peak (5,936 feet). The river seems very far away up here.

The trail then climbs along the north side of Hubbart. The singletrack looks more like the abandoned road that it is. It intersects with a lovely cascading waterfall streaming from Twin Peaks. (Incidentally, these peaks have nothing to do with the TV show *Twin Peaks,* whose credits were, however, shot in Snoqualmie at Snoqualmie Falls, closer to Interstate 90.) This is the usual turn-around point for heading back down. If you are looking for more adventure, consider following the trail yet a little higher to reach the end of the cirque and then hike to Poodle Dog Pass, right by Silver Lake, and then down to Monte Cristo, the historic ghost mining town.

The avalanche field.

Monte Cristo was quite the mining boomtown in the late 1880s, but foundations are all that remain of the town now. There used to be trams that carried the galena ore (silver and lead mixture) to a mill in town and then to an Everett smelter. All was running well until a huge flood in 1897 destroyed the Great Northern Railway tracks that ran through the Stillaguamish/Sauk River valleys. The big money investors (who included the Rockefellers) called in their loans, and the town of Monte Cristo quickly died. The Great Northern Railway returned sometime later to haul wood for the sawmills and occasionally to transport miners to the ore mines. Monte Cristo then became somewhat of a tourist attraction, though there are reputedly still active claims with minimal mining going on. Now, it's primarily a great place to hike and mountain bike.

To get there, you can ride your mountain bike up to the crossing of Silver Creek. This trail is rarely used from Monte Cristo down this far and can be tough to negotiate—it makes a more logical hike. After crossing the river, you essentially follow Silver Creek almost all the way up to Silver Lake, keeping to the east of the river. The trail then intersects with a two-mile trail heading to Twin Lakes. Follow the Silver Creek/Monte Cristo Trail straight to Poodle Dog Pass and then down to Monte Cristo. This makes a hefty trip though. It's easier to drive there via the Mountain Loop Highway. To do that, travel east from Everett on Washington 9 North to Washington 92 East. After passing through Granite Falls, continue east on the Mountain Loop Highway about 26 miles to Barlow Pass where the road turns into Monte Cristo Road.

Ride Information

❶ Trail Contacts:
Mount Baker/Snoqualmie National Forest, Skykomish Ranger District: (360) 677–2414

🕐 Schedule:
Open year round, but is best between April and October

💲 Fees/Permits:
No fees or permits required

❓ Local Information:
Monroe Chamber of Commerce, Monroe, WA (360) 794–5488

❾ Local Events/Attractions:
Fair Days, in late August, Monroe, WA (360) 805–6700 or (360) 794–5488

• **Sultan Summer Shindig Logging Show,** in mid July, Sultan, WA (360) 793–0983 • **The Columbia Winery,** Woodinville, WA (425) 488–2776 • **Chateau Saint Michelle Winery,** Woodinville, WA (425) 488–1133 • **Red Hook Brewery,** Woodinville, WA (425) 483–3232

🚲 Local Bike Shops:
Spokemotion, Monroe, WA (360) 794–4522 • **Centennial Cyclery,** Snohomille, WA (360) 568–1345 • **Woodinville ki & Bike,** Woodinville, WA (425) 483–2453

Ⓝ Maps:
USGS maps: Index, WA

Nason Ridge

Ride Summary

Nothing beats beginning a difficult ride with a hearty climb. This advanced ridge ride, overlooking Lake Wenatchee, takes you to the panoramic heights of Round Mountain. It's also highly regarded by cyclists who enjoy gonzo-abusive mountain biking. To reduce saddle fatigue, consider turning this loop into a shuttle ride, or possibly shortening the loop.

Ride Specs

Start: From the Merritt Lake trailhead
Other Starting Locations: Nason Ridge Campground or Nason Ridge trailhead
Length: 17.6-mile point-to-point
Approximate Riding Time: 5 hours
Difficulty Rating: Difficult due to long, steep climbs and ridge line riding
Terrain: Steep singletrack, doubletrack, and paved road (with the shuttle) across steep hills and rolling terrain
Land Status: National forest
Nearest Town: Leavenworth, WA
Other Trail Users: Hikers and equestrians
Canine Compatibility: Dogs not permitted
Wheels: Front suspension recommended

Getting There

From Stevens Pass: Drive east on U.S. 2 for 10.8 miles. Turn left onto Merritt Lake Road. Head up to the parking lot, after passing power lines and a spur road.

Shuttle Point: From Stevens Pass, drive east on U.S. 2 for 19 miles to Coles Corner. Turn left and head north on WA 207 to Nason Creek Campground, toward Lake Wenatchee. Nason Creek Campground is on the left at Cedar Brae Road. Cross the creek and park on either side of the road at the campground. *DeLorme: Washington Atlas & Gazetteer:* Page 82 B1

Nason Ridge runs parallel to U.S. Route 2 and is smack in between Lake Wenatchee and the Alpine Lakes Wilderness, just east of Stevens Pass. If you're into rockhounding, you might think about hanging out at Lake Wenatchee. Near the Ranger Station toward the end of Washington 207, there is a trail where you can find long green crystals of actinolite, multicolored talc, and soapstone. Lake Wenatchee, now a recreational getaway, just nearly escaped becoming a reservoir. The legislature (with the support of President Taft) passed a bond for construction, but luckily voters vetoed the project. Today Lake Wenatchee is a popular place to mountain bike, hike, fish, and camp. A state park, beach, and camping on either side of the lake provide ample recreational space.

Covering 306,000 square acres of wilderness in the Mount Baker-Snoqualmie National Forest, the pristine, moon-like Alpine Lakes Wilderness also stretches into the Wenatchee National Forest. At the alpine level, nothing but incredible rocks, lakes, and ptarmigans exist. White-gray rocks of all sizes blend with the sky on cloudy days, making it difficult to find the hiking trail at times. If it weren't for the cairns marking the trail as it winds around the icy cold, peacefully quiet alpine lakes, it would be quite easy to get lost up there. Be careful not to trip on a ptarmigan—a hearty variety of grouse, with feathers all the way down to their feet. These rugged, chameleon-like creatures change color according to the season. It can be difficult to spot them at first.

Looking toward Merritt Lake.

MilesDirections

0.0 START on The Merritt Lake Trail (Trail 1588).

2.3 Reach a junction with the Nason Ridge Trail (Trail 1583). (Rock Lake Trail is to the left.) Continue climbing to Merritt Lake.

2.9 Arrive at Merritt Lake (El. 5,083 feet). Follow the trail by the lake, but stay on the main trail to the right and head up the switchbacks to the ridge.

3.2 At the T-intersection, turn right to continue on Trail 1583 and up to the Alpine Lookout. *[FYI. The left goes to Lost Lake.]*

4.9 Arrive at a saddle with great views of the valley.

5.8 Begin a series of switchbacks after a narrow, technical descent down the steep hillside. *[FYI. The view is of the Nason Creek Valley.]* Head up to the ridge top on the switchbacks.

6.4 Encounter the final push up to the junction of the Alpine Lookout. Double back on your left for the lookout. The view is worth it. The trail continues around Round Mountain.

6.7 Reach the Alpine Lookout for 360 degrees of awesome views.

7.1 Back at the junction, follow the trail straight to Nine Mile Saddle and Round Mountain.

9.7 The trail is now heading around Round Mountain.

10.4 Reach the intersection of Trail 1529. Stay left on Trail 1583. *[**Note.** It isn't well marked so pay attention.]*

13.5 The trail turns into doubletrack and a gentle climb.

13.7 Turn right as the doubletrack crests the hill.

14.3 Turn left at the intersection and keep to Trail 1583. (FS 114 drops down to a saddle and goes off right.)

16.9 Arrive at the end of the trail. Cruise along the forest floor. Come to a gravel loop and follow it around to the main road.

17.0 Hit asphalt and turn left downhill on Golf Course Road.

17.1 Arrive at a fork from the right. Continue on the downhill fork.

17.3 Exit Kahler Glen Golf Resort. Turn right.

17.6 Arrive at the intersection with Cedar Brae Road and Nason Creek Campground Road. Pick up your shuttle. *[**Option.** To create a 30-mile loop and forget the shuttle, exit the campground and turn right on WA 207 and then right on U.S. 2 for a 13.4-mile return to the Merritt Lake Trail trailhead.]*

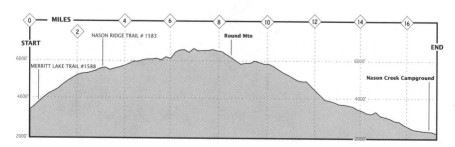

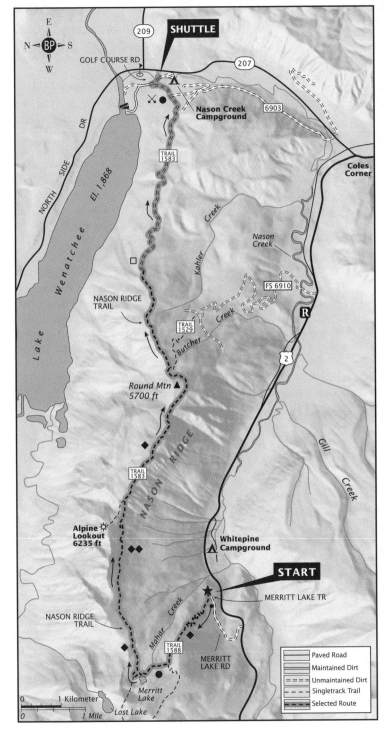

Nearby Stevens Pass was named for John G. Stevens who discovered the Nason Creek route over the Cascades. Crossed by U.S. Route 2, Stevens Pass is also a railroad route across the mountains. Trains don't travel over the pass but rather straight through it, via a tunnel carved into the mountains 1,900 feet beneath the summit. It took three years to construct the original 2.5-mile-long tunnel in 1900. The tunnel was replaced 29 years later with an eight-mile-long version about 900 feet lower than the original.

Stevens Pass has an older sibling—a route just to the north. The old pass is no longer a viable traveling road in most places but makes for a great road bike ride, with one large river crossing. To ride the old route, start out in Skykomish on the west side of Stevens Pass. Follow the road out of Skykomish that runs parallel to U.S. Route 2 along the Tye River. After about two miles, the road ends at U.S. Route 2. Ride on U.S. Route 2 for a little over two miles before crossing over to the north side of the highway, and continue traveling east on the old Route 2. The old road winds up the mountains, which are virtually deserted except for the occasional car where the road is still intact. After crossing the Tye River, the road is in serious disrepair—perfect for biking. The old pass leads right up to the Stevens Pass Ski Area. To return to Skykomish, ride down the newer U.S. Route 2. It is legal—folks do it all the time—and it's screaming fun. Except for the initial gravitational pull of the concrete and the counterbalancing you have to do because of the ferocious crosswinds, you'll love it. There's an adequate shoulder and plenty of lanes for cars, so you'll have lots of space.

For a thrilling singletrack ride, though, you'll want to go for the Nason Ridge ride. Now if you're a *super-biker*, you can probably ride the initial climb

of this ride. Mere mortals will most likely have to push a little. After leaving the parking area at the Merritt Lake Trail trailhead, the climb begins immediately, gaining a lot of elevation. (We recommend a brief warm-up on the road.) The trail reaches Merritt Lake at 5,083 feet after about three miles. There is a path around the lake, but this ride takes you up and away from the lake. Because of the incline, the ride can be pretty tough. There are a few short descents in which to catch your breath. After about five miles, the trail gives way to a slightly hairy descent and views of the Nason Creek Valley below. Continuing up, the switchbacks will likely be climbers and somewhat technical. The 360-degree view at the Alpine Lookout is divine and the descent following to Nine Mile Saddle and Round Mountain is worth the sweat of the climb.

Feeling a mite daunted by the intensity of this ride just by reading about it? Make an easier loop by driving up Forest Service Road 6910 to Trail 1529, from the rest stop on U.S. Route 2. Begin your ride at Trail 1529, making a loop by riding down to Trail 1583 and around Round Mountain to Lake Wenatchee and back. The Alpine Lookout is still accessible and the climb will be less harrowing. The most important thing is to have a good time.

Ride Information

❶ Trail Contacts:

Wenatchee National Forest, Leavenworth Ranger District, Leavenworth, WA (509) 548–6977 • **Wenatchee National Forest,** Lake Wenatchee Ranger District, Leavenworth, WA (509) 763–3103 or 1–800–452–5687

❷ Schedule:

Open year round, but best between May and October

❸ Fees/Permits:

$5 per car, per day ($30 for an annual pass)

❹ Local Information:

Leavenworth Chamber of Commerce, Leavenworth, WA (509) 548–5807 or www.leavenworth.org

❺ Local Events/Attractions:

Maifest, in May, Leavenworth, WA (509) 548–5807 • **Leavenworth Craft Fair,** in June, Leavenworth, WA (509) 548–5807 • **International Accordion Celebration,** in August, Leavenworth, WA (509) 548–5807 • **Washington State Autumn Leave Festival,** September-October, Leavenworth, WA (509) 548–5807

❻ Accommodations:

Mountain Home Lodge, Leavenworth, WA 1–800–414–2378 or www.mthome.com

❼ Local Bike Shops:

Der Sportsmann, Leavenworth, WA (509) 548–5623 • **Leavenworth Ski & Sports,** Leavenworth, WA (509) 548–7864 • **Leavenworth Outfitters Outdoor Center,** Leavenworth, WA (509) 763–3733 or 1–800–347–7934 or www.thrillmakers.com

❽ Maps:

USGS maps: Mount Howard, WA

Mountain Home Loops

Ride Summary

Nestled between the steep eastern slopes of the Cascade Range, the cross-country trails accessed from Mountain Home Road make great intermediate mountain biking loops in the summer. The forest road climbs are gradual at first, but they gain intensity the higher they go. Although the area is still recovering from a series of forest fires, the ponderosa pines still yield some *must-see* views. If you're staying at the Mountain Home Lodge, you can look forward to an incredible meal and a soak in the hot tub at the end of the day. If you aren't staying at the lodge, please park along Mountain Home Road.

Ride Specs

Start: From Mountain Home Road
Length: 12.1-mile loop from the lodge
Approximate Riding Time: 3–4 hours
Difficulty Rating: Moderate due to short, steep climbs
Terrain: Doubletrack, logging roads, and singletrack over rolling hills with a few steep climbs
Land Status: National forest
Nearest Town: Leavenworth, WA
Other Trail Users: Equestrians, hikers, cross-country skiers, and some motorcyclists
Canine Compatibility: Dogs permitted on trails but not at the lodge
Wheels: Front suspension recommended, but not required

Getting There

From Leavenworth: Take U.S. 2 East through town to North Leavenworth Road. Turn right to go south on North Leavenworth Road. Turn left immediately onto Mountain Home Road. Follow for 2.6 miles to the lodge on the left. *DeLorme: Washington Atlas & Gazetteer:* Page 82 D3

Leavenworth, *the Bavaria of the Cascades*, is home to anything and everything German—with the snow-capped, Alps-like peaks to boot. But Leavenworth hasn't always been that way. In the late 1800s, the promise of the Great Northern Railroad brought life to the small township of Icicle, built along the Icicle River. The town moved to the valley where the railroad tracks would run. Charles Leavenworth, a stockholder with the investment company, spearheaded the relocation. By 1897, the tracks were set and work began on tunneling through the Cascades. But by 1920, the country was heading into the Great Depression, and the railroad packed up and moved out of the valley. Orchards and sawmills saw hard times too, and

Leavenworth began to disintegrate. For the next 40 years, the town struggled to survive.

In 1960, Leavenworth citizens re-awakened to the beauty around them, realized their proximity to Washington's larger towns, and decided, in an effort to attract tourists, to go Bavarian. Although it took some time to get off the ground, the *new-and-improved* Leavenworth began booming oompah music and serving traditional Bavarian fare. And it worked. Leavenworth is now a destination town, a hub for winter and summer recreation. Backpacking, climbing, hiking, horseback riding, and mountain biking are

View of Leavenworth from Mountain Home Road.

continuing to grow in popularity, drawing a new kind of tourist and economy to Leavenworth.

Anyone would agree that an especially nice reward at the end of a tough day of mountain biking is a big meal and a soak in a hot tub. The Mountain Home Lodge in Leavenworth has both. Much more than a hotel or a sim-

MilesDirections

0.0 START from Mountain Home Road, just beyond the lodge. Head down the driveway and turn left onto Mountain Home Road.

3.7 Arrive at the Four Corners crossroads (El. 2,900 feet). Turn left on Boundary Road for Boundary Butte. *[Option. Turn right on Wedge Mountain Road to access the helicopter pad (El. 5,855 feet).]*

3.9 Pass a dead-end road on the right. Continue straight.

4.2 At the intersection, follow the road to the right.

4.6 Pass the intersection leading to the Canyon Crest Trail, continuing straight. At the next intersection turn right for the Boundary Butte Lookout.

6.0 Reach the top of the lookout. *[FYI. See Icicle Creek, the Enchantments, Peshastin, and Leavenworth.]* Turn around and head back down.

7.4 Reach the bottom of the road from the butte. Turn right at the fork and follow the doubletrack down and around to the intersection for the Rat Creek Trail and Canyon Crest Trail.

8.2 Arrive at the trailheads for the Rat Creek Trail and Canyon Crest Trail— they're well marked with signs. Turn right on the Canyon Crest Trail. (Continuing straight leads to the Rat Creek Trail.)

9.7 Stay straight at the fork.

11.2 See the sign for the Mount Stuart Lookout. Stay right at the fork.

11.4 Reach the intersection for the Overlook Loop and the end of the Ridge Ride Trail. Follow the Overlook Loop straight and then left at the intersection of Wapati Trail (hikers only).

11.9 Watch for a small sign on the right-hand side of the trail for the lodge. Follow it over the meadow and to the lodge. If you miss it, the trail exits onto the private road that is gated at the Mountain Home Road intersection, at which point you'll turn right and follow the sign for the lodge.

12.1 Arrive back at the Mountain Home Lodge.

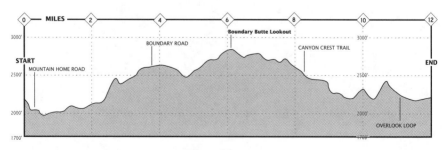

ple bed and breakfast, the Mountain Home Lodge is a home away from home. From its massive stone fireplace, both warm and inviting, to its spacious hot tub surrounded by tall, often snowy peaks, the Mountain Home Lodge is the perfect place to crash after a long day of pedal pounding. Brad and Kathy Schmidt, the inn's proprietors, are correct both figuratively and literally when they boast that their lodge is 1,000 feet closer to heaven. And this gives you a 1,000-foot advantage when taking off for the hills above.

The going is steady and not at all rough as you begin from the lodge up the Mountain Home Road. The forest of ponderosa pines adorn the roadside like memory lane: some trees are perfect, standing tall, branches reach-

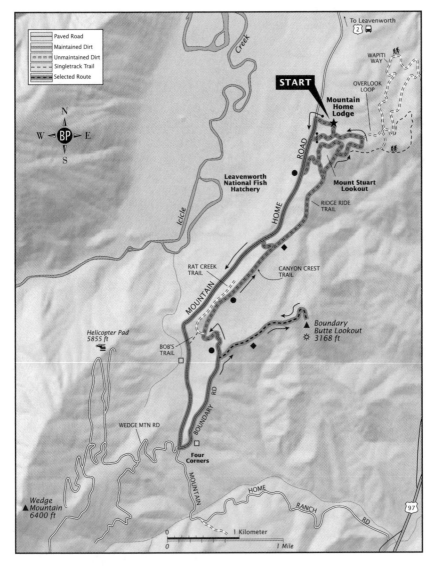

ing out to one another, and others are sadly scorched, ominously reminiscent of the huge and devastating fire that overtook this area in 1994. At the crossroads, called Four Corners, the route can take off in one of three directions. Heading up and right leads to the helicopter pad, used during forest fires. Turning left, the road leads to a lookout and the singletrack. Riding straight down, the road will eventually run into U.S. Route 97. The directions below will cover both routes—though not the road to the highway.

The climb up to the helicopter pad is steep, and if the road is at all wet, the mud will be thick and challenging to ride through. The views from the helicopter pad make the agony of the muddy climb worthwhile. The hillsides surrounding Leavenworth aren't the rolling kind you see on the western side of the Cascades. These mountains shoot straight up, making most every climb memorable.

After turning around, enjoy the downhill return to Four Corners. Then head up the road to the lookout. It is a steep climb, but the view is wide

open. You can see apple orchards and Icicle Creek Road. You'll be able to pinpoint the Enchantments and see cars drive along U.S. Route 2 and U.S. Route 97. The ponderosa pines stand like silent sentinels along the trails.

Getting down to the singletrack is great fun. The trails are well marked, so it's easy to find your way. The Ridge Ride Trail is a serious ridge-runner. Nothing flat about this trail: push up, fly down, push up, fly down. If you can manage to climb each and every rise, your quads will definitely be burning at the top. It's not too long, but it is a workout. The ridge trail travels to a couple of looping trails out behind the Mountain Home Lodge.

This is a good intermediate ride for mountain bikers who don't like to be too far out in the wilderness. The trails are fairly exposed most of the time, which lets you see exactly where you are. It's difficult to get lost, even without a map.

Ride Information

● Trail Contacts:

Wenatchee National Forest, Leavenworth Ranger District, Leavenworth, WA (509) 548–6977 • **Wenatchee National Forest,** Lake Wenatchee Ranger District, Leavenworth, WA (509) 763–3103 or 1–800–452–5687

● Schedule:

Open year round, but best between May and October

● Fees/Permits:

No fees or permits required

● Local Information:

Leavenworth Chamber of Commerce, Leavenworth, WA (509) 548–5807 or www.leavenworth.org • **Lake Wenatchee State Park,** Leavenworth, WA (509) 763–3409

● Local Attractions/Events:

Maifest, in May, Leavenworth, WA (509) 548–5807 • **Leavenworth Craft Fair,** in June, Leavenworth, WA (509) 548–5807 • **International Accordion**

Celebration, in August, Leavenworth, WA (509) 548–5807 • **Washington State Autumn Leave Festival,** September-October, Leavenworth, WA (509) 548–5807

● Accommodations:

Mountain Home Lodge, Leavenworth, WA (509) 548–7077 or 1–800–414–2378 or www.mthome.com • **Camping on the Icicle Creek Drainage:** 1–800–274–6104 • **Tumwater Campground:** 1–800–280–2267

● Local Bike Shops:

Der Sportsmann, Leavenworth, WA (509) 548–5623 • **Leavenworth Ski & Sports,** Leavenworth, WA (509) 548–7864 • **Leavenworth Outfitters Outdoor Center,** Leavenworth, WA (509) 763–3733 or 1–800–347–7934 or www.thrillmakers.com

● Maps:

USGS maps: Leavenworth, WA

13

Jolly Mountain

Ride Summary

Hot, dry, and *technical* describe the climb of this advanced ride to a T-intersection. Thrill-seekers will definitely appreciate the descent from Jolly Mountain. This 18-plus-mile route offers great views of nearby Cle Elum Lake, the Enchantments, and Mount Rainier. For this ride, you'll want to bring along plenty of food and water, and be prepared to ride hard.

Ride Specs

Start: From the Salmon la Sac Campground off WA 903
Length: 18.2-mile loop
Approximate Riding Time: 4–5 hours
Difficulty Rating: Difficult due to steep, technical singletrack
Terrain: Paved road, forest road, and singletrack over hills with a few steep climbs
Land Status: National forest
Nearest Town: Roslyn, WA
Other Trail Users: Hikers and equestrians
Canine Compatibility: Dogs permitted
Wheels: Hardtail is okay, but front suspension recommended

Getting There

From Seattle: Take I-90 East to Exit 80. Head north from the exit onto Bull Frog Road. Turn left onto WA 903 to Roslyn. Follow the main road through town into Ronald. Pass the Last Resort Restaurant on the right. Follow WA 903 for about nine miles to the Salmon la Sac Campground. Drive into the campground and over a narrow bridge. Park at this trailhead, which is close to where the ride finishes. *DeLorme: Washington Atlas & Gazetteer* Pages 65 A8

Head back in time, back to a place where simple living is revered and a sense of community has always been in vogue. Eight lanes of interstate narrow to four, slowing your pace considerably. You then pass through small towns with distinctly western flavors. You may even recognize Roslyn as Cicely, Alaska, the setting for the television show *Northern Exposure*. But Roslyn is more than just a TV celebrity town, it's also a prime location for weekend mountain biking, camping, boating, fishing, and just getting away from it all.

Roslyn was originally settled as a mining town and is actually built on top of a coal field. Coal produced in Roslyn once accounted for half of the coal produced in the state. The mining industry began here in 1884 with the

MilesDirections

0.0 START from the campground and ride over the narrow bridge to WA 903. Turn right on WA 903.

1.0 Turn left on FS 4315.

1.8 The road switches back left. Continue on the main road passing a spur road on the right.

2.9 The road switches left, heading east up the basin, then heads north again.

3.2 Pass a gated road on the right.

3.4 Pass a gate again.

3.8 The road switches right. Pass a spur on the left.

4.0 Zigzag up the hill.

4.6 Pass a gated road on the left and FS 121.

6.2 Keep heading up. Pass a spur road that heads down.

7.6 Round a bend *[FYI. Great view here of Mount Rainier, Lake Cle Elum, Mount Stuart, and the Enchantments.]*

7.7 Pass another spur on the right and climb up the spine of this ridge. Sasse Ridge Trail (Trail 1340) heads off to the right. Continue up the road, which will become Trail 1340 later. There will again be a trail marked 1340 that you'll pass shortly before the end of the road.

8.1 Wind up the edge of a clearcut. Stay right on the main road.

8.3 Come to the saddle. *[FYI. Great view of the Enchantments and Mount Rainier.]* Head over the rise and see the trail on your left.

8.5 Pass Trail 1340 on your right. Ride to the end of the road, onto the West Fork of the Teanaway Trail (Trail 1353).

8.9 The climb tops out and drops a little to the trail junction of Jolly Mountain Trail (Trail 1307), and in a little bit, Trail 1353 (on the right).

9.0 Head up to Jolly Mountain for a view.

9.3 Pass a junction on the right. Stay left to Jolly Mountain (one mile).

9.8 The trail to Jolly Mountain rounds the top of a drainage and gives you some incredible views of Mount Stuart and The Enchantments.

10.0 Pass the junction of Jolly Creek Trail (Trail 1355) on the left. Stay straight on Trail 1307. Ditch the bikes and hike 0.7 miles to the top (El. 6,443 feet) for a panoramic look at Ellensburg and the Stuart Range. Turn around for the descent and go back the way you came.

11.2 Arrive at the junction with Trail 1353. Continue straight.

11.5 Turn right on the Trail 1307.

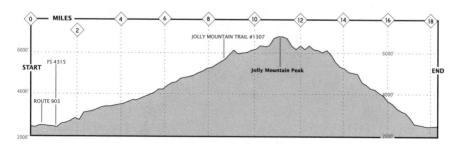

arrival of Nez Jensen. Jensen ran a small mining operation for two years before the Northern Pacific Railroad came to town. Because of existing land deals, it was easy for the railroad to take control of the town and Jensen's coal production. The land deals originated from President Lincoln's days in office. To push the railroads on the West Coast, the U.S. government offered the railroad companies incentive land: 40 square miles of land for every one mile of track. The coal mining areas in and around Roslyn happened to fall within the Northern Pacific's holdings, which is why it was easy for the company to own, operate, and run the town and its coal production.

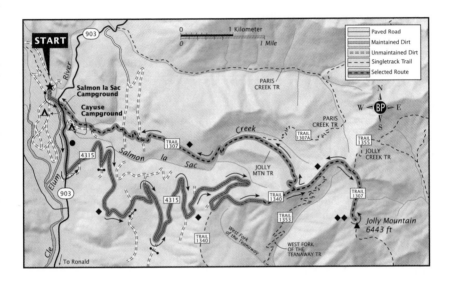

14.0 Reach the junction with the Paris Creek Trail (Trail 1307A). Continue straight on the Trail 1307.

14.7 Cross a tributary of Salmon la Sac Creek.

15.4 Great downhill ends at a clearcut. Look for the trail about 30 yards below. Rock cairns show you the trail on the left.

16.0 Cross the logging road. The trail is marked; just follow it across the road.

16.7 The trail crosses a spur road.

16.9 Back into the trees again. The river is just off to the left.

17.5 Come out at the top of Cayuse Campground. See the trail signs. Follow the main road straight and pass a number of spur roads. *[**Option.** Take the trail off to the right for a bit more singletrack. It drops to a creek with a short hike-a-bike climb into the horse camp and the trails for Jolly Mountain and the other trails.]*

17.9 Hit the paved road and turn right, heading back to Salmon la Sac Campground and your car.

18.1 Come to the campground intersection and turn left.

18.2 Arrive back at the parking lot.

Working in the coal mines paid well back then. People from all over the world came to Roslyn to get their piece of the action. The names on the headstones in the old cemetery in town illustrate the diversity of the work force; there you'll find Austrians, Croats, Germans, Italians, Hungarians, Scots, and Swedes. Coal mining itself ended when other, more efficient means of power were discovered, but huge deposits of coal still remain.

Today, Roslyn looks a lot like it did in the late 1800s. The Brick Tavern, (yes, it's "The Brick" from *Northern Exposure*) was built in 1899. It's got an old jail in its basement and a "gutter" spittoon running 23 feet along it's bar, complete with running water! The store on First Street and Pennsylvania still stands as it did in 1889. And many of the old homesteader cabins and houses still exist as well.

North of Roslyn is the small community of Ronald, named after a mine supervisor, Alexander Ronald. Watch your speed limit while driving through town: 25 mph. About a half mile outside of Ronald, you can see coal mine tailings on the hill. Six and a half miles down the road, you'll run into The Last Resort Restaurant—which it really is. There are no other restaurants or retail establishments past that point. The food is pretty good, too, especially after a hot and dusty mountain bike ride.

Continuing through Ronald, the road narrows along Cle Elum Lake. Long and blue, this lake stretches for about seven miles and has boat launches and campgrounds on its banks. If you look at a map, Cle Elum Lake, Kachess Lake, and Keechelus Lake all look like they were cut from the same mold. There is a fresh water spring toward the end of the lake (it's easy to miss), and Red Mountain stands at 5,722 feet to the north (it's hard to miss).

Jolly Mountain is located at the northeast end of Cle Elum Lake and Sasse Ridge. The peak is a spectacular point from which to view the natural sites of central Washington. The climb to this vantage, however, is a

tough, dry, and dusty mountain bike ride, with a thrill-seeker's descent. The ride to Jolly Mountain begins with a road climb, the long and steady kind. (The West Fork of the Teanaway ride begins in the same place.) The views of Cle Elum Lake, the Enchantments, and Mount Rainier are breathtaking from the top on clear days, and are well deserved after the last half-mile of ascent—the steepest and toughest part of the climb.

Arriving at the top of the road, you reach the junction with Jolly Mountain, the West Fork of the Teanaway Trail and the Sasse Ridge Trail. This is where the singletrack begins. There's still a little bit of climbing left to do, interspersed with a few short descents, and then the final climb to the top of Jolly Mountain. All your work won't have been for naught. The steep descent into the Salmon la Sac drainage is an exhilarating experience.

From then on, the trail crosses the Salmon la Sac Creek and travels through the uncut forest, alternating with passes through sparse clearcut meadows. The trail is dry and dusty, except by the creek, before arriving at the road leading back to the Salmon la Sac Campground and Cle Elum Lake. Remember to take a refreshing dip in the lake before you hit The Last Resort.

Ride Information

● Trail Contacts:

Wenatchee National Forest, Cle Elum Ranger District, Cle Elum, WA (509) 674–4411 • **Wenatchee National Forest Headquarters,** Wenatchee, WA (509) 662–4335 or *www.fs.fed.us/r6/wenatchee/*

● Schedule:

Open year round, but best April to October due to snow levels

● Fees/Permits:

$5 per car, per day ($30 for an annual pass)

● Local Information:

Cle Elum Chamber of Commerce, Cle Elum, WA (509) 674–5958 or *www.ohwy.com/wa/c/cleelucc.htm* • **Ellensburg Chamber of Commerce,** Ellensburg, WA (509) 925–3137 • **Central Sundries** (Roslyn's de facto Visitor Center), Roslyn, WA (509) 649–2210

● Local Events/Attractions:

Pioneer Days, in July, Roslyn, WA (509) 674–5958 • **Sweet Pea Festival,** in July, Roslyn, WA (509) 649–2758 • **Croatian Picnic,** in July, Roslyn, WA (509) 649–2714 • **Roslyn Miner's Celebration & Wing Ding Parade,** in August, Roslyn, WA (509) 649–2756 • **Whisky Dick Triathlon,** in July, Ellensburg, WA (509) 925–3137 • **Ellensburg Rodeo,** in August, Ellensburg, WA (509) 962–7831 or 1-800-637-2444

● Local Bike Shops:

Recycle Bicycle Shops, Ellensburg, WA (509) 925–3326 • **Central Sundries,** Roslyn, WA (509) 649–2210

● Maps:

USGS maps: Davis Peak, WA • **Green Trails:** Kachess Lake No. 208; Mount Stuart No. 209

West Fork of the Teanaway

Ride Summary

In the same neighborhood as the Jolly Mountain ride, this route along the West Fork of the Teanaway River has something a little different going for it: water. There are about a dozen creek crossings to contend with on this advanced ride, each a refreshing break on really hot days. The first third of the route begins with a road climb before hitting the trail. The trail ride down to the river is steep, narrow, and challenging. Following along the river, the singletrack passes a canyon filled with cool, inviting pools of water. Then the singletrack turns back onto a forest road about nine miles southeast of the start. As a shuttle or a round-trip, this is a ride you'll definitely want to try.

Ride Specs

Start: From the FS 4315 parking area
Length: 23.5-mile shuttle
Approximate Riding Time: 5–7 hours
Difficulty Rating: Difficult due to steep terrain and dry conditions
Terrain: Hilly land with a few steep sections crossed by forest roads, singletrack, and paved road (if you don't do the shuttle)
Land Status: National forest
Nearest Town: Roslyn, WA
Other Trail Users: Hikers and equestrians
Canine Compatibility: Dogs permitted
Wheels: Hardtail is okay, but front suspension recommended

Getting There

From Seattle: Take I-90 East to Exit 90. Head north from the exit onto Bull Frog Road. Turn left onto WA 903 to Roslyn. Follow the main road through town into Ronald. Pass the Last Resort Restaurant on the right. (Leave one car here for the shuttle.) Follow WA 903 toward the Salmon la Sac Campground. At 8.5 miles, turn right onto FS 4315 and park on the shoulder or farther up at the designated parking area. *DeLorme:* **Washington Atlas & Gazetteer:** Page 65 A8

The towns along the central Kittitas Valley are as interesting to explore as the mountains that surround them. Spend a little time in Roslyn, the home of the Emmy-award-winning television show *Northern Exposure*, or drive farther south to visit Cle Elum, where you can indulge in baked goods from its 1906 bakery. Travel even farther still to Ellensburg, host to Washington's finest rodeo.

Ellensburg is actually the largest town in the area. It was named in 1871 for Ellen Shoudy, the wife of John Shoudy, a man actively involved in improving the route over Snoqualmie Pass (the top of Interstate 90). In 1889, when Washington became a state, Ellensburg was in the running for

the capital city position, as were Yakima and Olympia. Although Ellensburg and Yakima initially received more votes from Washington's citizens, Olympia won in a runoff election. A financially strong farming community, Ellensburg is well known in Washington for its crop production, especially its timothy hay—the primary feed for racehorses all over the world. Ellensburg hosts the oldest and most popular rodeo in the state, held every year over Labor Day weekend.

Logging was also a major industry on this side of the Cascades. Until 1917, loggers used to float their felled trees down the Teanaway River to mills farther south in Yakima during springtime floods. This practice stopped after farmers complained and lawsuits ensued because the river frequently left big trees in their fields. Log transportation moved to rail after that, and the river is now left to its own devices, providing a refreshing backdrop to the trails running alongside it.

The trail along the West Fork of the Teanaway offers summer solstice cycling at its best. No matter how heated you become, the river will be there to cool you off. There are approximately 13 to 15 splashing opportunities along this ride as it crosses the West Fork of the Teanaway and its tributaries.

MilesDirections

0.0 START on FS 4315 with a gentle climb.

0.2 Pass FS 112 on the left.

0.3 Take the road heading up the hill.

0.8 The road switches back left, still heading up. Stay on the main road.

1.6 *[FYI. Enjoy views of the Enchantments to the north, Kachess Ridge to the west. Right behind is Sasse Mountain and Sasse Ridge.]*

2.0 Enjoy a little bit of a downhill here.

2.2 Pass a gated spur road on the left.

2.4 Cross a gate and a small trail on the left.

2.8 The road switches back right—still climbing. Pass a logging spur.

3.5 Pass FS 121 as you switchback left.

4.9 Passing a left switchback and another spur, you'll keep to the main road and keep heading up.

5.2 Pass a little spur on the left. Steep granny-gear climbing!

5.8 Hit a short and sweet downhill. *[FYI. The trail elevation is about 5,200 feet here.]*

6.5 After curling into the Salmon la Sac drainage, the trail switches back and around the Cle Elum Lake side of Sasse Ridge. *[FYI. Mount Rainier and Cle Elum Lake are visible.]*

6.7 Pass a spur road heading down to the right. Stay straight and continue up to the ridgeline. Fifty yards ahead, see a Forest Service marker for Sasse Ridge Trail (Trail 1340)—a strenuous trail. Keep to the road.

7.0 The road curves to the right on the edge of a clearcut. Pass a couple of spurs to the left and then to the right. Stay on the main road.

7.5 Reach the end of the road, Trail 1340. A sign indicates that Trail 1340, West Fork of the Teanaway Trail (Trail 1353), and Jolly Mountain Trail (Trail 1307) are ahead.

7.9 Start a white-knuckle descent into the next saddle where the Trail 1340 joins with Trail 1307.

8.3 Riding the ridge-top, arrive at the junction of the Trail 1353 and Trail 1307 (one mile ahead). Take Trail 1353.

8.5 Descend into a meadow. The sign posted on a huge fir tree indicates you are still on Trail 1353. *[FYI. Spring Creek Road is 10 miles back from this point.]*

10.4 The trail crosses the West Fork of the Teanaway. You may get your feet wet.

10.8 Cross a tributary of the river. Meander through the brush.

11.5 Cross another feeder creek of the river.

11.9 Cross the West Fork again and get your feet wet.

12.3 Hanging at the creek side, you'll cross again to the east side of the river. Cross another tributary.

12.5 Cross the river, yet again, to the west side.

12.9 Steep climbing on the west side of the river now. Keep going.

13.1 Cross another tributary. Keep going.

14.0 Cross another creek draining into West Creek.

This route should not be mistaken for an easy river trail. This is an advanced mountain bike ride. If possible, make this a shuttle trip. There are many convenient spots along Cle Elum Lake to leave a car while you take the second car to the top of the trailhead. Without a shuttle though, there will be a nine-mile paved road ride to tackle at the ride's end.

Oftentimes, after especially windy or snow-filled winters, the trail has more than its fair share of deadfall. The trailhead fees that were imposed a few years ago help eliminate this sort of hazard, but a quick call to the Ranger District before heading out will verify if this trail has been cleared, sparing you the time it takes to hike over logs and debris.

This day-long ride begins with a long, steady climb that eventually becomes intensely steep. In the summertime, add a little dust, heat, and elevation to the mix, and you've got a recipe for heat exhaustion. Bring along plenty of food and water, or at least a dependable water filter—you should NEVER drink straight from a river.

Like most road climbs, this seven- to eight-mile leg burner is a steady, semi-tough, granny-gear to middle ring event, but the views do a great job of distracting you from the pain in your legs and lungs. The last half-mile of the climb, before the singletrack, is the toughest section because of its steep grade. As you approach the crest of the climb, the Sasse Ridge Trail is to the

---

14.5 Cross the West Fork and a rocky chasm.

14.9 *[FYI. Promontory viewpoint overlooking the waterfall on the West Fork.]*

15.2 Cross over to the West Fork's west side.

16.8 Cross the river…for the last time!

18.1 Cross over the creek but stay on the left bank.

18.6 Reach the end of the Trail 1353. Turn right on FS 4305.

18.9 Continue on FS 4305 to a small clearing on your right. Cross the clearing and drop down to a dry wash and another creek. Continue up the road directly across, which may be blocked. If so, just go around the berm. Head up the road for about a half mile.

19.6 Pass a spur road on your left. Continue up the main road. Pass several spurs, keeping to the main road.

23.5 Reach WA 903 and pick up your shuttle. *[**Option.** Ride WA 903 back to the parking lot on FS 4315 for a 32.5-mile loop.]*

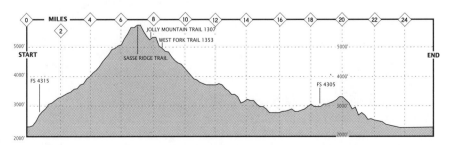

93

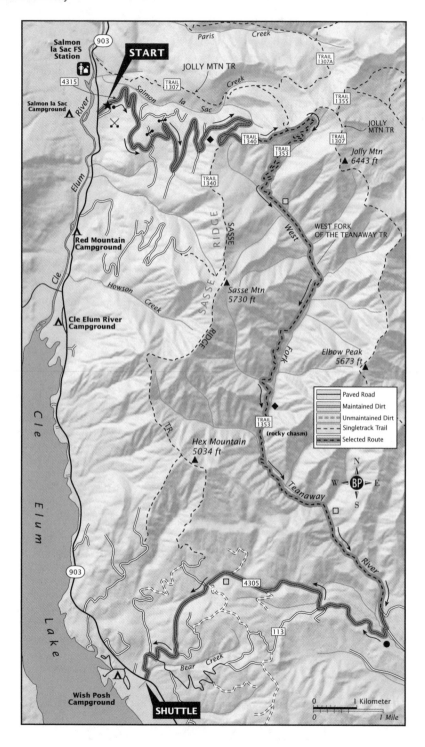

Paris Creek

Salmon
la Sac FS
Station

START

903

4315

JOLLY MTN TR

TRAIL
1307A

TRAIL
1307

la

Sac

Creek

TRAIL
1355

Salmon la Sac
Campground

River

Salmon

JOLLY
MTN TR

TRAIL
1340

TRAIL
1307

Jolly Mtn
6443 ft

Cle

Elum

TRAIL
1353

TRAIL
1340

West

WEST FORK
OF THE TEANAWAY TR

Red Mountain
Campground

SASSE

RIDGE

SASSE

Howson

Creek

Sasse Mtn
5730 ft

Cle Elum River
Campground

Fork

Elbow Peak
5673 ft

Cle

Elum

TR

Hex Mountain
5034 ft

TRAIL
1353

(rocky chasm)

	Paved Road
	Maintained Dirt
	Unmaintained Dirt
	Singletrack Trail
	Selected Route

N

W — BP — E

S

Teanaway

903

River

4305

113

Lake

Bear

Creek

Wish Posh
Campground

SHUTTLE

0   1 Kilometer

0   1 Mile

right. Portions of this trail are defunct; the road now runs where the trail once roamed. The Sasse Ridge Trail is still alive farther up, though, and starts again where the road intersects with it and the West Fork of the Teanaway Trail.

The singletrack of the West Fork of the Teanaway Trail begins with a short hike-a-bike then levels out and drops to a saddle. Following the saddle are some steep, descending switchbacks to the river that get very technical as the path travels along the narrow and steep hillside. There are an equal number of short climbs along the river, too. Remember—this is not a beginner's ride. Along the way there are many rewards for your work. The river canyon, for instance, has several refreshing pools for the weary, overheated mountain biker.

After tearing yourself away from the river's edge, the singletrack finally leads to a forest road climb and onto the road descent back to Cle Elum Lake. From there it's back to your car—either catch your shuttle or get started on the nine-mile ride back to your parking spot. Don't forget the bakery in Cle Elum on the way home.

Ride Information

● Trail Contacts:
Wenatchee National Forest, Cle Elum Ranger District, Cle Elum, WA (509) 674–4411 • **Wenatchee National Forest Headquarters,** Wenatchee, WA (509) 662–4335 or *www.fs.fed.us/r6/wenatchee/*

☉ Schedule:
Open year round, but best April to October due to snow levels

⑤ Fees/Permits:
$5 per car, per day ($30 for an annual pass)

❓ Local Information:
Cle Elum Chamber of Commerce, Cle Elum, WA (509) 674–5958 or *www.ohwy.com/wa/c/cleelucc.htm* • **Ellensburg Chamber of Commerce,** Ellensburg, WA (509) 925–3137 • **Central Sundries** (Roslyn's de facto Visitor Center), Roslyn, WA (509) 649–2210

♀ Local Events/Attractions:
Pioneer Days, in July, Roslyn, WA (509) 674–5958 • **Sweet Pea Festival,** in July, Roslyn, WA (509) 649–2758 • **Croatian Picnic,** in July, Roslyn, WA (509) 649–2714 • **Roslyn Miner's Celebration & Wing Ding Parade,** in August, Roslyn, WA (509) 649–2756 • **Whisky Dick Triathlon,** in July, Ellensburg, WA (509) 925–3137 • **Ellensburg Rodeo,** in August, Ellensburg, WA (509) 962–7831 or 1–800–637–2444

☙ Local Bike Shops:
Recycle Bicycle Shops, Ellensburg, WA (509) 925–3326 • **Central Sundries,** Roslyn, WA (509) 649–2210

❶ Maps:
USGS maps: Cle Elum Lake, WA; Teanaway Butte, WA • **Green Trails:** Kachess Lake No. 208; Mount Stuart No. 209

Kachess Ridge

Ride Summary

Located just east of Snoqualmie Pass, this ride offers a convenient adventure for Seattle-area mountain bikers. This route has a long, steep climb along a forest road before hitting the singletrack. The trail begins along a quickly eroding hillside, then becomes marvelous, jettisoning you across meadows and streams. The finale comes with steep, tight switchbacks. If you have the control, this racecourse-like trail is furiously fast and drops you into the parking area just a mile or so from where you began.

Ride Specs

Start: From the Kachess Lake area
Length: 19.7-mile loop
Approximate Riding Time: 3–5 hours
Difficulty Rating: Moderate to Advanced, due to steep climbs and descents
Terrain: Forest roads and singletrack over hills (one major climb gets pretty steep), creek-crossings, and meadows
Land Status: National forest
Nearest Towns: Easton, WA
Other Trail Users: Hikers and equestrians. ORVs are not allowed on this particular trail, but they do use the area adjacent to this ride.
Canine Compatibility: Dogs permitted
Wheels: Front suspension recommended

Getting There

From Seattle: Take I-90 east over Snoqualmie Pass to Exit 70 at Lake Easton State Park. At the stop sign, go left over the overpass to Sparks Road. Turn left onto Kachess Dam Road and head west (an I-90 feeder road). Go 0.4 miles and turn right. Take the fourth right onto FS 4818 (see sign for "Boeing Overnight Camp"). Head straight toward the power lines. Turn right on FS 203 and go under the power lines. Follow to any offshoot and park.
DeLorme: Washington Atlas & Gazetteer Page 65 B7

S ummers on Snoqualmie Summit are perhaps only slightly surpassed by spring and fall on the east side of the Cascade Range. Located a few miles east of Snoqualmie Pass, Kachess Ridge is situated neatly beneath the rain shadow of the Cascades, making this a drier trail than other rides on the neighboring western slopes.

Along the Interstate 90 corridor, nature and man have been at odds for some time. The forests surrounding this corridor resemble a colossal checkerboard, especially apparent when flying overhead. Squared sections of forest land, thick with trees, lie quietly next to other square sections stripped bare. A product of pure economics, the checkerboard exists not because of some devastating arboreal disease, but from years and years of

logging. The checkerboard effect now threatens the life of the forest and the trails recreationalists enjoy.

In 1864 President Abraham Lincoln offered over 40 million acres of federal land to the Northern Pacific Railroad (now part of the Burlington Northern system) in an effort to see that rail was extended west of Lake Superior to the Puget Sound. As it was figured, for every mile of track Northern Pacific laid, the federal government gave 40 square miles of land. The land grant was divided into alternating square-mile sections, mostly along the 2,000 miles of track. In the years since the agreement, the Plum Creek Timber Company, a subsidiary of Burlington Northern, has logged a

MilesDirections

0.0 START riding from the parking area back to FS 4818 along the dirt road. Turn right onto FS 4818.

2.2 Pass FS 111.

4.1 Pass the Boeing Overnight Camp.

6.0 Turn right on FS 4824.

7.6 The road switches back to the right, with an intersecting road on the left. Keep right.

8.0 Veer left at the switchback. Pass through the logging gate.

9.1 At the dirt spur road, continue on the left fork up the more noticeably traveled road.

10.0 Take the right fork up a really short, steep section.

11.0 Arrive at the saddle. Follow the road to the right. Look for the Kachess Ridge Trail (Trail 1315)—it can be difficult to find. *[Note. If you get to the parking area*

at the end of the road you've gone too far. FYI. Looking due south, there is another small saddle below the rocky crag. That is your destination. The trail intersection from the left is the Kachess Ridge Trail coming off Thorp Mountain.] Keep right.

11.5 Hike-a-bike!

14.8 Cross Silver Creek.

17.9 Take another switchback down left into the trees. *[Note. There is a blocked trail intersection here. If you take it you'll dead-end at a viewpoint of the I-90 corridor.]*

18.5 Finish more switchbacks heading down into the drainage.

19.0 Reach the end of Trail 1315. Stay on the main dirt road. Ride south back to the power lines.

19.7 Turn right and head west to reach your car.

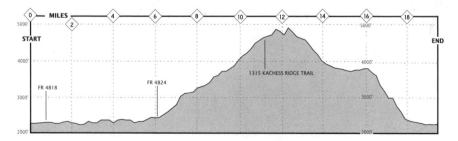

large percentage of their first holdings—bringing the checkerboard to life.

When the federal government began creating the national parks, large portions of land had to be traded between the government and the railroad.

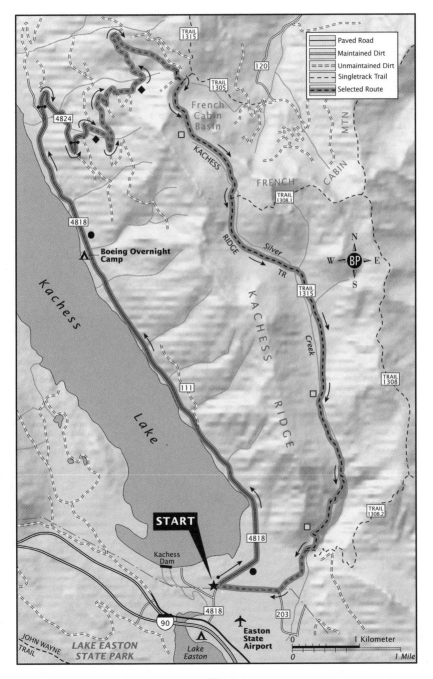

Significant stretches of parks like Mount Rainier National Park were owned by the Northern Pacific Railroad. In order to secure the land, the government had to exchange what were markedly treeless tracks around Mount Rainier for perfectly lush federal lands along the western Cascades. Northern Pacific then harvested the new squares of federal lands and promptly extended their railroads to the park systems to carry tourists.

When you fly over the Interstate 90 corridor, which travels east to west, you'll see where the Plum Creek Timber Company has logged this sprawling area for years. The alternating federal lands, now controlled by the U.S. Forest Service, have also seen their share of logging. Spirited discussions continue between loggers and environmentalists, and with every new proposal there's still hope that before the Pacific Northwest's last 15 percent of

old-growth forests are cleared, a peaceful balance between consumption and conservation can be found.

Responsible bicycling is mandatory in the area around Kachess Ridge. Walk carefully around areas where erosion is already taking its toll. As mountain bikers, we must do what we can to preserve these vanishing landscapes for future use and enjoyment. If that means walking our bikes every once in awhile, then that's the least we can do. Enjoy the incredible views, challenging terrain, and peaceful quiet. It's hard to believe you're so close to the big city.

The ride begins north of the parking area up Forest Service Road 4818. The climb starts on Forest Service Road 4824, eventually leading to overlooks of Lake Kachess (*kachess* meaning "many fish" or "more fish" in the native Yakima Indian language). Anglers will certainly appreciate knowing that neighboring Lake *Keechelus* means "fewer fish."

Finishing the rigorous climb, there is still a short, steep section of hike-a-bike to shoulder your bike down and then back up to reach the saddle. Once at the top, the true screaming-fun singletrack begins. You'll fly through meadows and pass over a couple of creeks for seven miles or so. Moving onto switchbacks running through the woods, you'll really pick up the pace. Technically challenging, these trails are more easily negotiated by the advanced mountain biker. When you hit the trailhead at the bottom, you're done. Just follow the dirt road back out to the power lines and to your car.

Ride Information

📞 Trail Contacts:
Snoqualmie Ranger Station, North Bend, WA (425) 888–1421

🕐 Schedule:
Open June through November, depending on snowfall

💲 Fees:
$5 per car, per day ($30 for an annual pass)

❓ Local Information:
Upper Snoqualmie Valley Chamber of Commerce, North Bend, WA (425) 888–4440

📍 Local Events/Attractions:
Grundig/UCI World Cup Race and State Championships, in June, The Summit at Snoqualmie, WA (425) 434–7669 • Snoqualmie Days and Bike Ride, in August, Snoqualmie, WA (425) 888–4440 • Snoqualmie Falls, Fall City, WA (425) 396–5200 • Snoqualmie Winery, Snoqualmie Pass, WA (360) 888–4000

🚲 Local Bike Shops:
Valley Bike Rack, Snoqualmie, WA (425) 888–4886 • Recycle Bicycle Shops, Ellensburg, WA (509) 925–3326

🗺 Maps:
USGS maps: Kachess Lake, WA

Cedar Creek Out-and-Back

Ride Summary

This picturesque trail provides a great diversion if you're heading east to Winthrop on the North Cascades Highway. Riding between the steep walls of the Gardner and Silver Star Mountains, the first few miles are steady and tough up to Cedar Creek Falls. The trail gets even a little tougher after that, but only briefly. The rest of the route is beautiful singletrack all the way across the valley and back.

Ride Specs

Start: From Cedar Creek Trail trailhead off WA 20
Length: 15.2-mile out-and-back
Approximate Riding Time: 3 hours
Difficulty Rating: Advanced, due to technical singletrack and climbing
Terrain: Smooth singletrack and two miles of technical singletrack through a wooded creek bed and deep into the forests of northcentral Washington
Land Status: National forest
Nearest Town: Mazama, WA
Other Trail Users: Hikers, equestrians, and cross-country skiers
Canine Compatibility: Dogs permitted
Wheels: Front suspension recommended

Getting There

From Winthrop: Follow WA 20 west for 17 miles, just past Mazama. Turn left at the sign for the Cedar Creek Trail (on the south side of the highway). Turn left again onto gravel FS 200, just west of the Early Winters Visitor Center. Follow the gravel road 0.9 miles to the trailhead parking area to the far left of the gravel pit. **DeLorme: Washington Atlas & Gazetteer:** Page 113 D5

Once you've passed the crests of Rainy and Washington Pass on Washington 20 (the North Cascades Highway), heading east into the Methow Valley (pronounced MET–how), you'll stumble upon the charming, Wild West community of Winthrop. The town is situated at the confluence of the Chewuch and Methow rivers. The great Methow River is an unusually straight and steep-walled river carving its way eastward through the Methow Valley. Both the river and the valley are the product of a glacier on the move during the last ice age.

Winthrop looks like a classically Western town—more the result of a 1960s facelift than a natural evolution, but attractive nonetheless. Between the wooden sidewalks and the false storefronts, you feel transported back in

Cedar Falls.

time. There's a saloon, a general store, and even hitching posts, should you need to tether your horse. But what makes this town special is its people, as friendly and laid back as any you can imagine. People who come to Winthrop come for its scenery, spectacular weather, and wide-open spaces, far away from the pulse of big city life.

The hillsides rising above the Methow Valley are dotted with a few houses and B&Bs and filled with miles of recreational trails. In an effort to ensure the integrity of these trails, a private, non-profit consortium of skiers, businesses, and families that promote non-motorized trail recreation came together to form the Methow Valley Sport Trails Association (MVSTA). The organization's goal is to "establish the finest and most interesting year-round trail recreation area in the United States." And they're doing a great job at it. Working with the U.S. Forest Service and many private landowners, the MVSTA is able to build new trails and repair older or abandoned trails in the national forest and on private property. In many cases, trails on private land connect with the national forest trails making the network in the Methow Valley quite extensive.

When heading to Winthrop for a weekend of mountain biking, Cedar Creek is a good place to start. If you're entering from the west, the Cedar Creek Trail is right on your way. The trail is just a little below Washington

MilesDirections

0.0 START from the Cedar Creek Trail (Trail 476) trailhead and head up the semi-steep singletrack.

1.8 Pass a pull-off with a view of Cedar Falls on your left.

4.1 The trail opens up into a clear meadow. *[FYI. The grove of aspens is gorgeous here in the fall.]*

4.2 Stay right at the fork. *[FYI. The left trail leads to a nice campsite.]*

5.1 Cross over a small creek.

6.0 Begin a series of creek crossings that stretch for 0.2 miles.

6.5 Cross a large creek crossing next to Cedar Creek.

6.7 Cross an even larger creek with beautiful falls.

7.6 Turn around here. *[**Note.** You're now entering the Lake Chelan-Sawtooth Wilderness, which is closed to bicycles at the ridge top.]*

15.2 Arrive back at the trailhead.

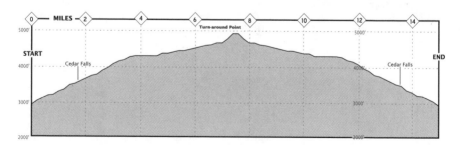

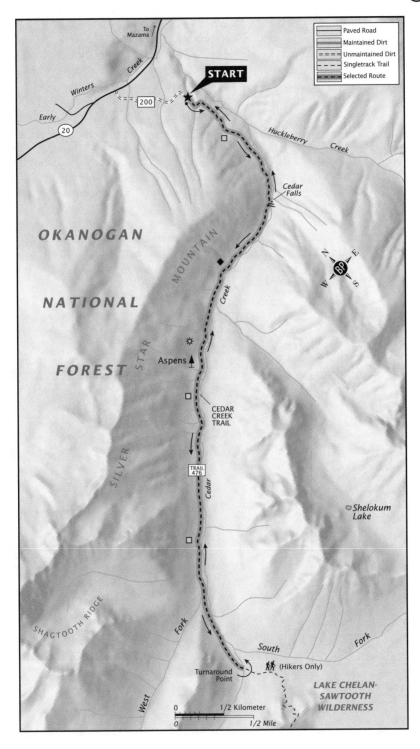

Paved Road
Maintained Dirt
Unmaintained Dirt
Singletrack Trail
Selected Route

To Mazama

START

Winters Creek

Early

20

200

Huckleberry Creek

Cedar Falls

OKANOGAN

NATIONAL

FOREST

MOUNTAIN

SILVER STAR

Creek

Aspens

CEDAR CREEK TRAIL

TRAIL 476

Cedar

N
E
BP
W
S

Shelokum Lake

SHAGTOOTH RIDGE

West Fork

South Fork

(Hikers Only)

Turnaround Point

LAKE CHELAN-SAWTOOTH WILDERNESS

0   1/2 Kilometer
0   1/2 Mile

Pass—a great place to stop and enjoy the view. Among the tallest peaks nearby are the Early Winters Spires (7,806 feet)—home of the Liberty Bell, a popular and moderately difficult rock climbing area. The hike to the Early Winters Spires makes a great short side-trip on your way to Winthrop. Head up the Blue Lake Trail, one mile west of Washington Pass. Proceed 1.5 miles up the trail to the open area below the lower slabs of the Liberty Bell.

The Cedar Creek Trail, a little farther east of Washington Pass, is heavily wooded and runs right next to Cedar Creek. In the summer, this ride will be a lot cooler than the trails down in Winthrop. The closer you get to town, the more arid the climate becomes. The first two miles of this ride are great for warming up. The next two, however, are highly technical, due to some incredibly rocky conditions. This short, two-mile section is challenging, especially when it's wet—which is a polite way of saying it's not that much fun. At the 1.7-mile point you come to a fantastic, roaring waterfall. You'll want to stop here for a rest before hitting the toughest part of the ride. If you climb down to the river from the trail, be careful; it's a steep embankment. The water crashing against the rocks below makes it hard to hear anything else once you get down there.

Most people drop out when they reach this section of the ride, but they're missing some of the best trail to come. The next three to four miles are wonderful, with very few rocky sections. The trail ahead is virtually untouched by anyone other than hikers, leaving it peacefully quiet and as smooth as a bike path. There are times when you'll be covered in the shelter and shade of the woods, and others when the trail is in the wide-open, giving a picture-perfect view of the interior of the valley and its steep walls. In the fall, the colors of the trees along the mountainsides are quite spectacular—the bright yellow larch and aspen are easy to spot.

Just after crossing the river—which is marked—you'll have to turn around and head back because the trail heads up the mountain and into Wilderness Area (where bicycles are not allowed). The trail on the return trip is a gas, especially the last two miles that were so tough to climb in the beginning.

Ride Information

◗ Trail Contacts:

U.S. Forest Service, Winthrop, WA (509) 996–4000 or *www.fs.fed.us* • **Okanogan National Forest,** Okanogan, WA (509) 826–3275 • **Winthrop Ranger District,** Winthrop, WA (509) 997–2131 • **Report forest fires:** 1–800–562–6010

◷ Schedule:

Open roughly June through October

⑤ Fees/Permits:

No fees or permits required

❓ Local Information:

Winthrop Chamber of Commerce Information Station, Winthrop, WA (509) 996–2125 • **Methow Valley Visitors Center,** Winthrop, WA (509) 996–4000

◉ Local Events/Attractions:

The Bone Shaker Mountain Bike Bash (a NORBA-sanctioned race), in May, Winthrop, WA (509) 535–4757 • **Winthrop Rodeo Days,** in May and Labor Day, Winthrop, WA (509) 996–2125 • **Mountain Triathlon,** second Sunday in September, Winthrop, WA (509) 996–3287 • **Methow Valley Mountain Bike Festival,** in early October, Winthrop, WA (509) 996–3287 • **"October-West,"** 2nd weekend in October, Winthrop, WA (509) 996–2125 • **MVSTA Ski & Sports Swap,** in November, Winthrop, WA (509) 996–3287

⊕ Organizations:

Methow Valley Sport Trails Association, Winthrop, WA (509) 996–3287 or *www.mvsta.com* – *Call 1–800–682–5787 for a seasonal snow report.*

⊛ Local Bike Shops:

Winthrop Mountain Sports, Winthrop, WA (509) 996–2886 • **D-Tours Bike & Board Shop,** Mazama, WA (509) 996–3673

Ⓝ Maps:

USGS maps: Mazama, WA; Silver Start, WA

The Cascade Loop Highway

The Cascade Loop is considered one of the hallmark driving trips in Washington. Practically speaking, it's the quickest way to get across the Cascades. What it actually amounts to is a series of connected highways. All told, the loop travels for some 400 miles past snow-covered peaks, pristine mountain views, and small, friendly, western towns.

Technically, the loop begins (or ends) with a ferry ride between Mukilteo and Whidbey Island. Washington 525 picks up at the ferry landing and runs half the length of Whidbey Island (which, incidentally, is the longest island in the continental United States.) before joining with Washington 20. Traveling east, Washington 20 crosses the Northern Cascades and safely deposits you in the Methow Valley. The towns of Winthrop and Twisp are the first real pit stops. The interesting name *twisp* comes from a slightly modified form of the Native American term *twips*, which means "yellow jackets." Apparently this area was once loaded with them.

Continuing east, leaving the mountains behind, Washington 20 merges with Washington 153 and U.S. Route 97, along the mighty Columbia River and into the Wenatchee Valley, the Apple Capital of the world. Here, the sun seems to shine a little brighter than it does on the western side of the Cascades. It's as if by crossing the mountains you've stepped into another world—a world of perpetual sunshine. The mountains form a physical barricade to the moisture that collects along the coast, making the eastern regions of the state ideal for growing all kinds of produce, especially crunchy, mouth-watering apples.

Turning back into the sunset, the Cascade Loop heads west leading directly through the towns of Cashmere and Leavenworth along U.S. Route 97 to U.S. Route 2. Leavenworth is a Bavarian village with Old World charm. It's also a gateway to the curvaceous Tumwater Canyon. Rapids and waterfalls adorn this spectacular section of highway. Be sure to use the pull-offs to get a good look at the raging Wenatchee River below.

After a most scenic drive, you'll arrive at the 4,061-foot high Stevens Pass—named after John F. Stevens, the builder of the Panama Canal. You're now in the heart of the Cascade Mountains and at the top of a great winter ski resort, Stevens Pass Ski Area. Not much biking is done at the resort itself, but Nordic trails just to the east of the pass are open to mountain bikers in the summer. To complete the Cascade Loop, U.S. Route 2 heads into the Everett area north of Seattle. Traveling north on I-5 will lead back up to Washington 20, beginning the loop again.

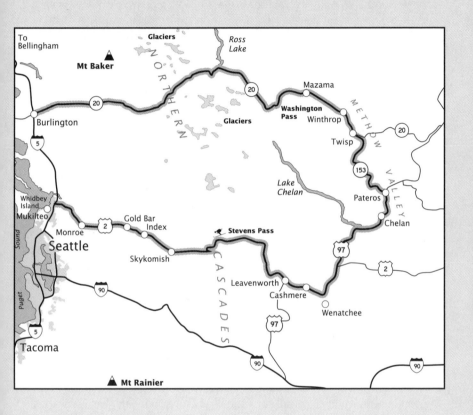

Along the Cascade Loop we've mapped a series of rides between Wenatchee and the Puget Sound that give a great sampling of what's available to mountain bikers. One of the most distinctive places to ride off the Loop is along Washington 20 about 20 miles east of Washington Pass, outside of Winthrop, back in the Methow Valley. There are tons of great rides in this area: Cedar Creek, Lightning Creek—just to name a couple from this book. But there's also Buck Mountain, Goat Wall, and many others that are waiting to be discovered.

Honorable Mentions

Northwest Washington

Compiled here is an index of great rides in the Northwest region that didn't make the A-list this time around but deserve recognition. Check them out and let us know what you think. You may decide that one or more of these rides deserves higher status in future editions or, perhaps, you may have a ride of your own that merits some attention.

(A) Lake Padden Park

Located near Bellingham and loaded with trails, this area offers rides for all skill levels. Warm up on the easy lake loop, following a wide gravel path for close to four miles. Or, increase the workout by heading up the trails into the hills, passing power lines along the marked trails. For an example of an especially challenging route, travel about one mile down the singletrack from the trailhead. Turn right at the intersection to follow a series of steep, banking switchbacks that are sure to test your technical skills. Always within a few miles of the parking lot, it's difficult to get lost.

Take I-5 to Bellingham. Exit at N. Lake Samish Road. Turn right on Samish Way, heading north away from Samish Lake. Travel for two and a half miles to the east entrance of Lake Padden Park. Turn left into the park. Follow the road to the end to the trailhead. For more information, there is a large, outdoor park map, or contact Bellingham Parks and Recreation at (360) 676–6985. See *DeLorme: Washington Atlas & Gazetteer:* Page 109, C5.

(B) Bellingham's Interurban Trail

An easy, seven-mile trail, the Interurban is a refurbished railroad grade that travels from the waterfront of Bellingham to the beaches at Larrabee State Park. This popular course is open to skaters, walkers, and joggers. In town, you can pick up the trail at Fairhaven Park, or farther east at Arroyo Park. Follow the trail, running parallel to Chuckanut Drive, on mostly level pathways all the way to Larrabee State Park, then turn around and head back.

Take I-5 north to WA 11 north into Bellingham. Turn right into Fairhaven Park. Call the Larrabee State Park at (360) 676–2093. See *DeLorme: Washington Atlas & Gazetteer:* Page 109, C5.

(C) Cranberry Lake in Anacortes

2,200 acres of community forest land surround Cranberry Lake (funded by local Anacortes tax payers), offering a great spot to stretch your legs while you wait for the ferry during the San Juan Islands' summer rush. Be aware that some trails prohibit bikes, so please heed the signs. Several moderate to advanced trails create loops ranging in length from a couple of miles to 20. The connecting trails are perfect for improvising your own route. From the Anacortes-Sidney, B.C. ferry terminal, ride a couple of miles up Oak Street (which turns into 12ᵗʰ). Turn right at Georgia Avenue and right onto West 4th Street. Follow that up to Cranberry Lake. For more information, contact Bob Vaux, Operations and Forest Lands Manager of Anacortes Parks and Recreation (360) 299–1953. Maps and info packets are available at many local businesses on Main Street, including Anacortes Cyclery and the Anacortes Chamber of Commerce Visitor Center. See *DeLorme: Washington Atlas & Gazetteer*: Page 94, A3.

(D) Sadie Creek

This area has two loop options, one that's moderate and another that's a little more difficult. After driving out past Port Angeles, time may dictate which loop you take. The longer, more difficult loop is about 18 miles long. Start at the parking area and take the trail heading into the forest. Turn right down to Sadie Creek, crossing the creek at the bottom. Turn right on the old road for a half-mile, then pick up the trail again on the left. Turn right at FS 3040 where the trail ends and then turn left on FS S1150 toward the Sadie Creek Trail, following the signs. Veer right with the path and begin the climb. Keep right at the Y-intersection, riding up steep, rocky doubletrack. Come upon harrowing switchbacks and veer right again at the next "Y" in the road. Arriving at the ridge after only four miles, the trail continues along the ridge over at least a dozen

summits. After another four miles, veer right at the Y-intersection and begin to descend, finally. Turn left of FS WA 100. Turn right on FS 1450. After a mile, turn left following a trail down the valley into the woods. Turn left on the old road. At the end, turn left up the logging road. At the Y-intersection, stay straight, following the old road. Turn left on the steep course descending to Susie Creek. Cross the logging road and follow the power lines. Turn left at the top, pass a spur and head down, staying right at the intersection. Continue on FS WA 1000 and ride ahead, crossing FS 3040 and onto the trail into the woods. Veer right to the parking lot and the end of the ride.

To ride the shorter, more moderate, 11-mile loop, begin at the same trail from the parking area. Cross FS 3040 on FS WA 1000. Stay left at the "Y" in the road and again at the spur. Climbing, veer left again where the road divides. Turn right onto the old road. Stay straight, cross Susie Creek, and ride up the valley. Turn right where the road ends, then right again back to the old road. Catch the trail on the right climbing just ahead. Turn right when the path ends, continuing up the logging road. Turn right back onto FS PA 1000. After about two miles, the road divides. Follow the left fork, even though it looks much less traveled. Two miles ahead, turn left at the intersection, cross FS 3040 and follow the trail back to the parking area.

From Port Angeles, head west on U.S. 101 then west on WA 112 to FS 3040. For more information, contact the Department of Natural Resources in Forks at (360) 374–6131 or 1–800–527–3305. See **DeLorme: Washington Atlas & Gazetteer:** Page 92, D2.

(E) Tahuya River Ride

Lots of racing goes on in Tahuya State Forest. Miles of trail await the beginner, intermediate, and advanced mountain biker. For a 10 to 12-mile moderate loop, take the Tahuya River Trail north from the campground to Twin Lakes Road and turn left. Quickly join the Howell Lake Trail on the left. Follow this rolling route all the way to the Howell Lake Loop, crossing both Bennettsen Lake Road and Belfair-Tahuya Road. Ride out to Howell Lake and continue until reaching Belfair-Tahuya Road again. Turn right on the road briefly and catch the Tahuya River Trail again, descending for about two miles back to the campground.

From Bremerton take WA 304 to WA 3. Follow to WA 300 at Belfair keeping to the north side of Hood Canal. Turn right on Sand Hill Road and left onto Goat Ranch Road. Continue to Tahuya River Road and park at the campground. For detailed maps, call the Department of Natural Resources at (360) 825–1631 or 1–800–527–3305. See **DeLorme: Washington Atlas & Gazetteer:** Page 78, D1&2.

(F) Tolt Pipeline Trail

One of the few in-city rides, the Tolt Pipeline Trail actually follows the Seattle waterline along a service road before branching off into a rather brief section of singletrack. About 14 miles round-trip, this is easily considered a moderate ride. From the parking lot, follow the Sammamish River Trail to the right, then turn right again onto the Tolt Pipeline Trail. Follow this over a couple of roads to the end. Turn right onto the singletrack. The course crosses a few more roads and a couple of streams before ending at an overlook of the Snoqualmie River, at which point, simply turn around and head back.

From Kirkland take I-405 to Monroe/Bothell, exiting onto WA 522. Take the Woodinville exit for WA 202. Turn right onto 131st Avenue NE and again at 175th. Turn left onto WA 202, see the Sammamish River Park on the left. For more information, contact King County Parks and Recreation at (206) 296–4136. See **DeLorme: Washington Atlas & Gazetteer:** Page 79, B&C7.

(G) Mad Lake

Bring plenty of water on your trek to Mad Lake. The 20-plus miles of advanced trails are usually hot and dusty and only open during the summer months. The ride begins by climbing up Chikamin Ridge on Trail 1561.

Turn right at the T-intersection onto Trail 1409.1. Ride past Marble Meadow, eventually reaching Mad Lake via a short trail to the right at the top of Mad Meadow. From there, turn around and head back, or wander off on your own adventure to Klone Peak, or loop around to Two Little Lakes.

From Lake Wenatchee, take WA 207 north to Chiwawa Loop Road. Veer right after the Wenatchee River. Turn left onto Chiwawa Road and cross the Chiwawa River. Turn left onto Road 62. Follow that for about 10 miles to Road 6210. Turn right onto 6210, and park about eight miles up at the trail intersection. For more information contact the Lake Wenatchee Ranger District in Leavenworth at (509) 763–3103. See *DeLorme: Washington Atlas & Gazetteer*: Page 82, A3.

(H) Mill Creek Valley

The Stevens Pass Nordic Center is a great area to ride and explore. From the Nordic Center you'll find the Walker Trail and many roads used for skiing in the winter that are smooth and fast for mountain biking.

From U.S. 2, head to Stevens Pass. Just to the east of the pass is the Nordic Center, on the south side of the highway. For more information, call the Stevens Pass Nordic Center (360) 973–2441. See *DeLorme: Washington Atlas & Gazetteer*: Page 81, B&C8.

(I) Money Creek Road #6420

Washington has thousands of logging roads, both abandoned and in-use, which make great rides in and of themselves, or they lead to incredible singletrack. This is one such area. From the Money Creek Campground, ride up FS 6420 (Money Creek Road) to Lake Elizabeth.

From U.S. 2 in Skykomish, head west to the Money Creek Campground. For more information, call the Skykomish Ranger District at (360) 677–2414. See *DeLorme: Washington Atlas & Gazetteer*: Page 81, C5.

(J) The Summit at Snoqualmie/Ski Acres Trails

This steep, rocky area is convenient to Seattle (only about an hour away), and the Ski Acres cross-country trails are great for mountain biking. There are many loop options, but the route around Mount Catherine is particularly good, encompassing beginner, intermediate, and advanced trails. Take the easy way up on the chair lift and turn left on Trail 1A, following it to Trail 15. The routes to the left (14 and 16) are easy to intermediate; the trails to the right (15 and 6) are advanced. All circle around the mountain and connects with intermediate trail 17, so take your pick and have a blast.

From Seattle, take I-90 east to any one of the exits to The Summit. Continue on the summit road a mile or so to Ski Acres on the right. For more information, call The Summit at Snoqualmie at (425) 434–7669, ext. 3372. See *DeLorme: Washington Atlas & Gazetteer*: Page 65, A5.

Southwest
WASHINGTON

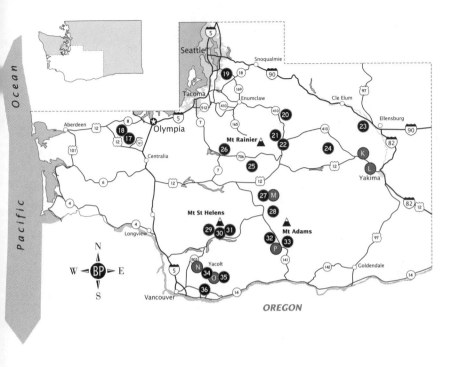

The Rides

Honorable Mentions

Southwest Washington

From Tacoma to the Columbia River and as far east as Yakima, Washington's southwest corner is a geologic playground and home to our own local chunk of mountain biking heaven. South of Interstate 90 sit three mighty volcanoes: Mount Rainier, Mount St. Helens, and Mount Adams. Among them are hundreds of miles of trails, years upon years of history, and countless Native American legends.

Mighty Mount Rainier will always be a point of reference and reverence. Magically evoking deep emotions in the hearts of all who see it, Mount Rainier remains the most majestic landmark in western Washington (to both locals and tourists). The national park surrounding Mount Rainier is off-limits to mountain biking, but around its periphery lay an abundance of trails, each providing incredible views of the glacier-covered behemoth.

Mount St. Helens, the hyperactive little sister of Rainier and Adams, awoke from her centuries-long slumber with a mighty eruption on May 18, 1980. Never before has the word makeover been used to such an extreme. Now, more than 20 years later, life has returned to this place, and Mount St. Helens is officially a National Volcanic Monument. New trails have been built around all sides of the mountain, enabling visitors to witness history in the making as the environment recovers.

Mount Adams, the loner, 50 miles east of St. Helens, is the second-tallest mountain within the Washington Cascade chain. Virtually undiscovered when compared to its sibling volcanoes, Adams keeps to himself, a sentry watching silently over southern Washington. The trails around this mountain are marvelously fun for mountain biking, and the weather is more dependable—more sunshine and less rain—than that farther north. Holding neither national park nor monument titles, Adams is pristine, remote, and the perfect place to "get away."

Capitol Forest–Lost Valley Loop

Ride Summary

This trail is especially nice for riders moving into the intermediate mountain biking skill level. Rolling along Capitol Forests' hillsides, the loop is fast, fun, and non-technical. With a variety of side trails to explore, you can tailor the mileage of this ride to suit any time or fitness constraints.

Ride Specs

Start: From the trailhead at the Mima Falls Campground
Length: 21.2-mile loop
Approximate Riding Time: 3.5–4.5 hours
Difficulty Rating: Moderate, due to hills and tricky terrain when it rains
Terrain: Singletrack and logging roads over rolling hills with a couple of climbs and one great downhill
Land Status: State forest
Nearest Town: Tumwater, WA
Other Trail Users: Hikers and equestrians (no motorized vehicles)
Canine Compatibility: Dogs permitted
Wheels: Come prepared for mud in spring and fall

Getting There

From Olympia: Take Exit 95 off I-5 onto WA 121 west to Littlerock. Follow to the T-intersection of Waddell Creek Road (to the right) and Mima Road (to the left). Turn left on Mima Road. Turn right on Bordeaux Road, then right again onto Marksman Road. Continue to the trailhead at the Mima Falls Campground. *DeLorme: Washington Gazetteer & Atlas:* Page 45 A7

Public Transportation: From the Olympia Transit Center, take Intercity Transit route 98 to 128th Avenue in Littlerock. Now on your bike, follow 128th Avenue to the T-intersection of Waddell Creek Road (to the right) and Mima Road (to the left). Turn left on Mima Road. Turn right on Bordeaux Road and then right again onto Marksman Road. Continue to the Mima Falls Campground and the trailhead. *[**Note.** Due to the bus schedule this is best done as an overnight trip.]*

Capitol Forest makes up some 90,000 acres of the Black Hills of western Washington. Micro-fossils found at the top of Capitol Peak (2,658 feet) remind us that the better part of Washington State spent some time under the waters of the Pacific Ocean. It's taken about 50 million years, through numerous fluctuations in the water level, for these *hills* to reach the heights to which they stand today. And so it's funny to think that these once water-soaked Black Hills got their name when the region's first settlers found the area blackened by forest fires. Where's water when you need it?

MilesDirections

0.0 START from the Mima Falls trailhead and head up Mima Porter Trail (Trail 8).

0.4 The trail turns into doubletrack and intersects with Greenline Trail (Trail 6). Sign reads: "Capital Peak 14.1 miles; Porter Creek Camp 23.5 miles; Wedekind 18.2 miles." Continue left on the Mima Porter Trail toward Mima Falls.

0.5 Keep straight on Trail 8. The Trail 6 is accessed off to the right.

0.7 Reach the intersection for Mima Falls 1.7 miles ahead.

2.1 Arrive at the intersection of Trail 10 and Mima Falls, 0.5 miles ahead. Stay on Trail 8.

2.4 Reach Mima Falls—check out the view!

3.0 Cross road D-6000, the trail begins on the other side.

3.5 Cross road D-6700 going down to Mima Creek.

4.4 Cross Mima Creek on a wooden bridge.

4.8 Come to the intersection of D-5000, climbing up out of Mima Creek.

5.9 You're almost at the top; check out the valley views.

6.3 Cross the road continuing on Trail 8.

6.8 Cross D-4000.

7.1 Arrive at West Mima Road. (See the sign for D-4000.) The trail is at the top of the T-intersection. Keep straight on the Trail 8.

7.7 Turn left at the intersection of Lost Valley Trail (Trail 20) at the T-intersection, staying left on Trail 8.

10.1 Arrive at the intersection of Trail 8. Turn right. Right goes to D-3000.

12.9 Cross a creek and start heading up Trail 6. Trail 8 heads north over D-3000. Continue east on Trail 6, crossing D-4300.

15.5 Reach the intersection with Trail 20. Stay on Green Line Trail 6. Turning right leads back to the trail you came out on.

15.8 Reach an intersection with roads D-4200 and D-4000. Stay east on the Trail 6, passing a sign about no motorized vehicles. Bikes are okay.

16.3 The trail hits D-4200 again and continues on the other side.

16.8 Cross D-4200 to a great downhill. See a great view of Mount Rainier.

17.0 Cross the road again.

17.1 The trail jumps onto the road again. Stay left.

19.2 Come to the junction of Trail 6 and Trail 10. Stay on Trail 6.

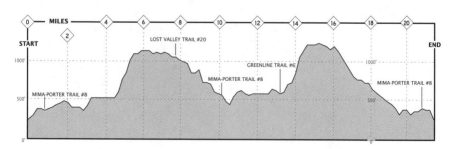

Scattered throughout the southwest side of the Black Hills, where the hills turn to prairie, are the mysterious Mima Mounds—*mysterious* because no one can say with any certainty how they got there. Some suspect that they are Indian burial mounds (though excavations have only revealed gravely soil). And in equal measure, there are those who insist that these mysterious earthen piles were left by prehistoric gophers (apparently the size of a Buick). Less radical theorists assume that they are gravel-filled deposits from the last glacial melt. Though the glacier theory seems perfectly reasonable, the mounds occur in areas that were never glaciated. At any rate, these mounds have excited enough interest to earn designation as a Natural Area Preserve. The mounds range from five to 10 feet tall and 15 to 25 feet

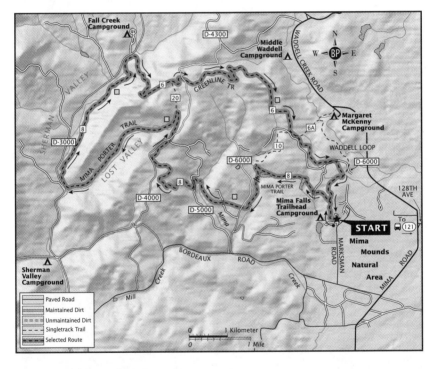

19.7 Come to the intersection with Trail 6A; McKinney Camp is to the left one mile on Trail 6A; Trail 8 is ahead two miles. Stay on Trail 6.

20.1 The trail crosses D-6000.

20.3 Again, the trail crosses D-6000. Arrive at the intersection of the Waddell Loop Trail and Trail 6. Follow Trail 6 to the right, toward the Mima Falls Campground.

20.8 At the next intersection, a trail comes in from behind to the left and joins up with Trail 6. Continue straight.

21.1 The trail crosses a small road section. Continue on the trail across the road to another road crossing cut during recent logging. Just ignore it.

21.2 Come to the intersection of Trail 6 and Trail 8 and the trail back into the campground parking area

in diameter and spread out across several hundred acres near the Black Hills. The best time to visit is from April through June when the wildflowers are in full bloom. Self-guided tours are available.

Capitol Forest is a working forest. Logging has been active here for a number of years, and continues even today. A good number of the trails, rivers, and creeks within the forest are named for historical figures who worked in the logging industry during the late 1800s and early 1900s. Porter Creek and the Porter Creek trails are named for a man who ferried commuters across the Chehalis River. There was also a small logging community (also called Porter), complete with its own mill. Up Bordeaux Road, just past the entrance to the Lost Valley Loop ride, is where the French-born Bordeaux brothers (Joe, Tom, and Leo) started their family logging business

in 1890. Incorporated under the name Mason County Logging Company, the Bordeaux brothers remained in the business for 40 years.

The town of Bordeaux was situated just below the junction of the Big Mima and Little Mima creeks. The Bordeaux family was well known and respected among their peers in the industry, and their sons, reared into the business, took over when their fathers retired. In the early 1920s, the family business grew steadily until logging in general hit hard times. By the 1940s, the forests were stripped of all the old-growth trees, and forest fires began to rage, devastating the Black Hills. Bordeaux, once a prosperous logging town, quickly became a ghost town. The Bordeaux entrance of Capitol Forest still has a few reminders of the logging heyday of the early 1900s. The old concrete vaults mark the site of the Mason County Logging Company store where the Bordeaux's payroll was kept, and the original Bordeaux home still stands nearby. (It's privately owned.)

This is a great loop for the beginner to intermediate mountain biker. There's only a moderate amount of climbing, and the trails are in good shape. The singletrack begins as a smooth, wide trail, shared only with hikers and horseback riders. There are a few rooty sections, but on the whole, this is a well-maintained, fun ride. There are several optional loops, too. Contact the Department of Natural Resources for a free copy of the latest Capitol Forest recreation map.

Ride Information

◐ Trail Contacts:
Department of Natural Resources: (360) 748–2383 or 1–800–527–3305

◑ Schedule:
Open year round

◉ Fees/Permits:
No fees or permits required

❓ Local Information:
Tumwater Chamber of Commerce, Tumwater, WA (360) 357–5153 • Olympia/Thurston County Chamber of Commerce (360) 357–3362

◔ Local Events/Attractions:
Mima Mounds Interpretive Area, near Tumwater, WA www.ohwy.com/wa/m/mimamnap.htm • Tumwater Bluegrass Festival, in May, Tumwater, WA (360) 357–5153

◑ Local Bike Shops:
Deschutes River Cyclery, Tumwater, WA (360) 352–4240 • Bike Stand, Olympia, WA (360) 943–1997 • Bike Tech, Olympia, WA (360) 754–2453 • Cobb Works, Olympia, WA (360) 352–7168 • Falcon Schwinn, Olympia, WA (360) 943–2091

◐ Maps:
USGS maps: Little Rock, WA

Capitol Forest– Larch Mountain Loop

Ride Summary

The mainstay for mountain biking on the western side of the Cascades, Capitol Forest will always be a popular site for recreation. This ride starts with a hefty forest road climb and moves into rolling singletrack at the top. There are many trails out here, so follow the signs and our directions to avoid getting lost.

Ride Specs

Start: From the Rock Candy Mountain entrance to Capitol Forest
Length: 20.5-mile loop
Approximate Riding Time: 2–4 hours
Difficulty Rating: Moderate to Advanced, due to technical sections
Terrain: Fire roads and singletrack (which are frequently muddy) over rolling hills with moderate ascents and semi-technical descents
Land Status: Department of Natural Resources land
Nearest Town: Tumwater, WA
Other Trail Users: Motorcyclists, mostly on weekends
Canine Compatibility: Dogs permitted
Wheels: Front suspension a good idea, and bring mud tires

Getting There

From Olympia: Take Exit 104 off I-5 onto U.S. 101 north, then pick up WA 8 west toward Aberdeen. Follow WA 8 for just over 10 miles. Turn left on Rock Candy Mountain Road (small sign). This road turns into gravel. Turn right at the fork and follow the main gravel road for 0.1 mile to the parking lot. *DeLorme: Washington Atlas & Gazetteer:* Page 45 A7 & 8

Throughout the year riders flock to Capitol Forest, all anxious to take on the challenging trails of Larch Mountain. And yet, as popular as this area is, especially to Seattlites, you'll rarely come across another rider on the trails, even when the parking lot suggests otherwise. This is chiefly because there are so many trails to explore—you'll want a compass and a good map. The trail options may even overwhelm you. Weather is a big fun-factor at Capitol Forest. If it has rained at all in the last 48 hours, you'll more than likely encounter thick, sticky mud. But rain or shine, these wonderful trails provide a great workout.

This ride begins on a logging road with a gradual incline, partially canopied by the forest. The side roads along the way may tempt the curious,

but we recommend staying to the main road for now. At the saddle is a junction of road, hills, and power lines. The signs here will tell you where you are and where you're heading (the Department of Natural Resources is good about keeping you informed). The road takes you to a large clearing resembling a gravel parking lot (it's actually just a large intersection of roads). At the apex you'll see a hillside that seems to be missing a chunk of land. The singletrack trail starts here, across from the parking area, and the loop portion of the Larch Mountain ride begins.

Short climbs and descents, with patches of rooted trail, carry you along as other trails shoot off in a variety of directions, inviting those with a sense of adventure to explore. By the time you're heading down again, you'll hardly realize you've gone 10 miles. Following Capitol Forest's excellent signage, complete the loop and head downhill in the direction of the forest road. If you're up for more, spur off onto more singletrack. It's not all downhill, but you'll still get back pretty quickly.

MilesDirections

0.0 START from the Rock Candy entrance, heading up B-Line Road west.

0.2 Follow B-Line Road past B-8000.

0.7 B-8000 forks left. Stay on B-Line Road.

1.5 Pass the North Rim Trail (Trail 1) crossing.

2.3 Pass a road to the left. Follow the main road.

2.5 Reach Porter Pass, intersecting with road B-5000. Stay on B-Line Road through the saddle. See the North Rim Trail. Ride through the saddle and turn left on B-1000—toward Capitol Peak.

3.1 Turn left on C-4000. B-1000 follows to the right.

5.0 Stay left following C-4000 at the T-intersection.

5.9 Come to an intersection of C-4700 (Army Road). Stay right on C-4000.

6.9 Pass a gravel pit on the left.

7.0 Begin the Larch Mountain Loop. Look for the trail to the left of C-4000 that runs straight through this intersection. The trail goes down into the woods and the loop will take you to the east side of Larch Mountain and back on the west to this very same point. Follow the trail a little ways to the sign reading "Mount Molly Porter #3 for Bordeaux Camp and Mount Molly Camp." At the first intersection, follow Mount Molly Trail (Trail 4). Take the right fork. *[Note. The left fork is Trail 20, which you'll take back to Rock Candy.]*

7.3 The trail hits C-4000 briefly. Follow the trail.

8.9 At the Intersection, Trail 40 heads south to Bordeaux. Follow the right-hand trail, Trail 30, up toward Capitol Peak.

9.3 Arrive at C-4000—stay on the trail.

9.9 Take C-4400 briefly to the rock pile at the main intersection. C-4400 continues left. Turn right up the hill. One hundred yards ahead is a sign for Trail 30. Follow Trail 30.

11.4 Cross a logging road. Keep to the trail.

11.9 Follow Trail 30 straight. *[FYI. The other trail (Trail 3) goes west to Porter Creek Camp.]*

15.0 Turn left at the junction. The trail straight ahead leads to C-4000. The left trail follows C-5000.

15.3 The Larch Mountain Loop comes back to join C-4000 and C-5000. This is where the singletrack began earlier. Head back down the trail turning left instead of right. Follow the signs for Trail 20 down the east side of Rock Candy Mountain. One hundred feet into the trail the left leads to Trail 40 and then to Trail 20.

15.6 Turn left on Trail 20 at the intersection.

17.1 After crossing C-4700, the trail continues across the road about 20 feet away.

17.9 Cross entrance. Continue down toward Rock Candy.

19.0 See North Rim Trail 1. Stay left, keeping the road on your left. Access the trail about 100 feet down the road.

19.3 Come to an intersection. Stay right on the narrower trail.

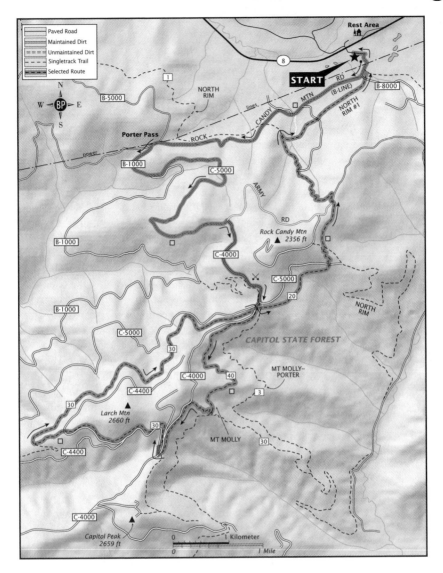

19.4 Cross a small creek.

19.5 Hit a slight junction. Keep to the main trail on the right.

19.8 Cross B-8000, but stay on the trail heading down.

20.4 Cross B-8000 again, staying to the trail.

20.5 Hang a left and head toward the parking lot.

Capitol Forest is situated next door to Washington's capital city, Olympia. Home to some 37,000 people, Olympia has a surprisingly small-town appeal, with friendly faces, elegant homes, and tree-lined streets. Settled in 1846 by Edmund Sylvester and Levi Lathrop Smith (and briefly called Smithfield), Olympia had a meteoric rise to fame. In 1853 it was named the capital of the newly formed Washington Territory. But nearly 40 years passed before Olympia could rest comfortably with the title. Seattle, North Yakima, Port Townsend, Centralia, Vancouver, and Ellensburg all vied for the position. A rather presumptuous Ellensburg even went so far as to build a state capital building. It wasn't until 1889, when Washington became the 42nd state, that the case was finally settled. The White House sent a telegraph to Olympia informing them of their official title and welcoming the state into the Union. Rather unceremoniously, however, they sent the wire collect. Olympia couldn't read the message until the charge was paid. Welcome to the U.S., indeed.

The area in and around Olympia was far from uninhabited prior to Smith and Sylvester's claim. Coastal tribes such as the Chinook, Nisqually, and Puyallup had lived in the region for years. Allowing for this, the U.S. government, with its so-called noble intentions, planned to relocate the tribes (in bulk) to the Olympic Peninsula. The treaties of 1854–55 saw to this, giving the Indians the right to fish, hunt, and gather at all of their "traditional" locations in exchange for U.S. ownership.

Many of the tribes chose to fight rather than sign these treaties. The very next year saw such tribes as the Puyallup and Nisqually still battling American volunteers and the U.S. Army. In August of 1856, another compromise was drawn. Sadly though, this agreement was not much different from the Medicine Creek Treaty of 1855. It's remarkable, then, if not gratifying, to see so many of these tribes still living along rivers and towns that bear their names.

In a grove of trees by Medicine Creek stands the *Treaty Tree*—the site on the Nisqually Delta where the Medicine Creek Treaty of 1855 was signed. Contained in a no-access area of the Nisqually Wildlife Refuge, you can see this tree from a protected area within the wetlands. Take Exit 114 from Interstate 5 and follow the signs for the refuge. There are five and a half miles of walking trail through the delta that are open during daylight hours year-round. Bikes and dogs are not allowed, and there is a small admission fee per family.

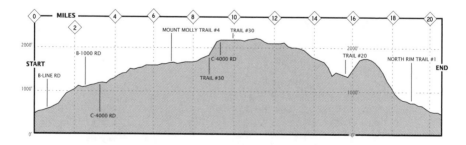

Ride Information

🕐 Trail Contacts:
Department of Natural Resources: (360) 748–2383 or 1–800–527–3305

🕐 Schedule:
Trails closed to ORVs and horses from November 1 through March 31

💲 Fees/Permits:
$2 admission per family

❓ Local Information:
Tumwater Chamber of Commerce, Tumwater, WA (360) 357–5153 • **Olympia/Thurston County Chamber of Commerce,** Olympia, WA (360) 357–3362

💡 Local Events/Attractions:
Coffee Fest and Swap Meet, in March, Olympia, WA (360) 753–8380 • **Art Walk,** in April, Olympia, WA (360) 753–8380 • **Swede Day,** in June, Rochester, WA (360) 786–5595 • **Lake Fair,** in July, Olympia, WA (360) 943–7344 • **Capital Lakefair,** in mid–July, Olympia, WA (360) 943–7344 • **Harbor Days,** in August, Olympia, WA (360) 352–4557 • **Music in the Park,** Saturdays in August, Rochester, WA (360) 786–5595 • **Washington State Capitol Museum,** Olympia, WA (360) 753–2580 • **Longhouse/Evergreen State College Campus,** Olympia, WA (360) 866–6000

🚲 Local Bike Shops:
Deschutes River Cyclery, Tumwater, WA (360) 352–4240 • **Bike Stand,** Olympia, WA (360) 943–1997 • **Bike Tech,** Olympia, WA (360) 754–2453 • **Cobb Works,** Olympia, WA (360) 352–7168 • **Falcon Schwinn,** Olympia, WA (360) 943–2091

🅝 Maps:
USGS maps: Little Rock, WA; Capitol Peak, WA

Tiger Mountain

Ride Summary

One of the few neighborhood trails in the Seattle area still open to mountain bikers, this mountain is very popular and has a lot to offer. The forest roads lead up to the singletrack, which in turn leads to the woods, over technical trails darkened by the thick canopy of trees overhead. The singletrack at Tiger Mountain is a great training ground for those learning how to ride technical trails, and is especially challenging on wet days.

Ride Specs

Start: From the Tiger Mountain parking lot
Length: *Preston/NW Loop:* 11.5 miles; *Short Loop:* 4.0 miles
Approximate Riding Time: *Preston/NW Loop:* 2 hours; *Short Loop:* 30 minutes to 1 hour
Difficulty Rating: *Preston/NW Loop:* Moderate; *Short Loop:* Easy
Terrain: Logging roads and singletrack through second-growth forest, passing recent logging areas
Land Status: Department of Natural Resources land
Nearest Town: Issaquah, WA
Other Trail Users: Hikers and equestrians

Canine Compatibility: Dogs permitted
Wheels: Front suspension recommended, but not required

Getting There

From Seattle: Take I-5 to I-90 east. Take Exit 25 onto WA 18 west toward Auburn and Tacoma. Travel 4.5 miles to the summit and turn right into the parking lot of Tiger Mountain State Forest. *DeLorme: **Washington Atlas & Gazetteer:*** Page 64 A1

S o you've come to Seattle to check out the sights and go for a couple of radical mountain bike rides. You'll need a little elevation training, right? Just pack up the car and head east on Interstate 90; Tiger Mountain is waiting to kick your unsuspecting butt. Part of what are known as the *Issaquah Alps*—a range that's even older than the Cascades—Tiger Mountain is one of Washington's most popular hiking and mountain biking destinations. Greenbelt areas connect it to nearby parks, creating a seemingly endless system of trails and explaining how the town of Issaquah came to be called the *Trailhead City*.

This particular trail is great because it's challenging and not too long. You can ride these trails in any direction depending on the workout you want to achieve. Most trails can be individually covered in a couple of hours—locals use them for after-work night rides. During rainier times, it's

likely to be muddy and slick. The occasional mud-bogs can be very deep and some instances do require a bit of hike-a-biking.

Most of the trails, like this one, start out with a road climb on fire roads no longer open to vehicles. The roads can be rather steep. On the way up, you'll pass a couple of trails that you should definitely explore if you've got the time. After about three miles of climbing, you'll reach the Preston Railroad Trail. It's a bit dark and ominous when the sun is hidden, but you'll be having too good of a time to be bothered by it. The trail is well worn, so there are many exposed roots to catch you if you aren't paying attention. No matter what time of year, there always seems to be standing water somewhere along the way. Just beware—you never really know how deep some of those holes can be.

MilesDirections

Preston/NW Loop (Moderate)

0.0 START from parking lot and take the Tiger Mountain Road on the far right.

2.8 At the T-intersection, turn left onto Road 4000, toward West Tiger Summit. Sign reads: "East Tiger Summit 1.4 miles to the right."

3.2 Turn right onto the Preston Railroad Trail.

4.7 Switchback left. There are old trails dying in the woods. Keep to the main trail.

5.2 Switchback right.

5.7 Switchback left.

6.0 Switchback right again.

7.0 Arrive at Road 5500/Crossover Road. Turn left heading downhill.

7.1 Turn right at the T-intersection onto Eastside Road.

9.1 Arrive at the NW Timber Trail, turn right at the fence.

11.5 Reach the bottom of NW Timber Trail at the Tiger Mountain Road. Turn left for the parking lot.

Short Loop (Easy)

0.0 Head up the West Side Road to the left of the gate at the end of the parking lot.

1.5 Turn right on the Iverson Railroad Trail.

3.5 Turn left at the NW Timber Trail to head back to Tiger Mountain Road, or turn right onto West Side Road. At Tiger Mountain Road turn right toward the parking lot.

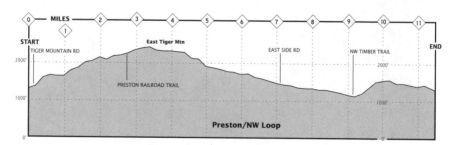

On the southeast side, you'll catch the Northwest Timber Trail, which is comfortably smooth. It takes you into a ravine-like section with a couple of fun surprises. Watch out for hikers, in particular, along this trail. Since it's in such good condition, it seems to be a favorite of hikers. There are horses to contend with as well, so be courteous. Some of these horses are unfamiliar with mountain bikes and can become skittish. Always dismount and stand between the horse and your bike as you pass.

This is one of the few remaining trails still open to mountain bikers in the Seattle area. The Backcountry Bicycle Trails Club (BBTC) has been fighting for some time to keep the Tiger Mountain trails open to mountain bikers. Thus far, they've been successful, but biking in this area always seems to hang in the balance. The BBTC and the Sierra Club will have the most current information about which trails in the area are open, closed, or under construction.

Except for the road climb up, the trails are protected by thick forest. It gets dark rather quickly at the end of the day. Make sure you are prepared

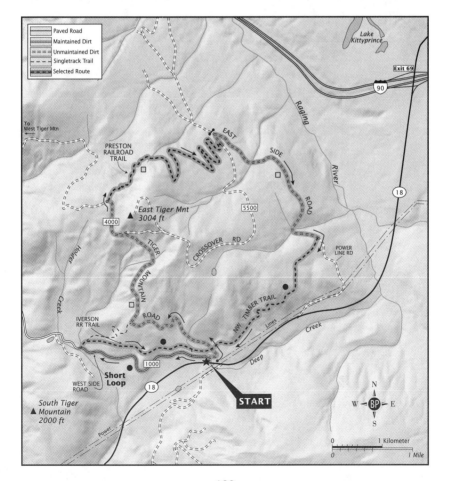

for bad weather—around here you never know when it will hit. This area is known as a convergence zone, where low-pressure zones that rise counterclockwise from Alaska and Canada converge with high-pressure zones that fall clockwise from the mid-Pacific. As the two come together over the region in and around Seattle, they produce cloudy conditions and—you guessed it—rain!

Don't let a little rain get you down though. There's plenty of Gore-Tex® to go around. And after your ride, you can always go for a little of Seattle's

A common trail hazard.

liquid sunshine. Depending on your taste, you could go for a coffee or a beer or some juice—Seattle aims to please. There are plenty of juicebars and great coffeehouses in virtually every neighborhood; this is, after all, the home of the Starbucks® revolution. And there are just as many local brewpubs and breweries, many of which offer daily tours. You might try the Redhook Brewery (where they've redefined the term "micro") or the Hales Brewery—just to name a few.

Ride Information

🌕 Trail Contacts:

Department of Natural Resources: (360) 825–1631 or 1–800–527–3305 • **Backcountry Bicycle Trails Club:** (206) 283–2995 or *www.bbtc.org*

🕐 Schedule:

Open April 15 through October 15 (closed in winter)

❓ Local Information:

Seattle/King County Convention and Visitors Bureau: (206) 461–5840 • **Issaquah Visitor Information Center,** Issaquah, WA (425) 392–7024

💡 Local Events/Attractions:

Seattle International Film Festival, in mid May to early June, Seattle, WA (206) 324–9996 • **University District**

Street Fair, in May, Seattle, WA (206) 547–4417 • **Northwest Folklife Festival,** over Memorial Day weekend, Seattle, WA (206) 684–7300• **Bite of Seattle,** in mid July, Seattle, WA (206) 684–7200 • **Seafair,** from mid July to mid August, Seattle, WA (206) 728–0123 • **Bumbershoot,** over Labor Day weekend, Seattle, WA (206) 684–7200

🚲 Local Bike Shops:

The Bicycle Center of Issaquah, Issaquah, WA (425) 392–4588

Ⓝ Maps:

USGS maps: Hobart, WA; Fall City, WA

Ranger Creek

Ride Summary

On a quest for the quintessential mountain bike ride? You just might find what you're searching for at Ranger Creek. Combining every element of the "ideal" ride, this course includes a couple of creek crossings, a long road climb, and technical singletrack with lots of roots, rocks, switchbacks, drop-offs, thread-the-needle gaps, and steep sides. Some trail sections are smooth, while others are a little rough. Stunning scenery, elevation gains, and an incredible descent are just a small selection of what you'll get with the Ranger Creek Ride northeast of Mount Rainier.

Ride Specs

Start: From FS 72
Length: 23.0-mile loop
Approximate Riding Time: 4–5 hours
Difficulty Rating: Difficult due to high elevations and challenging singletrack downhill
Trail Surface: Forest Service road, singletrack, and short paved road section over extreme hills, occasionally under the cover of trees
Land Status: National forest
Nearest Town: Greenwater, WA
Other Trail Users: Hikers and equestrians
Canine Compatibility: Dogs not permitted
Wheels: Front suspension recommended

Getting There

From Puyallup: Take WA 167 to WA 410 East. Follow WA 410 for 38.2 miles to FS 72. Turn left and go 50 yards. Park on the side of the road at the fork. The ride begins to the right up FS 72. ***DeLorme: Washington Atlas & Gazetteer:*** Page 64 D4

> *"A wilderness, in contrast with those areas where man and his own works dominate the landscape, is hereby recognized as an area where the earth and its community of life are untrammeled by man, where man himself is a visitor who does not remain..."*
>
> (from the Wilderness Act of 1964)

I f you're looking for a long, technically challenging ride, with a good road climb and hair-ball descents, then you'll love Ranger Creek. Roots, rocks, switchbacks, drop-offs, thread-the-needle gaps, steep sides—this trail has it all. While some sections are carpet-smooth, others will rattle the bolts right out of your joints. And as always, you can bank on stunning scenery: an array of Douglas fir, western red cedar, and western hemlock, all intertwined with glacier-fed creeks and rivers and all in the shadow of the magnificent Mount Rainier.

Forest Service Road 72 takes you up the first three miles of the ride. You'll encounter challengingly steep inclines, with the exception of a small

descent traveling south to north along the first ridge. Lightning Creek intersects your path a few times in the first few miles. The road up is fairly smooth, packed with dirt and gravel. The elevation tops out around 5,500 feet. Bring appropriate clothing in case the weather decides to take a turn. Packing an extra shirt is a good idea, too. After crossing Ranger Creek, several rather steep switchbacks will initiate your final descent.

If you take out a state map, you'll notice a lot of land in this region tagged "Wilderness Area." You may not realize it, but mountain bikes are not permitted within these areas. The reason for this is the Wilderness Act of 1964, signed into law by President Lyndon Johnson. This act spawned a program called the National Wilderness Preservation System. The charge of this system, to a certain degree, is to keep "man" out of prescribed areas, so that the wilderness may remain wild. There is no building of roads or logging of trees

MilesDirections

0.0 START from the Y-intersection where you parked, heading up FS 72.

1.5 Pass FS 7290.

2.4 Pass an unmarked road on the right. Stay straight, crossing Lightning Creek a couple of times.

3.5 Cross Boundary Creek at 3,750 feet—you've covered about 1,500 feet already.

4.1 Cross around the west end of the ridge, and begin heading southeast.

5.2 Pass spur roads on the right and left. Continue straight on the most traveled road.

5.3 Another spur road is on the right. Keep straight. See the Viewpoint sign ahead of the intersection.

5.5 Pass a viewpoint on the left side of the road, with views of Mount Stuart, The Enchantments, and Mount Pilchuck.

5.6 Pass another unsigned spur on the right.

6.4 Pass a spur from behind on the right. The sign for FS 72 assures that you're on the correct route. Continue climbing.

6.8 Pass another spur from behind on the right. Head downhill a bit around the next drainage.

6.9 Pass another spur.

7.1 Pass signed FS 138.

7.4 FS 72 begins to descend. Take FS 7250 on the right, climbing up.

7.7 Pass spur FS 102 on the right. Stay left on FS 7250 through a road cut.

8.6 At the Y-intersection, stay to the right continuing on FS 7250. The left is FS 110.

9.6 Come to a four-way intersection. Stay straight, gently climbing up FS 210. The right goes down. The left doubles back behind you and ends shortly.

10.2 FS 210 ends at the Dalles Ridge Trail (Trail 1173). Climb up the trail into the ridge.

10.7 Look for the sharp right-hand turn for Ranger Creek Trail (Trail 1197)—it's hard to catch so beware. Trail 1173 continues straight ahead. The Ranger Peak viewpoint is 3.0 miles ahead; the White River Trail, 6.0 miles; and WA 410, 7.0 miles. Hang onto your brakes; there are some quick switchbacks coming up.

11.9 Arrive at Ranger Creek Shelter. The trail is to the left in the back. In the front is the Palisades Trail (Trail 1198). Follow Trail 1197 left behind the cabin, downhill.

14.2 Come to a junction for Ranger Peak viewpoint. Continue down the Trail 1197.

16.8 At the three-way intersection, take the hard right, down the White River Trail (Trail 1199). Don't go straight unless you want to take WA 410 back now.

16.9 Come to a new spur down to WA 410. Continue along the trail paralleling WA 410 northwest.

17.0 Trail 1199 comes right up on WA 410. Since they've widened FS 410, the trail runs right next to the highway. Ride along Trail 1199, toward Camp Shepherd (2.0 miles ahead). The trail basically parallels the highway. Keep the highway on your left.

17.3 Pass a small wooden bridge over a creek. Continue rambling next to WA 410.

17.6 Cross another creek.

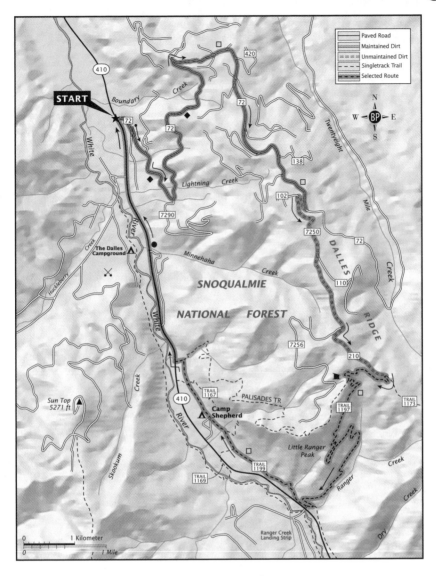

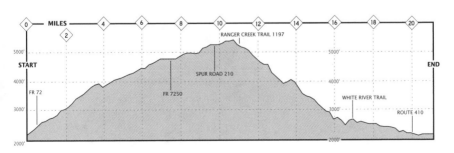

18.2 Come to a junction with the Buck Creek Trail (Trail 1169) on the left. To the right is Snoquera Falls Trail (Trail 1167). Skookum Flats is across the highway. Continue straight on Trail 1199.

18.5 Reach the junction with the Snoquera Falls Loop (closed to bikes) at a four-way intersection.

18.6 Cross a bridge and come to a four-way intersection. Go straight. The left heads to WA 410, the right goes to the falls.

18.7 Come to another four-way at Camp Shepherd. Take the soft right, staying right of the camp. If you start climbing

too much you're not on the correct trail. Or, you can head left to WA 410 and ride back.

18.8–18.9 Cross three clearing sections.

19.4 Come to another four-way. Stay straight. Trail 1167 is looping into the White River Trail again here.

19.8 Pass Dalles Creek Trail (Trail 1169) back from the right. Go straight, following down the side of the drainage. Turn right on Powerline Way, heading to WA 410.

20.0 Turn right on WA 410 for a paved, gentle downhill back to FS 72.

23.0 Turn right on FS 72.

---

within the wilderness areas, and anything mechanized is forbidden—from chainsaws to mountain bikes (unfortunately).

Washington has 4,287,875 acres of designated wilderness areas—724,700 acres of which are in the Mount Baker-Snoqualmie National Forest. The Norse Peak Wilderness Area—one of eight in the Mount Baker-Snoqualmie National Forest—has 51,300 acres of high ridges, mountain lakes, and forested valleys—and approximately 52 miles of hiking trails. This wilderness is home, in part, to the famous Pacific Crest Trail that stretches a staggering 2,600 miles from Mexico to Canada—through four of Washington's national forests and two of its national parks. Recreational miners might want to venture into the Norse Peak Wilderness to take a stab at panning for gold (Morse and Crow Creeks are said to be fruitful locations).

With such a definite presence in this area, we would be remiss to not say just a little about the fourth tallest mountain in the Lower 48, Mount Rainier. From the start of this ride, you're only five miles, as the crow flies, from the northern edge of the Mount Rainier National Park. By car, it's a little farther. With over 230,000 acres of glacier-filled crevasses, flower-studded prairies, old-growth forests, and cascading waterfalls, Mount Rainier is an adventurer's paradise. Though relatively quiet for the last 2,500 years, Mount Rainier's volcanic core is hardly tame. Scientists, however, say the mountain's greatest threat to man is not its molten core but rather its potential for mudslides. To put a gauge on a mudflow's destructive power: 5,700 years ago, triggered perhaps by an earthquake, Mount Rainier shed an unwanted 2,000 feet off its summit, sending mud and debris racing through the White River Valley to just shy of the Puget Sound, completely inundating what today are the towns of Buckley, Enumclaw, Puyallup, and Kent.

A Word of Caution Concerning Bees

Whether hiking or mountain biking along wooded trails, avoid disturbing fallen trees. These decaying logs are nurseries for new trees, but more importantly they are home to bee colonies, snakes, and all sorts of varmints. If you come in contact with a hive of bees in particular, the scenario that ensues will most likely not be pretty.

The most obvious thing to do if you've upset a hive of bees is to run like crazy. In some cases you may have to leave your bike behind—as we did once. You'll want to wait at least a half-hour before retrieving it. At a safe distance, examine your sting(s) to make sure there are no bees clinging to your clothing. And above all, remember to relax. Drink some water and collect yourself. Being stung by one bee can be annoying but being stung by a swarm of bees can be downright frightening. Emergency treatment for stings begins with the stinger, which needs to be removed very gently if it is still in the skin. Then, apply a paste of baking soda, a cold, wet cloth, or ice cubes to reduce the pain and swelling—mud works great out in the woods. If you remembered to bring an antihistamine, take it—this will slow down your reaction to the venom.

About one in 10 people are allergic to insect stings. For some, being stung by a bee or another insect can be life-threatening and can cause an anaphylactic reaction. If you're not sure whether or not you're allergic to bees, some of the symptoms may include: a swollen tongue or throat; swelling about the eyes and lips; difficulty breathing; coughing or wheezing; numbness; cramping; hives; slurred speech; anxiety; mental confusion; nausea or vomiting. If anaphylactic symptoms occur, get the victim to a hospital as quickly as possible. You should know before heading into the woods whether you are allergic. Consult your physician, who might suggest that you carry an emergency epinephrine injection called an Epi-Pen (which costs about $50).

Ride Information

● Trail Contacts:

U.S. Forest Service White River Ranger District, Enumclaw, WA (360) 825–6585 • **Department of Natural Resources:** (360) 825–1631 or 1–800–527–3305

● Schedule:

Open year round, depending on snow levels

● Fees/Permits:

$5 per car, per day charge ($30 for an annual pass)

● Local Information:

Enumclaw Visitor Center, Enumclaw, WA (360) 825–7666 • **Radio AM**

530, Enumclaw, WA – the latest weather and road conditions, plus mountain area information • **Mount Rainier National Park Service,** Ashford, WA (360) 569–2211 – call for maps and brochures

● Local Events/Attractions:

King County Fair, in July, Enumclaw, WA (360) 825–7666 • **Pacific Northwest Highland Games**, in July, Enumclaw, WA (360) 825–7666

● Maps:

USGS maps: Sun Top, WA

Skookum Flats

Ride Summary

Across the highway from Ranger Creek, this popular trail runs along the riverside in a virtual dance with the drainage that requires a lot of effort in the technical skills department. Rolling along, this trail doesn't gain any elevation, but you will still have to contend with lots of roots and rocks. It's a great ride to build your skills, and if necessary, there are several points at which to leave the trail for higher routes, or to return to the start.

Ride Specs

Start: Skookum Flats Trail trailhead
Length: 14.9-mile loop
Approximate Riding Time: 4–5 hours
Difficulty Rating: Moderate with lots of roots
Trail Surface: Singletrack and paved road over rolling terrain along riverfront under the cover of huge fir trees
Land Status: National forest
Nearest Town: Greenwater, WA
Other Trail Users: Hikers and equestrians
Canine Compatibility: Dogs not permitted
Wheels: Front suspension is a good idea due to large rocks and tree roots

Getting There

From Puyallup: Take WA 167 to WA 410 East. Follow WA 410 for 39.1 miles. Take a right on to FS 73. Go over the bridge and follow 0.4 miles to the parking lot on the right. The Skookum Flats Trail (Trail 1194) is on the left side of the road. *DeLorme: Washington Atlas & Gazetteer:* Page 64 D4

N ative American influence is strong in the Pacific Northwest. Although tribal names and words are easy to learn, their translations are often difficult to decipher. *Skookum*, the name used in this ride, comes from Chinook jargon, an Indian trade language—a particular way of speaking created by different tribes to *talk business* amongst themselves. Skookum has been translated to mean "strong" or "strength." In some translations, this word also means "ghost," "evil spirit," or "demon." Such heavy words make one curious, but according to one expert at the University of Washington's Northwest Special Collections Library, it's important not to read too much into this cobbled language. What you see is what you get.

The White River, glacially fed from Mount Rainier's icy crown, runs through the Skookum Flats. Following the river's course from the northeastern base of Mount Rainier to its western terminus, Commencement Bay in Tacoma, there are more than a few sights to see.

MilesDirections

0.0 START at the Skookum Flats Trail (Trail 1194).

1.1 Pass a small trail coming in from the right. Follow the river.

1.3 Begin traversing a series of wooden bridges for the next 0.2 miles.

2.2 Cross a stream, trying not to get wet.

3.5 Notice the huge trees on this section of trail.

3.7 Pass over a wooden bridge with rails.

4.1 Come to a trail intersection with a sign that reads: "Road 73: 4.1 miles; Skookum Falls: 2 miles." To the left is the suspension bridge crossing the White River. Check it out,then continue along Trail 1149. *[**Bail-Out Point:** Cross the bridge and take Buck Creek Trail up to WA 410, and then back to the start.]*

5.5 Turn left and continue along the White River. Pass an uphill spur and FS 7160 on the right.

5.6 Come to a Y-intersection. Turn left up the river.

5.8 To the right of the airstrip is Silver Springs Campground along the White River.

5.9 Pass the right-hand spur leading to the Ranger Creek State Airport.

6.2 The river curves to the left and the trail is a little rough for a couple hundred yards.

6.5 Pass Ranger Creek Camp off to the right. Arrive at a T-intersection. The trail to the right goes to the campground. Turn left heading toward the White River and the trail after the washout.

6.7 Reach an intersection with the old washed-out trail.

7.1 Pass a horse camp and a forest service road. Turn right along FS 210 and follow it to the concrete bridge, paralleling the airstrip.

8.3 At the top of the airstrip turn right toward the Trail 1194, White River, and WA 410.

8.5 Come to WA 410. Turn left, heading toward Enumclaw. Take the White River Trail (Trail 1199) on the right, paralleling the road. Ranger Creek Trail (Trail 1197) is behind you.

10.1 Intersect with Buck Creek Trail (Trail 1169) and Snoquera Flats Trail (Trail 1167) one mile ahead. Continue straight.

10.4 Reach an intersection for Trail 1167 (closed to horses and bikes). Stay straight on Trail 1199. Cross a bridge ahead.

10.5 Turn right at the Y-intersection. The lower trail goes to Camp Shepherd. Continue straight past a spur trail.

10.8 Cross an open clearing. Look for big elk. Cross a couple of clearings ahead.

11.3 Arrive at a four-way intersection with Trail 1167, the power line, the trail to WA 410, and Trail 1169. Stay on the Trail 1199.

11.7 Reach the junction of the Dalles Creek Trail (Trail 1198), plus many other trails to the right. Stay straight.

11.8 Reach the junction of Power Line Way. Follow the trail as it curves down to WA 410.

11.9 Arrive at WA 410. Turn right and continue along WA 410 back to FS 73.

14.4 Turn left on FS 73.

14.5 Stay left at the Y-intersection.

14.7 Cross a bridge over the White River.

14.9 Arrive at the parking lot.

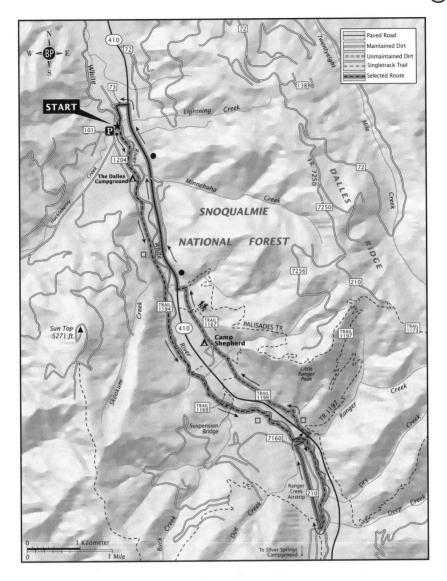

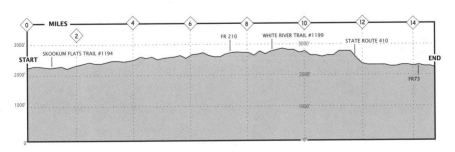

Mount Rainier is the most impressive site, by far, along White River. At Rainier's base, the White River Campground is a great location for hiking near the glaciers. Mountain biking is prohibited in national parks, but being so close to the goliath Rainier is an experience unparalleled in the Northwest, where there are many trails and campgrounds from which to choose.

Following the White River northward from the mountain is the town of Greenwater, just a few miles from the start of the Skookum Flats mountain bike ride. A small town, Greenwater is home to the Catherine Montgomery Interpretive Center. The center showcases Washington's flora and fauna within the Federation Forest State Park's 612 acres of virgin timber. Greenwater is also close to the starting point for an historic route that Native Americans once traveled to cross the Cascade Mountains. This route, Naches Pass, can only be accessed on foot. Travel 10 miles east from Greenwater along Forest Road 70 to a trailhead just past Pyramid Creek for a short five-mile (one-way) hike to the pass.

From Greenwater the river flows west toward Enumclaw, a town named in 1885 by Frank Stevenson after a nearby mountain. Native Americans used this word to refer to the mountain, too, believing that the Thunderbird, who lived in a cave in this mountain, changed a tribesman into thunder. *Enumclaw* has been translated to mean "loud rattling noise" or "thundering mountain."

Although Enumclaw Mountain can't be seen from Washington 410, evidence of the town's prominent industries can. Timber mills and dairies have been in operation since the 1800s in Enumclaw. Passers-by will easily notice the logged roadsides and the lumberyards, just as they are sure to take notice, with only a whiff, of what the locals call their *dairy air*.

The White River joins with the Puyallup River near Tacoma (which is known for its pulpy aroma). Home to about 170,000 people, Tacoma is Washington's third-largest city, behind Seattle and Spokane, and began as a settlement surrounding a sawmill.

Water and erosion from the White River creates a challenge for mountain bikers who ride the Skookum Flats Trail. A root-riddled experience, the Skookum Flats Trail winds up and down drainages alongside the river. The mileage is short and the elevation gain is nil, but this ride is extremely technical and challenging. The trail follows the river for about four miles until it crosses a suspension bridge, at which point mountain bikers can bail out if necessary.

The singletrack continues down the Buck Creek Trail on the opposite side of the White River, along similar rooty terrain, for another four-and-a-half miles until it too intersects with a bailout option to Washington 410. To complete the final third of the Skookum Flats ride, take the White River Trail; it's easier to negotiate than the other two trails. The trip ends with a three-mile ride on Washington 410 back to Forest Service Road 73.

Ride Information

ⓒ Trail Contacts:
U.S. Forest Service White River Ranger District, Enumclaw, WA (360) 825–6585 • **Department of Natural Resources:** (360) 825–1631 or 1-800-527-3305

ⓞ Schedule:
Open year round depending on snow levels

ⓢ Fees/Permits:
$5 per car, per day charge ($30 for an annual pass)

ⓠ Local Information:
Washington State History Museum, Tacoma, WA (253) 272–3500 • **Enumclaw Visitor's Center,** Enumclaw, WA (360) 825–7666 • Radio AM 530, Enumclaw, WA – the latest weather and road conditions, plus mountain area information

ⓠ Local Events/Attractions:
King County Fair, in July, Enumclaw, WA (360) 825–7666 • **Pacific Northwest Highland Games,** in July, Enumclaw, WA (360) 825–7666

ⓖ Local Bike Shops:
Enumclaw Schwinn Cyclery, Enumclaw, WA (360) 825–4461 • **Enumclaw Ski & Mountain Company,** Enumclaw, WA (360) 825–6910 • **Valley Cyclery,** Auburn, WA (253) 833–4910

ⓝ Maps:
USGS maps: Sun Top, WA

Crystal Mountain Loop

Ride Summary

Of all the rides along the Cascade Range, this is the *must-do* course for Washington mountain bikers. Situated on one of Washington's most popular ski resorts, this ride features an extremely aerobic advanced climb up forest road and singletrack, a 7,000-foot view of three volcanoes, and world-class singletrack downhill. Few rides compare to the rush this route can provide. There are more moderate, alternative routes that will get you to the top, too, and as long as you get there, you'll find it very difficult not to have a sensational day on the mountain.

Ride Specs

Start: From the FS 510 parking lot
Other Starting Locations: From Crystal Mountain Resort
Length: 14.5-mile loop
Approximate Riding Time: 4 hours (shorter hour-long option with chairlift ride up to the top)
Difficulty Rating: Difficult ascent/ Moderate descent
Terrain: Singletrack, doubletrack, fire roads, sand, creek crossings, and a short section of paved road. Extreme uphill and screaming downhill.
Land Status: National forest and private property (Crystal Mountain Resort)
Nearest Town: Greenwater, WA

Other Trail Users: Hikers and equestrians
Canine Compatibility: Dogs not permitted
Wheels: Front suspension recommended, and full-suspension is a good idea.

Getting There

From Puyallup: Take WA 167 to WA 410 East. Follow WA 410 for 47 miles to Crystal Mountain Road. Turn left and travel five miles to FS 510 (a dirt road). Turn right between mile markers 4 and 5. Follow down into the parking lot.
DeLorme: Washington Atlas & Gazetteer: Page 49 A5

Washington 410 is one of the main avenues to Mount Rainier, with many incredible trails and sights along the way. A few miles south of the turnoff for Crystal Mountain Road, along Washington 410, is Cayuse Pass. This portion of the highway closes in the winter because of snow. In the summertime, however, the drive up to Cayuse Pass is as breathtaking as seeing an eagle soar or a sunset over the Pacific Ocean.

At the top of Cayuse Pass and with a quick turn to the left, Washington 410 takes two deep switchbacks up and over Chinook Pass, between Sourdough Gap and Dewey Lake. Trailheads for both the gap and the lake

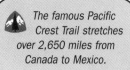

The famous Pacific Crest Trail stretches over 2,650 miles from Canada to Mexico.

are on either side of Chinook Pass. The hike to Dewey Lake is a popular trail because it has an easy grade and follows the Pacific Crest National Scenic Trail. Camping is permitted along the trail. The hike to Sourdough Gap is great for backpacking. The trail passes Sheep Lake and travels along the Pacific Crest Trail, too. Mountain bikes are prohibited on the Pacific Crest Trail, which also crosses into wilderness areas.

There are three ways to tackle Crystal Mountain in the summertime. First, there's the heart-pumper route: up Forest Service Road 184 and the Silver Creek Trail for a relatively short, steep climb; and then down the

MilesDirections

0.0 START from the parking lot at the trailhead on FS 510 and ride back up to Crystal Mountain Road (FS 7190).

0.4 Turn left onto Crystal Mountain Road.

0.8 Turn right onto FS 184, the first intersection with a dirt road.

1.1 Pass the Norse Peak Trail, which heads into wilderness area and is closed to bikes.

3.1 At the four-way intersection, the road goes left. Stay straight to the doubletrack on the Silver Creek Trail (Trail 1192), toward the Crystal Mountain Trail (Trail 1163).

3.5 The doubletrack ends and the singletrack begins to the right. Follow the trail signs and the singletrack, leading under a chairlift.

3.6 On the left, a bridge crosses the creek at the abandoned Silver Creek Mine.

4.5 Reach a junction with a spur trail that leads to Bullion Basin and the Pacific Crest Trail. These trails are hiker-only trails. Cross over the creek to the right, heading toward the ski resort.

4.8 Veer right at the fork, following the signs.

5.0 Turn left at the junction.

5.1 Arrive at Henskin Lake. Stay on the main path curving around Henskin Lake. Keep the lake to the right.

5.2 Reach the intersection of the Bear Gap Trail and Trail 1163. Stay on Trail 1163.

5.7 Stay right at the intersection. *[FYI. The left path heads up to a small lake.]*

6.2 Cross the creek to the right, heading toward the chairlifts.

6.3 Cross the cat track and continue up.

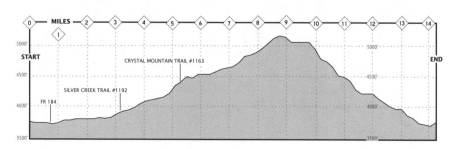

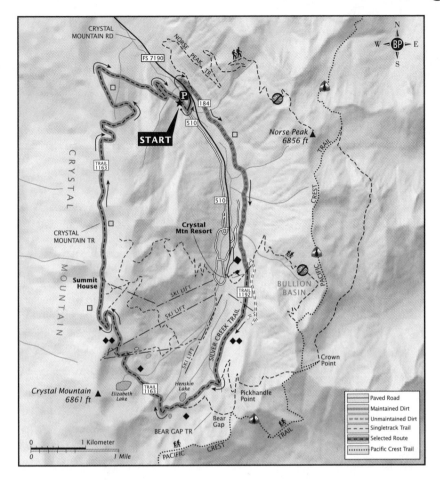

6.5 Encounter a short, flat meadow and ride under two chairlifts.

7.5 Skirting the southwest side of a bowl in the mountain, you'll encounter a long switchback up to the saddle.

7.6 There is a healthy climb from the saddle to the top of the mountain. You can follow the lesser climb on the left.

8.1 Turn right up the dirt, doublewide track toward a large boulder field. You can see the Summit House Restaurant at the top a few yards away.

9.5 Begin the descent over the boulder field. The junction to the left makes a steeper downhill, but the trail in front of you meets with the left hand trail in just a of couple yards.

11.2 For close-up views of Mount Rainier, head left to the edge of the ridge. Continue along the switchbacks of the Crystal Mountain Trail.

14.5 Arrive at the trailhead and parking area on FS 510.

Crystal Mountain Trail for a world-class downhill experience. This is not the easiest way up, by any means, but it offers a challenging, exhilarating, cardiovascular workout. Of course, there is the *traditional* route, too. By climbing up the Crystal Mountain Trail and coming down the Silver Creek Trail through the ski resort, you save more of the technical trail for the descent. Just follow our instructions in reverse, starting at the trailhead in the parking lot. The third option involves a meager fee. Take the chair lift up and ride down the Crystal Mountain or Silver Creek Trails, or even down the absurdly steep cat tracks. It's much harder without the chairlift, but it's also worth the effort.

When temperatures rise, this ride can get pretty warm. Scaling the gravel road up into the trees, there is little escape from the sun. The Crystal Mountain Resort lies to the right—you should be able to see the chair lifts from here. (Just keep telling yourself that this grueling climb is saving you $10.) The singletrack traverses the bunny slope and leads into the woods where the trees give much needed relief from the unrelenting sun. And as if the sun weren't bad enough, expect on your typical summer day to confront a welcoming committee of biting flies. Without some form of insect repellent, these inhospitable hosts will keep your rest stops to a minimum.

Well into the hills, the trail passes the abandoned Silver Creek Mine— a highly unadvisable side-trip. It is here that the terrain breaks from super

steep to super technical. The deep ruts come from the hard pounding this portion of the trail used to get when it was host to an annual cross-country mountain bike race. Some of these sections are tough enough to negotiate when you're going downhill, but heading up, they are almost unbearable . . . *almost*.

After completing the toughest and most technical portion of the ride, the trail leaves the forest and rounds a bluff, coming face to face with the bowls carved into the side of Crystal Mountain. Crossing a few cat tracks along the way, the trail encircles one of the bowls and begins the slow traverse up the hillside into some gnarly, rocky terrain. At the top, just below 7,000 feet, the Summit House and outdoor picnic tables are a welcome sight. The Summit House happens to be the highest restaurant in Washington and offers a picturesque setting for any meal of the day.

Leaving the crest of the mountain, head down along the ridge, over the large boulders in the direction paralleling Mount Rainier. It's best to walk over the boulders. The singletrack picks up at the bottom of the boulder field and then just screams. It's a blast the entire way down. You'll pass meadows and overlooks, Mount Rainier and Mount Adams, and sometimes even Mount Hood's crystalline peak. The views along the ridgeline of the Crystal Mountain trail are truly entrancing, and the trail surface couldn't be more perfect.

Ride Information

● Trail Contacts:
Crystal Mountain Ski Area: (360) 663–2265 or 1–888–754–6199 or *www.crystalmt.com* • **U.S. Forest Service:** (360) 825–6585 • **U.S. Department of Natural Resources:** (360) 825–1631 or 1–800–527–3305

● Schedule:
Ride after snow melt in June through October. Lift operates weekends only, Memorial Day through Labor Day.

● Fees/Permits:
Chairlift is $14 for one ride for adults, $9 for children 10 and younger

● Local Information:
Campground reservations: 1–800–280–2267 • **Radio AM 530,** Enumclaw, WA – *the latest weather and road conditions, plus mountain area information*

● Local Events/Attractions:
Summit House, Crystal Mountain, WA (360) 663–2300

● Local Bike Shops:
Rainier Rides Mountain Bike Rentals, Crystal Mountain, WA (360) 663–0182 or *www.rainier-rides.com* • **Enumclaw Schwinn Cyclery,** Enumclaw, WA (360) 825–4461 • **Enumclaw Ski & Mountain Co,** Enumclaw, WA (360) 825–6910 • **Valley Cyclery, Auburn,** WA (253) 833–4910

● Maps:
USGS maps: White River Park, WA; Norse Peak, WA

23 Taneum Creek Loop

Ride Summary

Ready to climb? Ready to career downhill? Ride up one fork of Taneum Creek, up and over the ridge to an elevation of 4,200 feet, and then traverse Fishhook Flats before dropping down to the other fork of Taneum Creek. Depending on the time of year, be prepared for high-elevation snow or rain-slicked trail conditions.

Ride Specs

Start: From the Taneum Junction Forest Camp
Length: 15.0-mile loop
Approximate Riding Time: 3–4 hours
Difficulty Rating: Moderate to Difficult, due to hard climbing and elevation gains.
Terrain: Gravel road and singletrack, which can be rocky in places. Creekside riding with some hard climbing and downhills, mostly under the cover of trees.
Land Status: National forest
Nearest Town: Cle Elum, WA
Other Trail Users: Hikers and motorcycles
Canine Compatibility: Dogs permitted
Wheels: Front suspension recommended

Getting There

From Cle Elum: Take I-90 eastbound to Exit 93 for Elk Heights Road. Turn left at the end of the off-ramp, then right at the stop sign on the north side of the highway onto Elk Heights Road. Follow Elk Heights Road for four miles, and then turn right onto Taneum Road. Cross over the highway, and then turn right onto Taneum Creek Road. Go about nine miles to FS 3300, just past FS 3330. Park in the parking area after crossing a small bridge at Taneum Junction Forest Camp. *DeLorme: Washington Atlas & Gazetteer:* Page 66 D1

Enter into the heart of the Wenatchee National Forest through the Taneum Valley. Formed by the north and south forks of Taneum Creek, the valley was originally homesteaded around the same time as the neighboring towns of Cle Elum, Thorp, and Ellensburg. The road that leads into the national forest land borders the L.T. Murray Wildlife Area, so be on the lookout for elk, deer, and all sorts of birds.

Like many of the rides along the eastern foothills of the Cascade Mountains, riding along Taneum Creek offers a quick escape to the backcountry. The rocky trail sets out along the south fork of the creek, departing from the main gravel road onto a run-down road paralleling the creek. History unfolds just a few miles into the ride, as the trail winds past an old log cabin—likely an old homesteader cabin or hunting outpost. There isn't

much left of the cabin today, but it does offer some cover if you get caught in the area during a rain squall.

The cabin marks the point where the trail departs from the south fork of Taneum Creek and starts the long climb up and over Taneum Ridge. Some sections of the trail get a bit steep, so don't be surprised if you need to dismount and walk the bike uphill. While you're walking, look to the left to view the crags and rocky mountaintops to the south. Among the peaks of the Manastash Ridge in the distance is the Frost Mountain Lookout, used by the Forest Service as a fire lookout during summers. The trail continues climbing after rejoining the main Forest Service road, and it tops out near the turnoff point for Fishhook Flats Trail. Contrary to its name, not much is flat in this neighborhood. And at an elevation of 4,200 feet, you need to be prepared for just about any kind of weather at the top of the ridge. Snow or heavy rain storms can turn the strenuous ride into an endurance contest. The trail can turn from hard-pack to a slick mess, sending riders sliding off the trail. In summer months, obstacles along the trailside can include bee nests and the occasional snake. And since this is true backcountry, keep an eye out for a rare bear sighting.

There isn't much rolling to these hills as the trail descends from Fishhook Flats down to the north fork of Taneum Creek—this is one of those hang-onto-the-handlebars-for-dear-life-and-be-sure-to-dodge-those-rocks-or-be-bounced-off-the-trail-and-down-the-canyon kind of downhill sections. As you descend along the creek bed, glance off to the trailside now and then to see the enormous sections of silvery, flaking rock. Schist, a metamorphic rock that shows the volcanic origins of this stretch of the Cascade Mountains, is common rock here. Pick up a piece of the rock that

has broken from its parent rocks and you can see the layers and lines that make up schist. Its mica content makes it shine.

Continuing down the hill back toward the Taneum Junction Forest Camp, the singletrack levels out in spots and, when wet, it can get nearly as muddy as western Washington riding. This ride offers a little bit of everything.

MilesDirections

0.0 START from Taneum Junction Forest Camp and head up the hill on FS 3300.

0.3 Turn left and descend closer to the South Fork of Taneum Creek on an old gravel road.

1.7 Pass an abandoned log cabin on the right and continue along the road, starting to climb.

2.9 Climb a steep hill, turning away from the creek.

3.1 The trail intersects FS 3300. Go left onto the road and continue up hill.

4.7 Pass the Taneum Ridge Trail on the right.

4.9 Turn right onto Fishhook Flats Trail.

8.0 Drop into a steep canyon and cross a small stream.

8.2 Turn right onto Trail 1377 and head down the North Fork of Taneum Creek.

Ride Information

Trail Contacts:
Wenatchee National Forest, Cle Elum Ranger District: (509) 674–4411 • **Wenatchee National Forest Headquarters,** Wenatchee, WA (509) 662–4335

Schedule:
Open year round, but best between April and October, depending upon snow levels

Fees/Permits:
$5 per car, per day ($30 for an annual pass)

Local Information:
Cle Elum Chamber of Commerce, Cle Elum, WA (509) 674–5958 or *www.ohwy.com/wa/c/cleelucc.htm* • **Ellensburg Chamber of Commerce,** Ellensburg, WA (509) 925–3137

Local Events/Attractions:
Thorp Mill, Thorp, WA (509) 964–9640 – *a National Historic Site* • **Olmstead Place State Park,** Ellensburg, WA (509) 925–1943 – *a state park set on a pioneer homestead established in 1875*

Local Bike Shops:
Cle Elum Bike & Hike, Cle Elum, WA (509) 674–4567 • **Central Sundries** (Roslyn's de facto Visitor Center), Roslyn, WA (509) 649–2210 • **Recycle Bicycle Shops,** Ellensburg, WA (509) 925–3326

Maps:
USGS maps: Frost Mountain, WA; Quartz Mountain, WA; Ronald, WA; Cle Elum, WA

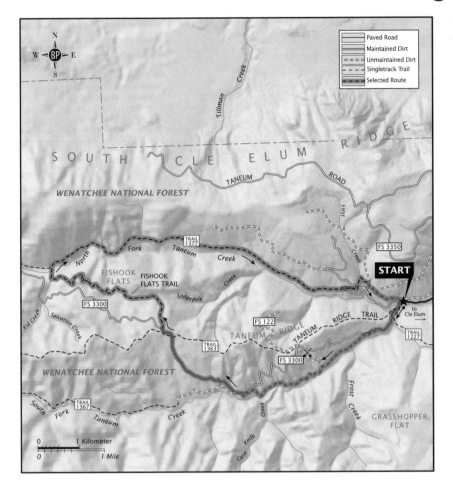

13.5 Cross the road and pick up the trail on the other side.

14.3 Turn right on the old logging road and head downhill.

14.98 Take a sharp right onto the trail to the Taneum Junction Forest Camp and drop the final few yards down to the road.

15.0 Arrive back at the Taneum Junction Forest Camp.

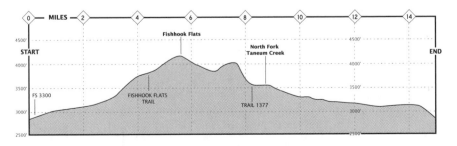

Fifes Ridge

Ride Summary

Located in the middle of prime recreational territory, Fifes Ridge is within reach of Mount Rainier, camping spots, a slew of rivers, and Bumping Lake. Heading up one of the most scenic forest roads in the state, this ride begins with a smooth nine-mile climb that's not too strenuous. Skirting the edges of a wilderness area, it's important to keep to the designated ridge trail. The views are stupendous, and the singletrack is impressive and fun with brief, moderately technical sections.

Ride Specs

Start: From the campground at FS 1902
Length: 14.4-mile circuit
Approximate Riding Time: 3 hours
Difficulty Rating: Moderate with steady ascent and technical descents
Terrain: Singletrack and forest road up and down steep hills
Land Status: National forest
Nearest Town: Cliffdell, WA
Other Trail Users: Hikers and equestrians
Canine Compatibility: Dogs permitted
Wheels: Front suspension recommended

Getting There

From Chinook Pass: Head east on WA 410 to FS 19 north toward Little Naches Campground and Horsetail Falls. Pass FS 1901 to Quartz Creek. Follow signs for Raven's Roost 14. Turn left on FS 1902. Cross the bridge over the river. See FS 1920 Fifes Ridge sign ahead. Park in adjacent camping areas along the river. *DeLorme: Washington Atlas & Gazetteer:* Page 49 A6

Remnants of volcanoes dating back 40 million years have been found along the lower edges below Mount Rainier. This trail along Fifes Ridge runs atop a vestige of the second volcanic episode Mount Rainier experienced. Although it doesn't look like one, neighboring Fifes Peak is a volcano as well. It is believed to have erupted about 25 million years ago. Rocks found around Mount Rainier contain fossil plants, like palms and other warm climate trees, which are evidence that, at one time, temperatures here were on the balmy side.

Over the last 20 million years, Mount Rainier has had some time to cool off, and now shoulders 26 glaciers. Rising to 14,411 feet, Mount Rainier has been, and will continue to be, a landmark from which to navigate and a beacon for aspiring mountain climbers. Each year this mountain draws nearly 8,000 eager climbers who use ropes and ice axes for their two-day ascent. Day One gets climbers to Camp Muir where they rest, eat, and pre-

Looking east from the top of Fifes Ridge.

pare to continue to the summit. Between midnight to 2 A.M. of the following day, climbers depart Camp Muir and continue to Rainier's peak for a 14,000-foot sunrise view of the world, which also gives them enough time to descend during daylight hours.

Permits are required to climb Mount Rainier and are issued at the mountain. The park service allows a rather large number of people per day to head

MilesDirections

0.0 START from the Crow Creek camping/parking area and turn right up FS 1920, which begins with pavement and turns into gravel almost immediately.

1.3 Pass FS 1922 the on right and a spur road on the left. Continue up the gravel road.

1.7 Pass a side trail. Continue up the road.

2.1 Pass FS 94 on the left.

2.7 Pass Trail 955. This is the junction for the West Quartz Creek Loop. Stay straight up the road.

3.4 Pass Trail 955. Continue ascending.

4.1 Pass FS 820 on the right. Still climbing.

5.5 Pass FS 822 on the right. Continue traversing the contours of this ridge.

6.5 Rounding a drainage on the ridge, look off to the right, north and northeast, to the Manashtash Ridge, Panther Ridge, and Peaches Ridge—all in one long succession. The tallest peak is Quartz Mountain.

8.2 Intersect with the West Quartz Creek Trail (Trail 952) and FS 828. FS 828 takes you into wilderness area. Take Trail 952 left to the top of the ridge. *[Option. Turn right for a six-mile downhill.]*

9.3 Arrive at the top. See the wilderness area signs and the Trail 954 to the right (hiker only). Stay left on 952.

10.0 Cross FS 823.

10.3 Keep straight at the intersection, closest to the drainage. Pass a road cut on the left.

10.5 Pass road crossing of FS 1920.

11.5 Trail 955 crosses over the ridge to WA 410.

11.6 Cross FS 824.

12.9 Arrive at the intersection for the loop of Trail 952 and FS 1920. Turn right on FS 1920.

13.4 Reach the intersection of FS 1920.

14.4 Arrive at the Crow Creek Campground.

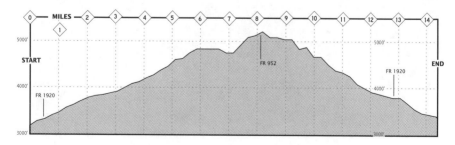

up, but on the weekends, climbers should get there early. The National Park Service recommends that prospective climbers be educated in crevasse rescue and ice ax arrest (stopping a slide by using an ice ax.) No matter how good the other climbers are, you'll want to know what to do if they get into unexpected trouble.

Climbing Mount Rainier fascinated early European settlers, but not the local Native Americans. They believed that attempting the summit would anger the mountain spirit—though Native American legends speak of medicine men, and others, reaching the peak. In August of 1870, General Hazard Stevens and Philomen Van Trump made the first successful summit attempt. An Indian named Sluiskin led Stevens and Trump to within a day of the summit, but turned back at the last minute, citing the "evil spirit who dwelt in a fiery lake on the summit" as reason enough. The first women to summit Mount Rainier were Kay Fuller in 1890, and 13-year-old Susan Longmire in 1891.

Captain George Vancouver of the Royal British Navy discovered Mount Rainier in 1792 and named it after his friend Rear Admiral Peter Rainier. Mount Rainier became the nation's fifth national park in 1899. James Longmire, owner and operator of Mount Rainier's first *tourist attraction*, is credited with exciting the popular interest in the mountain that ultimately lead to its protected park status. It was while leading his third successful summit climb of Mount Rainier in 1883 that Longmire, resting for the night next to steam vents for warmth, discovered hot mineral springs. He quickly filed a mineral claim and developed the area into the mountain's first mineral hot springs resort, called Longmire Springs (also known as Longmire's Medical Springs).

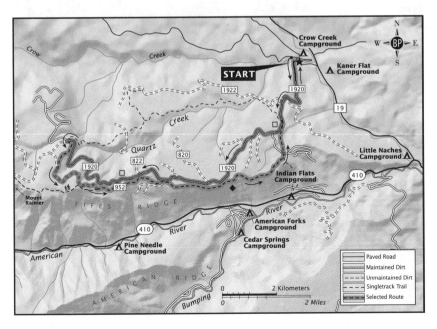

The Longmires are well known for their explorations on Mount Rainier. Martha Longmire named Paradise Valley—the most famous of all sites on the mountain—in 1885. And the Longmire family is credited with identifying and naming hundreds of places along the mountain, as well as creating miles and miles of trail. There are over 300 miles of hiking trails now, which in winter can have up to 30 feet of snow.

This area around Mount Rainier offers some spectacular mountain biking terrain. The Fifes Ridge Ride is one that anyone with a little determination can complete. The climb is fairly long, but it isn't that strenuous. The road itself is in great condition—hardly a washboard wrinkle to be found. The trail situation seems to be a bit unsettled, though, in that certain trails, once open to mountain bikers, are now considered part of the Norse Peak Wilderness Area—where mountain biking is prohibited. Some of the trails you'll really want to explore now happen to be within the wilderness area. Leave your bike, or carry it, and hike along the ridge for a couple of miles to catch the excellent views of Mount Rainier's eastern face. From the ridge you can climb out onto some rock formations for the best views—a great spot for lunch, too!

The ridge trail is in good condition. Horses and motorcycles do leave some sections chewed up, but for the most part, it is fast and a ton of fun. Conditions range from packed dirt to sand, with a few technical, rocky sections. It then descends onto doubletrack with huge motorcycle ruts—a slight challenge to navigate. These trails will lead you right back to the campground.

Ride Information

● Trail Contacts:
Wenatchee National Forest Headquarters: (509) 662–4335 • Naches Ranger District: (509) 653–2205

● Schedule:
Open during summer months

● Fees/Permits:
$5 per car, per day ($30 for an annual pass)

● Local Information:
The Mountaineers, Seattle, WA (206) 284–6310 • Rainier Mountaineering Inc., Halls Lake, WA (253) 627–6242

● Local Bike Shops:
Sagebrush Cycles, Yakima, WA (509) 248–5393 • Valley Cycling and Fitness Equipment, Yakima, WA (509) 453–6699

● Maps:
USGS maps: Goose Prairie, WA; Old Scab Mountain, WA • USFS maps: Naches Ranger District Map • Green Trails: Bumping Lake No. 271 and Old Scab Mountain No. 272

Osborne Mountain

Ride Summary

This is another advanced mountain biking loop that can be categorized in the gonzo/abusive realm. The *climb that never ends* really does find a stopping point—it just takes a while. And, gads! The scenery is spectacular. Right between Mount Rainier within the Sawtooth Ridge, this route is both challenging and rewarding. The descent is filled with switchbacks and requires a lot of technical skill, wiping out any unsuspecting mountain bikers if they aren't careful.

Ride Specs

Start: From the Big Creek Campground
Length: 24.4-mile loop
Approximate Riding Time: 6 hours
Difficulty Rating: Difficult due to steep, unrelenting climbs
Terrain: A forested road climb opens the ride and then it's singletrack, paved road, and forest road. Be prepared for a white-knuckle, switchback-filled descent.
Land Status: National forest
Nearest Town: Ashford, WA
Other Trail Users: Hikers and equestrians
Canine Compatibility: Dogs permitted
Wheels: Front suspension recommended

Getting There

From Ashford: Head east on WA 706 toward the southwest entrance of Mount Rainier. (See Osborne Mountain ahead, dominating the skyline. High Rock Lookout is on the other side of the mountain.) Turn right onto FS 52 into the Gifford Pinchot National Forest. Head toward Big Creek Campground and FS 85 on the right as the road curves left. Turn right toward Osborne Mountain Trail (Trail 250) on FS 29. Parking is available in the campground or any other pull-off. *DeLorme: Washington Atlas & Gazetteer:* Page 48 C2

L ong before there were any modern modes of transportation, Washington 706 and the roads leading east out of Ashford to Mount Rainier were Native American trails laid out by tribes traveling east to the Yakima country. By the 1880s, as homesteads began springing up and sawmills became the primary employers of the area's residents, the trails quickly became wagon roads.

Homesteading began in the late 1800s in this region. The community of Ashford was established in 1891. The National Mill operated near Ashford, serving as the region's primary employer, and specialized in the production of especially long and especially large timbers. It might have taken loggers days to find trees that were tall enough for their purposes. But in those days, the turn of the century, there were still plenty of old-growth trees to choose

from. The Ford Motor Company reportedly purchased three enormous planks of wood from the mill for their mid-west factory. Each timber measured 3'x3'x150'—all from one tree! To see old-growth forest of this size, visit the Grove of the Patriarchs on the eastern flank of Mount Rainier National Park. From Paradise, follow the Stevens Canyon Road east, almost all the

Sawtooth Ridge.

MilesDirections

0.0 START from Big Creek Campground. Head back out and cross the bridge to paved FS 52 and turn left toward Ashford. As the road curves right, turn left onto FS 85 following the sign for Osborne Road.

0.1 Cross a one-lane bridge.

1.0 Pass a spur road: No trespassing.

1.4 The climb begins on the paved road.

2.5 Pass an unmarked spur on the left.

5.0 See one of the points of the Sawtooth Ridge directly in your line of vision.

6.2 Pass the remains of a spur road on the left.

6.3 There may be water over the road at this point.

7.3 Reach the intersection of FS 8440 (to High Rock Lookout) and FS 85 (to Randle). Turn left toward High Rock Lookout (five miles ahead). The road has turned to gravel.

9.5 Pass FS 064.

10.6 Intersect with FS 54 on the right. Switchback to the right up the ridge. The road will switchback a few times up ahead.

12.5 Arrive at Towhead Gap where the road curves to the left. *[FYI. See High Rock Lookout, the upward jutting rock*

overlooking Mount Rainier. Goat Rocks Wilderness is ahead of you. Optional side-trip. At this time, you can take the 2.6-mile round-trip hike to the top of High Rock Lookout. It's worth it.] Descend into the big right-hand turn.

13.4 Round the turn and turn left onto Big Creek Trail (Trail 252), climbing up to the saddle.

13.9 You're now on singletrack, climbing up through a nice section of old-growth.

14.2 The trail switches back again and intersects with old overgrown double-track. The trail heads off to the left. You're almost to the top of the gap.

14.3 Just as you push up this last section, Mount Rainier jumps into view. The trail descent is steep, narrow, and tends to be overgrown.

14.8 At the trail intersection, take Trail 251. The sign reads: "Granite Lake: 2 miles; Bertha May Lake: 3 miles." Begin to climb again.

15.1 The climb tops out at a sharp corner underneath High Rock.

15.6 The climb tops again for the descent to Granite Lake.

16.3 The descent stops and the trail starts climbing again around a saddle.

17.2 Climbing out of the cirque is a long, arduous process. When the trail is in the

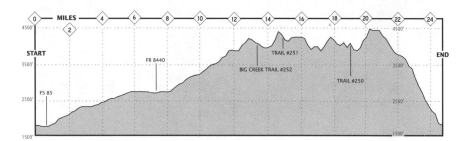

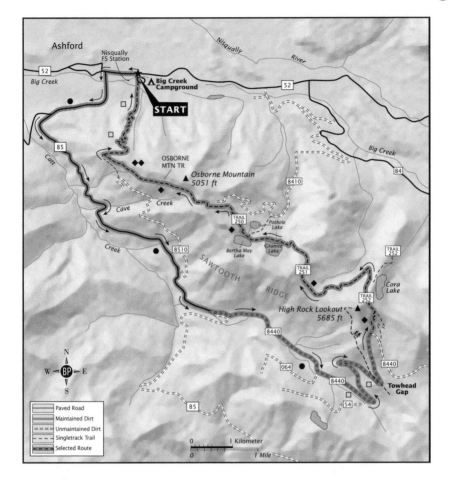

woods, it's clean, but a first gear grind. Out in the open, the trail is covered in briar bushes.

17.6 Reach Granite Lake. The trail heads toward a saddle and Bertha May Lake.

18.2 Come down to Bertha May Lake—an emerald green mountain jewel. The trail winds away from the lake on the other side. Go around the lake.

18.6 Reach the junction of Trail 251, which drops down to the road and Pothole Lake. Climb up from the junction, now on Osborne Mountain Trail (Trail 250).

18.7 The trail opens up to almost doubletrack. Cross an old road cut and then head into a sandy gully that turns steep.

18.9 Here, the super steep gully section turns into nice singletrack—a first-gear climb.

19.3 The singletrack comes out next to a road that curves up and right. Brush by the road. The trail turns away a little to the left.

19.5 Trail 250 comes to FS 8410. The trail across it peters out, so turn left up the road and climb a little.

19.8 Take the trail to the left that comes up shortly, heading into the saddle, as the road switches back right. The trailhead is signed on your left and the trail, somewhat faint at first, traverses a clearcut of Osborne Mountain.

20.1 The trail heads back into the trees.

20.3 The singletrack becomes well groomed. The trail now meanders through a few clearcuts on the west side of Osborne Mountain.

21.7 After some excellent downhill, come to Cave Creek Trail (Trail 911A or 255). Switchback right and continue heading down Osborne Mountain.

23.5 Cross a drainage, making sure you cross to the right side. You'll switch back and forth on the way down.

24.3 Cross a wooden bridge.

24.4 End of the ride. Back at the campground.

---

way to Washington 123. The grove is open between the end of May (or after snowmelt) to mid October (or before snowfall).

Timber companies pumped out a lot of cut lumber in those days. The largest timbers were used as factory roof supports. Steel beams were used occasionally, but when the heat rose, the steel beams got hot enough to actually burn the roofs they supported. Heavy, wooden beams were used in place of steel because they could absorb more heat.

Ashford became a terminal for the railroad around 1907 and actually was a decent sized shipping center and service area for travelers heading up to visit Mount Rainier from the Paradise entrance on the southwest side of the mountain. Following the steps of early settlers, it's a short drive up to Paradise, where visitors can have a face-to-face with Mount Rainier and its several glaciers. Once there, forest rangers at the national park's visitor center can provide information on the best views, the wildlife, Mount Rainier's history, and much more. There are also a few superb, short hikes that leave from the Paradise Visitor Center up to the glaciers. Glacier Vista is a three-mile round-trip hike, perfect for getting a taste of the mountain. A worthy

reminder: dogs and bicycles are not allowed on national park trails, but they are allowed on the trails at Osborne Mountain.

Heading east from Ashford the road leads to a marvelous area for mountain biking in the foothills of Mount Rainier. Just outside the national park boundaries is Rainier's neighbor, Mount Osborne, where mountain bikers can expect to get one of the most difficult rides of their cycling careers. Beginning at Big Creek Campground, the road climb is fairly easy. Climbing gently up a paved road, the forest canopy provides a shady cover for most of the way. The saw blade ridge of the Sawtooth mountains cuts sharply into the sky ahead as the road beneath you changes from asphalt to gravel on the way up to High Rock Lookout. But the trail is where all the action is. It is the singletrack that brings the most challenge to this ride, offering a great place to practice your technique. Littered with switchbacks, the trail is steep. Its rolling route traverses bowls and around mountain lakes on a very technical path that seems to go on forever. Rapidly descending the mountain, you may smell the rubber from

Native Names

Many tribes have lived along the base of Mount Rainier: the Nisqually, Puyallup, Upper Cowlitz, Muckleshoot, and Yakima. The Native Americans tribes had other names for Mount Rainier, like Takhoma and Ta-co-bet. Translations of these names include "big mountain," "snowy peak," or "place where the waters begin." The name Little Tahoma has been preserved as a place name for the conspicuous rock outcropping seen on the east side of Mount Rainier.

your brakes heating up and feel the metal begin to quiver beneath your deteriorating brake pads. As you continue to succumb to gravity's pull, your fingers may crimp and your forearms moan, echoing the scream from your calves and your quads begging for relief. And then, all of a sudden, you'll arrive back at the Big Creek Campground, exhausted but rewarded.

Ride Information

Trail Contacts:
Gifford Pinchot National Forest, Packwood Ranger District: (360) 494-0600

Schedule:
Best between late May and early October

Fees/Permits:
$5 per day, per car ($30 for an annual pass); appropriate campground fees for overnight camping

Local Information:
Mount Rainier Visitor Center, Paradise, WA (360) 569-2211 • Mount Rainier Scenic Railroad, Elbe, WA (360) 569-2588 • Forest Service Outdoor Recreation (206) 470-4060

Local Bike Shops:
The Sports Hut, Packwood, WA (360) 494-7321

Maps:
USGS maps: Sawtooth, WA • Green Trails: Randle, WA No. 301

Elbe Hills

Ride Summary

Bring extra clothes and your best mud tires for this ramble through a second-growth forest. After a long climb up a fire road, the 12.4-mile route veers into the woods on soft, root-strewn trail. Beware when you reach the bottom of the hills as bike-swallowing mud holes offer obstacles that can turn the ride into a messy swim with one wrong slip.

Ride Specs

Start: From the Elbe Hills ATV Park
Length: 12.1-mile loop
Approximate Riding Time: 3–4 hours
Difficulty Rating: Moderate to Advanced, due to technical sections, climbs, and extremely muddy terrain
Terrain: Rolling hills, alternately covered with second-growth trees, a few old-growth trees, and a host of recovering clearcuts. The singletrack and fire roads can get extremely muddy.
Land Status: Department of Natural Resources land
Nearest Town: Elbe, WA
Other Trail Users: ORV users, including motorcycles and jeeps
Canine Compatibility: Dogs permitted (best to bring them on weekdays if at all)
Wheels: Come ready for mud, with wide tires

Getting There

From Tacoma: Take I-5 to the WA 7 exit and then follow WA 7 South through Spanaway. When the road forks, stay to the left and continue on WA 7 toward Elbe. Head east 6.3 miles on WA 706 and then turn left across from the Rainier Lions Club sign onto 278th Avenue East. Follow the paved road 0.6 miles until it switches to gravel, and then turn left onto the DNR road. Continue on this main road 3.1 miles and then turn left at the fork in the road. In 0.1 miles veer left and continue 100 yards to the parking area, 5.3 miles from the turn off of WA 706.
DeLorme: Washington Atlas & Gazetteer: Page 47 B7

A trip into the wilds of the Elbe forests is an exercise in mud. This 12-plus mile ride offers a little bit of everything you'd expect in a western Washington mountain bike ride: fire roads, hills, root-covered technical trails, and scary downhills. But more than anything else, count on Elbe to offer year-round mud.

As any Washington mountain biker will tell you, there are many different kinds of mud in this state. There is the sandy, wet mud offered in places like the Tahuya State Forest, near Belfair, and there is sticky mud on the Capitol Forest trails that can build up on your knobby tires and turn a bike

ride into a mud removal project. In Elbe, the challenge of super-slick mud is taken to another level, thanks to motorcycle and ATV users who create mud holes that can swallow a bike and rider in a quicksand sort of slurry. Consider the shade from the second-growth forest and the ever-present moisture from fog and clouds overhead, and you recognize why Elbe is a major mud challenge.

This ride starts midway up a hillside in a small parking area and sends riders climbing along a fire road for the first four miles. Along the way, take in the view of the Nisqually River Valley to the left below the hill. The valley has been shaped by a combination of the effects of water draining from Mount Rainier's Nisqually Glacier and by ancient mudslides from Mount Rainier. It may be hard to imagine, but throughout the geologic history of the Elbe area, mudslides have come rushing down this val-

MilesDirections

0.0 START From the parking area, ride to the logging road and turn left down Busy Wild Road for 4.4 miles.

4.4 Turn right onto the Rainier Vista Trail and continue south along the ridge.

5.0 Ride down a steep downhill that may require a dismount for some riders.

5.2 Turn left at the bottom of the downhill.

5.3 Left onto a fire road, then a quick right onto the Gotcha Trail.

6.5 Back into the woods to a T-intersection in the trail. Go straight on the Gotcha Trail, avoiding the Swamp Trail.

7.0 Keep left on the gravel road in a clearing with a view of the valley below to the right.

7.4 Veer left off the Gotcha Trail onto the Mainline Trail and go deeper into the woods.

8.0 Stay left on the Mainline Trail.

8.2 Stay left and head up the hill on the Busy Wild Trail exit.

8.3 Head right on the Mainline Trail that is marked with silver triangles on nearby trees.

9.5 Stop on this hill and you can hear water rushing down the Busy Wild Creek. From here the trail emerges from the woods along a clearcut area. Take an unmarked right turn into the woods down a short downhill section to return to Busy Wild Road.

12.1 Turn left on Busy Wild Road to pedal back to the parking area.

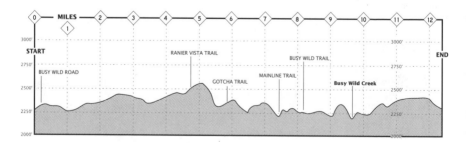

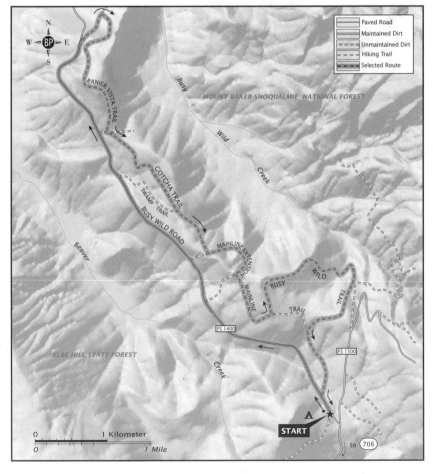

ley off the flanks of Mount Rainier to bury the area in countless feet of mud and volcanic debris.

None of that volcanic debris is readily apparent along this ride. After riding up the fire road for four miles, the trail turns to the right and runs through second-growth forest and recently logged, rolling hills to the north. The trail is well marked and easy to follow for the first six or seven miles, but it requires a rider's careful attention to stay on track when the trail turns from a fir needle-covered path to a winding, muddy mess formed by years of ATV use. Don't be surprised if you encounter jeeps and their drivers stuck up to their hubs and deeper in the muck. Despite the hardship of dodging the deep mud holes, the ride offers some great technical sections and the charming sights and sounds offered by the nearby Mashel River and Busy Wild Creek.

Undoubtedly it was these sights and sounds that led German pioneer families to settle the Elbe area in the 1880s. Just shy of the border of Mount Rainier National Park, the small town serves as the gateway to the park as well as to cross-country skiing and mountain biking in the folded mountains that lead to Mount Rainier.

Figuring into Elbe's history are some of Washington's earliest logging and mining railroads; in fact, the town is probably best known for its historic tourist train, the Mount Rainier Scenic Railroad. From Memorial Day through September, this vintage steam train carries passengers 14 miles from the heart of town along a winding track. Elbe is also home to one of the most unique churches in the state: the Evangelische Lutherische Kirche, a white clapboard church that measures just 24 feet by 18 feet. It's worth a peek inside the tiny church's exterior windows on the way through town.

Ride Information

◑ Trail Contacts:
Department of Natural Resources: (360) 748–2383 or 1–800–527–3305

◐ Schedule:
Open year round, but most rideable May through October

⑤ Fees/Permits:
No fees or permits required

❷ Local Information:
Singletrack Mind Mountain Biking Club at http://members.aol.com/STMClub/stmclub.html

◐ Local Events/Attractions:
Mount Rainier Scenic Railroad, Memorial Day through September, Elbe, WA (360) 569–2588 or 1–888–783–2611 or www.mrsr.com

🚲 Local Bike Shops:
Rainier Cycle Sports, Tacoma, WA (253) 756–2116

ⓝ Maps:
USGS maps: Ashford, WA; Elbe, WA

Tongue Mountain

Ride Summary

The super fast trail lies in the heart of timber country. Ridden as a loop or a shuttle, the climb up forest road is gentle, but the singletrack above is challenging. A quick jaunt will take you to a view on the mountain itself, while the trail actually circles around before heading down. The descent is steep and relatively smooth. This ride can be done fairly quickly by advanced riders, and is frequently the finale of the Juniper Ridge route that connects to the Tongue Mountain Trail to the south.

Ride Specs

Start: From FS 29 (or FS 2904 for the shuttle)

Other Starting Locations: From the intersection of Cispus Road and Spur Road 2801

Length: 11.1-mile point-to-point (17.0-mile loop)

Approximate Riding Time: 2–3 hours

Difficulty Rating: Moderate climb, difficult singletrack descent

Terrain: Steep ridgetop riding on singletrack (some smooth, some technical), forest roads, and optional pavement (on the round-trip return) with a descent through thick forest

Land Status: National forest

Nearest Town: Randle, WA

Other Trail Users: Hikers, equestrians, and motorcyclists

Canine Compatibility: Dogs permitted

Wheels: Front suspension recommended, but not required

Getting There

From Chehalis: Take U.S. 12 east to Randle. Turn right onto Woods Creek Road/ FS 25 and then left on to Cispus Road. Follow Cispus Road over the Cispus River. Park along FS 2801 to the left for the round-trip ride, or leave one car here and continue for almost a mile to a fork in the road. Turn left on FS 29. Follow about three miles to any pull-off or on to FS 2904 to begin the ride. *DeLorme: Washington Atlas & Gazetteer:* Page 34 A2

O ne of the most scenic driving tours in Washington is the loop around our famous lady volcano, Mount St. Helens. There are two loop routes, both originating from the town of Randle on U.S. Route 12. Loop One is 75 miles and heads south from Randle down Forest Service Road 25. Winding southward on paved forested roads, this loop takes Forest Service Road 26 and Forest Service Road 99 to the perch of the awe inspiring Windy Ridge Viewpoint, facing the great mountain and Spirit

Tongue Mountain rising up ahead.

Lake. From Forest Service Road 99, head back to Forest Service Road 2560 leading back to Forest Service Road 25 northward to Randle. Loop Two is over twice as long, heading west on U.S. Route 12 to Interstate 5 South. Take Exit 21 at Woodland and travel east on Washington 503 to Cougar, picking up Forest Service Road 90 to return northward to Randle on Forest Service Road 25. There are all kinds of photo opportunities along this route, as well as a slew of hiking and mountain biking trails.

Surrounded by mountains, the town of Randle is located on what used to be an ancient glacial lake that once stretched for 30 miles. A town of farmers and loggers, Randle saw its first sawmill go into operation in 1866. To the west and east of Randle are the towns of Morton and Packwood, both

MilesDirections

Shuttle Ride starting on FS 2904:

0.0 START the ride by heading up FS 2904.

1.2 Begin crossing the drainage and traversing to the other side of the valley.

1.9 Pass FS 604 on the left.

3.0 Round the corner to see Tongue Mountain in full view.

4.1 Intersect with the Juniper Ridge Trail (Trail 261) on the right and the Tongue Mountain Trail (Trail 294) on the left. Turn left onto Trail 294.

4.5 Ride along the ridge, downhill to the next saddle and then into another climb.

5.6 Climb to the next ridge of Tongue Mountain. From there it's all downhill!

5.7 Take a 0.8-mile hike up to a viewpoint at the top of Tongue Mountain, or continue straight toward FS 2801.

5.8 Pass a small trail berm off to the right. From here you can see Tower Rock and the whole ridge ahead of you.

6.2 Intersect with the Highbridge Trail (Trail 293A) on your left. Turn right at the Y-intersection, staying on Trail 294.

6.7 Just finishing an A+ section of downhill—fast.

7.6 Encounter a super tight switchback—be careful.

8.9 The trail starts a long descent down the ridgeline of Tongue Mountain: sweet, smooth downhill with little humps.

9.7 Reach FS 2801, and turn left to continue to your shuttle point.

11.1 Reach shuttle point at Cispus Road and FS 2801.

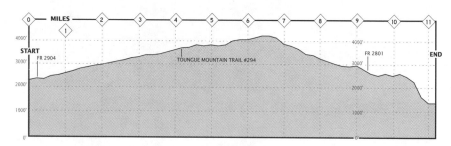

of which were settled in the late 1800s. Pioneering farmers from Kentucky and Tennessee populated these towns after growing weary of their southeastern homelands. Coming west in droves, they hoped to find homes in which to raise their families, where fish and wildlife were plentiful, and where there was room to grow.

Packwood was named after William Packwood, a well-known explorer who traveled the Cascade Range with James Longmire in the 1850s in search of a better crossing over the mountains from the Oregon Trail to Puget Sound. Together they cut the trail for Cowlitz Pass on the east side of Mount Rainier. In Packwood you'll find Hotel Packwood, which has been operating since 1912. President Theodore Roosevelt stayed here while attending the christening ceremonies of Mount Rainier National Park. This cozy hotel has nine rooms, two with private baths, and is furnished in antiques. It's open year-round, and rooms are very reasonably priced. Across the street is the Timberline Library. Built during the same time period, this small log library is set in a grove majestic Douglas firs alongside a city park.

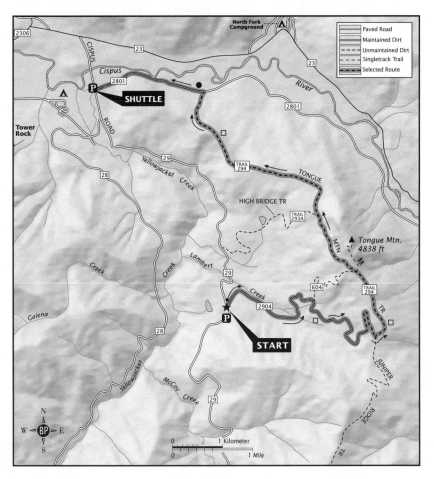

Southeast of Randle down Forest Service Road 25 is the Tongue Mountain Trail. One of the many ridge-top trails in the Gifford Pinchot National Forest, the trail to Tongue Mountain is at the north end of an epic ridge-runner along Juniper Ridge. Included in this book as an *Honorable Mention*, Juniper Ridge is a longer and tougher route. The Juniper ride circles east of four peaks along the Cispus River before climbing up to the ridgeline and around Jumbo, Sunrise, and Juniper peaks, finishing out with the trail to Tongue Mountain—all in one ride.

The Tongue Mountain ride begins by climbing a well-graded forest road up the Lambert Creek drainage. The road climb is only four miles to the Juniper Ridge Trail at 2,200 feet. (The trail climbs to 3,600 feet.) Logging trucks tend to run pretty fast out here, so be on the lookout. The climb can be made longer by starting lower on the logging road. It's not a tough climb so doing this ride as a loop is a good option if you're looking for more miles.

After climbing about three miles, the first peek at Tongue Mountain comes into view before you hit the singletrack. Remember, this is a ridge ride. The trail is steep at first and has intermittent downhills. There are several small climbs before the real descent begins after about four-and-a-half miles. The descent can be incredibly fast due to its steep grade in places. Under the cover of the dense forest canopy, the trail is technical and deeply rutted in places. Equestrians and motorcyclists also use this trail, so it does have its choppy moments. The last few miles of trail make an incredible mountainside descent. At the intersection with Forest Service Road 2801, it's all downhill on forest road to the Cispus River. A couple of pull-offs along the river make for nice picnic spots.

Ride Information

● Trail Contacts:
Gifford Pinchot National Forest, Randle Ranger District: (360) 497–1100

● Schedule:
June through October

● Fees/Permits:
$5 per car, per day ($30 for an annual pass); appropriate camping fees at the campgrounds

● Local Information:
Forest Service Outdoor Recreation Information: (206) 470–4060 • **Hotel Packwood,** Packwood, WA (360) 494–5431

● Maps:
USGS maps: Greenhorn Buttes, WA
USFS maps: Gifford Pinchot National Forest, Randle Ranger District Map
Green Trails: McCoy Peak No. 333

Chain of Lakes
Figure Eight

Ride Summary

This fantastic loop covers rolling singletrack and a forest road descent while weaving around an actual chain of lakes. Although Mount Adams rarely comes into view, two river crossings and great singletrack make this moderately difficult ride one you will want to do again and again.

Ride Specs

Start: From the Chain of Lakes Campground
Other Starting Locations: Takhlakh Lake Campground
Length: 16.5-mile figure eight
Approximate Riding Time: 3–4 hours
Difficulty Rating: Moderate to Difficult due to semi-technical singletrack and intermediate climbs
Terrain: Singletrack, forest road, and short pavement sections over rolling hills with occasional water views
Land Status: National forest
Nearest Towns: Randle, WA; Trout Lake, WA
Other Trail Users: Hikers and equestrians
Canine Compatibility: Dogs permitted
Wheels: Front suspension recommended

Getting There

From Chehalis: Take U.S. 12 east to Randle. Turn right onto Woods Creek Road/FS 25, and then left on to Cispus Road. Follow Cispus Road to a fork just before crossing the Cispus River. At the fork, follow FS 23 to the left. Follow FS 23 south at least eight miles to the fork with FS 21. Veer right to stay on FS 23; stay on FS 23 for about 10 miles until the intersection for Takhlakh Lake and FS 2329. Turn onto FS 022 and park near the Chain of Lakes Campground.
DeLorme: Washington Atlas & Gazetteer: Page 34 B4

ount Adams. Now this is the place to mountain bike. Though remote when compared to its high-traffic sister volcanoes Mount St. Helens and Mount Rainier, Mount Adams offers spectacular trails, interesting geologic traits, and warm, dry weather—not to mention plenty of elbow room. Since Mount Adams has no national park designation, mountain biking is allowed just about everywhere (except in the wilderness areas, of course). For those who are willing to venture a little off the beaten path, Mount Adams is an exquisite oasis for all kinds of fun.

Standing at 12,276 feet, Mount Adams is Washington's second highest peak and home to the second largest glacier in the Cascade Range, the

Killen Creek.

MilesDirections

0.0 START from FS 022 at the Chain of Lakes Campground, ride back up the gravel road to FS 2329 toward Lake Takhlakh.

1.0 Turn right on FS 2329.

1.5 Turn right on FS 5601.

1.6 Pass Squaw Creek Trail (Trail 265) on the left.

1.7 Turn right on High Lakes Trail (Trail 116)—see mile marker #6. Chain of Lakes is two miles ahead on this trail.

3.2 Complete a short descent heading to the Chain of Lakes, passing one on the left. Follow the trail left toward the lake and arrive at the camping area; or, follow the right turns and cross FS 022 to the connecting trail across the road.

3.6 The lake trail ends at the campsite. Turn right on the road and pick the trail up on the left a few hundred feet up. Take Trail 116.

5.3 Cross Adams Creek. There should be a log to walk over.

6.3 Wade across Killen Creek.

7.0 Intersect with Trail 115 and Keenes Horse Camp Trail. Follow the Keenes Horse Camp Trail to the right.

7.1 Pass a spur to the right leading to the lake. Ahead 50 yards, pass signs for Horseshoe Camp. Take Trail 116 on the left, or bail to the road if you've had enough.

7.6 Turn right onto Trail 120. Follow it toward Keenes Horse Camp. In 0.1-mile, at the fork, turn left heading up.

8.1 Cross a wooden bridge.

8.3 Cross another wooden bridge.

8.5 Cross another wooden bridge into Keenes Horse Camp. Leave the horse camp to the right heading to FS 2329. Turn right on FS 2329. There are a few trails off to the right of the road that you can take for extra singletrack riding.

9.7 Pass Killen Forest Camp on your right.

10.2 Pass Killen Creek Trail on your left.

11.6 Cross the East Fork Adams Creek (El. 4,300 feet).

12.3 Cross the Middle Fork Adams Creek.

12.5 Cross the West Fork Adams Creek.

12.8 Pass Divide Camp Trail 112 on the left.

13.7 Pass Takh Takh Meadow. The trail is open to hikers only.

14.9 Come to an intersection with FS 26. Continue straight.

15.2 Turn right on FS 022 to the campground.

16.5 Arrive back at the Chain of Lakes Campground.

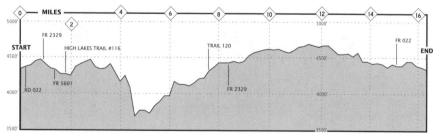

Klickitat. Though Mount Adams has been dormant for about 10,000 years, there are acres of evidence, easily spotted along this ride, to suggest that the mountain has not always been so well behaved. As you ride the Chain of Lakes loop, look for the ancient basalt surrounding the mountain's periphery, especially on the descent to Adams Creek. The black clumps of rock are hard to miss. Also, keep on the lookout for hawks and ravens riding the warm air currents of the mountain thermals.

Of all the Cascade volcanoes, Mount Adams is probably the least understood, due in part to its attention-getting neighbors, but also due to its remoteness. The few geologic studies that have been conducted draw some interesting conclusions. David Alt and Donald Hyndman, authors of *Roadside Geology of Washington*, describe the mountain as being "broadly squat in form, which looks distinctively different from every direction." This is different from the other volcanoes, indicating that there is more to

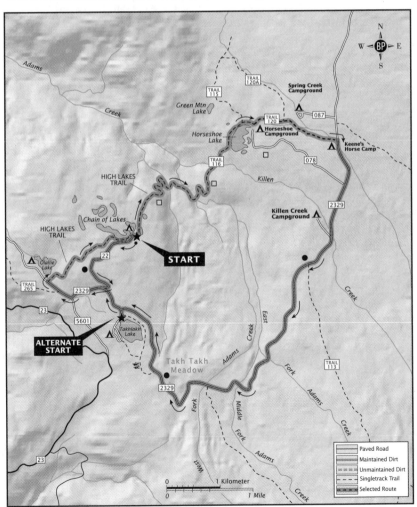

Adams than meets the eye. One theory to explain the difference in shape is that Mount Adams may be made up of more than just one volcanic cone—quite possibly several. This is of no real consequence to your safety, but geologists find it interesting and enjoy speculating about the shape of the mountain's lower half.

Mount Adams may be dormant on the inside, but there's certainly a lot of activity on the outside. The entire area surrounding Mount Adams has a labyrinth of awesome trails; however, not all are open to mountain bikes. The weather is dry and warm on summer days and cool and crisp at night, making this a fantastic place to ride and camp. Even in August you can ski, climb, and snowboard on the frozen, white fields above the treeline. The forests are dense with hemlock, Douglas fir, and some silver fir. These dry, needle-bedded forests are considerably different from the lush, wet forests west of the Cascades.

The Chain of Lakes trail officially begins at the Chain of Lakes Campground, a secluded area next to one of the placid mountain lakes in the chain. There are only a few camping pull-offs and an outhouse up the road. The High Lakes Trail laces its way around a few small lakes connecting with the Chain of Lakes Trail at the Chain of Lakes Campground. After a moderate climb into the woods and around a few more small lakes, the

Adams Creek.

scenery changes upon entering what looks like a graveyard of igneous rock deposits. The trail tightly hugs the hillside and drops quickly to Adams Creek, a fairly large creek. You will probably get wet at some point along this ride—either here or farther up the trail. There are no bridges along this portion of the ride, just a downed log over Adams Creek, and nothing else over the stream ahead.

Climbing up from the creek requires strong legs and a bit of tenacity. Fortunately, the trail is smooth. It's a long climb, though, flattening briefly before arriving at Killen Creek. Much smaller than Adams Creek, Killen Creek is still a great place to dunk your head to cool off. After crossing the creek, the ride is pretty easy. Continue to Keenes Horse Camp around Horseshoe Lake, and the singletrack ends shortly thereafter. At the horse camp there's a gravel forest road that winds down along the wilderness boundary of Mount Adams all the way back to Takhlakh Lake.

Camping is available at either Takhlakh or Chain of Lakes. There are three peaceful sites at Chain of Lakes. There is no running water and only one outhouse, a short walk from the lake. Takhlakh Lake sites do have running water in a few central areas and room for RVs. It can get a bit crowded at this campground, but it's right on the lake facing the mass of Mount Adams. You just can't beat the view.

Ride Information

ⓒ Trail Contacts:
Gifford Pinchot National Forest, Randle Ranger District: (360) 497-1100 • **Gifford Pinchot National Forest Headquarters,** Vancouver, WA (360) 891-5000 • **Mount Adams Ranger District**, Trout Lake, WA (509) 395-2501

ⓒ Schedule:
Open in the summer and fall months before and after snowfall

ⓢ Fees/Permits:
$5 per car, per day ($30 for an annual pass)

ⓠ Local Information:
Weather Radio: AM 1340

ⓠ Local Events/Attractions:
Arts Festival & Volkssport Walk, in July, Trout Lake, WA (509) 395-2294 • **Community Fair and Dairy Show,** in August, Trout Lake, WA (509) 395-2241 (or 395-2289) • **Huckleberry picking,** in August, all over the Mount Adams area. Ask at the Ranger Station for a permit and map of the legal areas in which to pick.

ⓒ Local Bike Shops:
Dick's Bicycle Center, Vancouver, WA (360) 696-9234 • **Excel Fitness,** Vancouver, WA (360) 834-8506 • **Discovery Bicycles,** Hood River, OR (541) 386-4820 • **Mountain View Cycles & Fitness,** Hood River, OR (541) 386-2888

ⓝ Maps:
USGS maps: Green Mountain, WA

Mount St. Helens

For years it was said that Mount St. Helens had no rival in the Cascade range when it came to beauty—just as mythology's Helen had had no rival in all of Greece. Ranked a modest fifth in height among Washington's landmark peaks, the volcano derived its allure not from age or size or vertical achievement but from its flawless symmetry and its graceful, glacier-trimmed slopes. It was proudly dubbed the Mount Fuji of America. And then one day, rather unexpectedly, the sleeping beauty began to rumble. Geologists rightly feared that the volcano was about to blow and set to warning the surrounding communities. The gravity of the geologists' concern could not have been imagined by Washingtonians, since no living soul had ever witnessed a Cascade eruption. For two months the mountain was rocked with nearly 10,000 localized earthquakes and hundreds of steam explosions. The pressure had swollen the north flank by more than 270 feet. On the morning of May 18, 1980 (8:32 A.M.), the once serene volcano awoke to a magnitude 5.1 earthquake. The swollen north flanks immediately collapsed, in mass, amounting to the largest recorded landslide in history. Within seconds the mountain blew. The eruption lasted, without pause, for 9 hours. But it was the initial lateral blast, which lasted only the first few minutes, that cause the most destruction. Steam and rock debris shot from the mountain at 670 miles per hour, leveling 150 square miles of forest and killing virtually everything in its path—a number of pocket gopher actually survived the blast. All told, the mountain shed 1,312 feet off its crown, killed 57 people and countless animals, destroyed 96,000 acres of timber (a good deal of it old-growth), and deposited 490 tons of ash on 22,000 square miles of land.

Ape Canyon

Lava Dome

Sasquatch Steps

Plains of Abraham

Mount St. Helens: McBride/Kalama Loop

Ride Summary

This popular route skirts the base of Mount St. Helens and is frequently used by horseback riders. Its trail, thick and mucky along the river, climbs steeply to meet very deep and sandy singletrack. Although it is not a long loop, the ride is quite fulfilling. The trail heads into the woods and around McBride Lake through prime Sasquatch-viewing territory, so keep your eyes peeled for big, hairy men (not to be confused with your riding partner).

Ride Specs

Start: From the Kalama Horse Camp
Other Starting Locations: From the Red Rock Pass
Length: 12.0-mile loop
Approximate Riding Time: 1 hour
Difficulty Rating: Easy to Moderate due to sandy singletrack and mild grade climbs on forest road
Terrain: Forest road and sandy singletrack over rolling hills through second-growth forests, with a few sandy sections
Land Status: National forest
Nearest Town: Cougar, WA
Other Trail Users: Hikers and equestrians
Canine Compatibility: Dogs permitted
Wheels: Front suspension suggested, and come prepared for mud and loose, sandy soils

Getting There

From Vancouver: Take I-5 North to Woodland. Take WA 503 East (Lewis River Road). After 34 miles, turn left on to FS 83. Pass FS 8303 and take FS 81 all the way to Red Rock Pass and FS 8123. Turn left onto FS 8123, and follow it approximately 2.5 miles to the Kalama Horse Camp. *DeLorme: Washington Atlas & Gazetteer:* Page 33 C6

M other Nature. Would you think to call her Helen? Whether blowing her top or providing incredible landscapes to explore, Mount St. Helens certainly knows how to put on a show. You can't beat the adventures to be had at this historic site.

This first ride starts off in the trees surrounding a trail that has become very sandy. So sandy in fact, you may think you're at the beach—except the seagulls are now bald eagles. You'll be heading up and away from the river in a bit, but for the early section of the ride you'll feel the cool and somewhat clammy dankness of the

Nothing like a good author pose.

river drainage. The climb out of the drainage is tough. You'll probably need to push your bike up.

At the top, the air clears and the tree cover opens. Occasionally along the trail you'll run across horse treats; be careful. If the weather's at all warm, these *treats* draw flies to the trail—though you can usually depend on a pleasant breeze to keep them away. Once on top, you may think you're still climbing because of the sandy trail conditions. If you stay on the upper sides of the trail, it'll be easier. The horses have made the path soft, so try to spin through as best you can. This might actually make a nice downhill ride.

As you meander through these forests, be attentive; you're in perfect Sasquatch-spotting territory. Better known to Americans, at least since the 1950s, as Bigfoot, Sasquatch is believed by some to be the so-called *missing link*, a possible relation of the believed-to-be-extinct race of Neanderthals. This is an even more curious theory when we look at how long humans have been spotting these creatures. The Kwakiutl Indians of British Columbia carved the ferocious human-like face of *Bukwas* (Wild Man of the Woods) into their popular masks. And Sasquatch, the giant cannibal, is spoken of frequently in the tales of the Salish Indians.

The Indians relayed their stories to some of the areas earliest Anglo-explorers, many of whom were skeptical, but nonetheless curious. In 1792 explorer Jose Mariano Mozino wrote:

MilesDirections

0.0 START by taking the Toutle Trail (Trail 238) at Kalama Horse Camp up along the Kalama River.

0.4 Intersect with the Kalama Ski Trail. Keep to the Trail 238.

2.9 Cross FS 8122 at the campground and continue on the Trail 238.

4.2 Pass FS 600. Follow the river one-and-three-quarter miles toward Red Rock Pass.

4.6 Climb above McBride Lake.

5.0 Climb tops out. Descend to Red Rock Pass.

6.0 Arrive at the junction of FS 8100. Turn left and follow it down for about three miles.

9.0 At FS 8123, turn left and ride back to the Kalama Horse Camp.

12.0 Arrive at the Kalama Horse Camp

Note: *For a smoother climb, a more interesting descent, and an easier ride overall, try this route in reverse.*

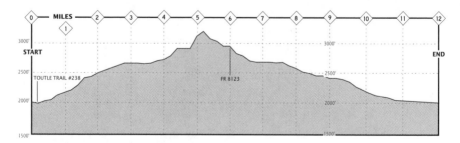

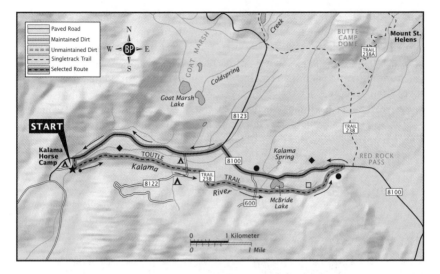

I do not know what to say about the matlox [Sasquatch], inhabitant of the mountainous districts, of whom all have an unbelievable fear. They imagine his body as very monstrous, all covered with stiff black bristles; a head similar to a human one but with much greater, sharper, and stronger fangs than those of the bear; extremely long arms; and toes and fingers armed with long curved claws. His shouts alone (they say) force those who hear them to the ground, and any unfortunate body he slaps is broken into a thousand pieces.

In 1811, while crossing the Rockies near the Athabasca River in British Columbia, David Thompson reported finding unusually large animal tracks that would not fit the characteristics of a bear. His men insisted they were the tracks of the "young Mammoth" the Indians had spoken of, but Thompson held that the tracks were simply left by an abnormally large bear whose claws had worn away from age. He admitted, though, that he had no explanation for the balls of the feet.

Some other notable accounts of brushes with Sasquatch include a report in 1884 by a British Columbian newspaper about a four-foot, hairy, ape-man creature they called "Jacko"—maybe a teenage Bigfoot. In the early 1900s, Fraser River in British Columbia seemed to be the place for spotting Sasquatch. The Seattle Times ran a story on July 16, 1918, about a band of Sasquatch that attacked a man in Kelso, Washington, while he searched for gold. People had a tough time believing the story, even though the man provided "eye-witnesses."

One of the most famous stories about Sasquatch involves a retired lumberman, Albert Ostman. In 1924, Ostman was on Vancouver Island searching for gold. On the second night of his trip, he was awakened by someone (or something) dragging his sleeping bag (with him in it) from his camp. He lay still in the bag for some 25 miles before slipping out. His escape attempt failed. In no time he found himself surrounded by a Sasquatch family. Ostman said he was not harmed by the animals, and thought the family of four was actually intrigued by him. It was a full six days before Ostman escaped. It was another 33 years, however, before he was willing to tell anyone his story, which he swore to before a justice of the peace at Fort Langley, British Columbia.

Whether fact or fiction, hundreds of Sasquatch sightings have been reported between northern California and British Columbia. It's worth noting, though, that there have been no known sightings in this area for over 20 years. But you never know when Sasquatch might reappear. In the interest of preparedness, if you happen to spot an eight-foot tall, hairy creature that looks half-human/half-ape, our expert advice is: take a picture and ride like hell!

Ride Information

🕐 Trail Contacts:
Mount St. Helens National Volcanic Monument office: (360) 247–5473 • Mount St. Helens National Volcanic Monument, Amboy, WA (360) 247–3900

🕐 Schedule:
No winter riding

💲 Fees/Permits:
$5 per car, per day ($30 for an annual pass); campground fees

❓ Local Information:
Visitor Centers around Mount St. Helens from WA 504 are: **The Mount St. Helens Visitor Center:** (360) 274–2100 • **The Cowlitz County Hoffstadt Bluffs Rest Area and Visitor Center** at milepost 27: (360) 274–7750 • **The Forest Learning Center,** May through October only:

(360) 414–3439 • **The Coldwater Ridge Visitor Center:** (360) 274–2114 • **The Johnston Ridge Observatory,** five miles from the crater: (360) 274–2143

🚲 Local Bike Shops:
Jack's Restaurant and Sporting Goods, Ariel, WA (360) 231–4276 – limited bike supplies, mostly backpacking gear • **Chelatchie Store,** Amboy, WA (360) 247–5529

📖 Suggested Reading:
Sasquatch/Bigfoot The Search for North America's Incredible Creature by Don Hunter and Rene Dahindenk • *Sasquatch: Wild Man of the Woods* by Elaine Landau

🅝 Maps:
USGS maps: Goat Mountain, WA; Mount St. Helens, WA

Mount St. Helens: Blue Lake Ride

Ride Summary

The route along Blue Lake showcases some of Washington's most vivid landscapes. Traveling along the still-forested sections of Mount St. Helens, this non-technical ride keeps to the trees, making a trail that cyclists of any skill level will enjoy—until the descent into Sheep Canyon. For those new to the sport, take caution entering the canyon. You might have to push your way back up. Pay close attention to the posted signs, as some of the trails are unfortunately not open to mountain bikes.

Ride Specs

Start: From the Redrock Pass trailhead
Other Starting Locations: From the Kalama Horse Camp
Length: 12.8-mile out-and-back (12.0-mile loop)
Approximate Riding Time: 3–4 hours
Difficulty Rating: Moderate, except for one steep climb on non-technical single-track
Terrain: Sand and gravel singletrack and dirt roads cross rolling hills with some steep climbing, all through the trees
Land Status: National forest
Nearest Town: Cougar, WA
Other Trail Users: Hikers and equestrians
Canine Compatibility: Dogs permitted
Wheels: Front suspension recommended, but not required

Getting There

From Vancouver: Take I-5 North to Woodland. Take WA 503 East (Lewis River Road). After 34 miles, turn left on to FS 83. Pass FS 8303 and take FS 81 to Redrock Pass. The road turns to gravel after a few miles and the trailhead is on the right next to Mount St. Helens.
DeLorme: Washington Atlas & Gazetteer: Page 33 C6

A thick evergreen canopy covers the trails along Mount St. Helen's southwestern flank. From here, one might not realize that Mount St. Helens ever erupted. But on May 18, 1980, this serene mountain, which had been quiet for over a century, did, in fact, *wake up*. The blast from Mount St. Helens scorched everything in its northeastern path, stripping trees of their branches, bark, and needles, and flattening them to create thousands of acres of giant toppled toothpicks. Lakes moved or disappeared as others were created by the accelerated melt of Mount St. Helen's glaciers. Even though their homes were decimated, deer and elk

were seen wandering within the destruction zone just days after the event—they soon left for greener pastures. Within a year, plant-life began to spring from the scorched earth, and today, more than 20 years later, many animal species have returned to their homes. Though the toothpicks remain, the hillsides become greener every year, and trees have begun to grow once again. In 1982, 110,000 acres of land on and around Mount St. Helens received its official national monument designation and is now known as the Mount St. Helens National Volcanic Monument.

The Blue Lake Trail is located on Mount St. Helen's southwest side, shielded by the mass that was not lost in the eruption. This is a moderately challenging trail, due mostly to the ravine that leaves you gasping for breath at the top. It's a popular route, too, because it displays a different side to the mighty mountain, one that is still green and tree covered, reminiscent of the way it used to be all the way around.

The ride begins out in the open at first, in a field of huge, black boulders at Red Rock Pass, which are quite impressive. There may be a little pushing involved, but not much; and soon afterward, the trail begins to roll into the woods. Skirting the edge of the mountain, past a couple of intersections, the trail then leads to Blue Lake and beyond. The lake is actual-

ly more of a swamp by late summer and adds thick moisture to the air inside the forest. The trail climbs gently for about six miles until it drops like a rock into Sheep Canyon. At this point, there are a couple of options for the return trip.

The easiest ride back involves only the retracing of your tracks back to Red Rock Pass. A longer, more difficult option is to continue on down into the canyon and following the Loowit Trail back to Redrock Pass. Since the mountain's eruption, trail development has been growing steadily. Depending on the progress made on the Loowit Trail you may have no choice but to turn around. Since the area is still under development, it is difficult to accurately predict which trails you can use. Please check at the trailhead or at one of the four visitor information areas to make sure the Loowit Trail is open to mountain bikers if you plan to ride the loop option.

MilesDirections

0.0 START at the Red Rock Pass trailhead (Trail 238) and head into the huge boulder field.

1.5 Pass Butte Camp Dome, behind and on the right.

3.1 Intersect with Blue Horse Trail (Trail 237). Continue straight.

3.4 Arrive at FS 170 and the parking area for the Blue Lake Trailhead. Follow the trail over the wooden bridge and up alongside Coldspring Creek.

3.8 Arrive at Blue Lake. Take the trail up away from the lake.

4.0 The trail traverses and climbs into the forest.

6.4 Trail 240 is on the right and goes across the bridge over the creek. Loowit Trail (Trail 216) picks up in 1.5 miles. This is the trail loop option that travels around the entire mountain. To the left is the Toutle Trail (Trail 238) continuing on. Turn around here and retrace your tracks back to Red Rock Pass. *[Option. If the signs indicate that bikes are permitted, follow Trail 240 to the right and up the mountainside to make a 12-mile loop. At Trail 216, turn right and follow it along the northeast side of Butte Camp Dome. At Trail 238A, turn right and take major switchbacks to Trail 238. From there it's left and then back to Red Rock Pass.]*

12.8 Arrive back at the Red Rock Pass trailhead.

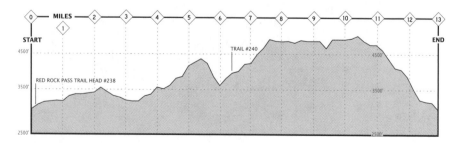

198

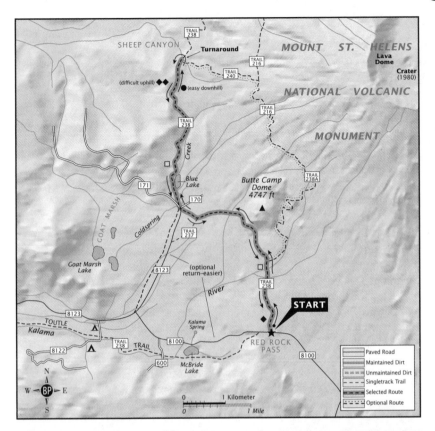

Ride Information

📞 Trail Contacts:
Mount St. Helens National Volcanic Monument office: (360) 247–3900

💲 Fees/Permits:
$5 per car, per day ($30 for an annual pass); campground fees

❓ Local Information:
Visitor Centers around Mount St. Helens from WA 504 are: **The Mount St. Helens Visitor Center:** (360) 274–2100 • **The Cowlitz County Hoffstadt Bluffs Rest Area and Visitor Center** at milepost 27: (360) 274–7750 • **The Forest Learning Center,** May through October only:

(360) 414–3439 • **The Coldwater Ridge Visitor Center:** (360) 274–2114 • **The Johnston Ridge Observatory,** five miles from the crater: (360) 274–2143

🚲 Local Bike Shops:
Jack's Restaurant and Sporting Goods, Ariel, WA (360) 231–4276 – *limited bike supplies, mostly backpacking gear* • **Chelatchie Store,** Amboy, WA (360) 247–5529

🅽 Maps:
USGS maps: Goat Mountain, WA; Mount St. Helens, WA

Mount St. Helens: Plains of Abraham

Ride Summary

Riding straight for the blast zone, the trail to the Plains of Abraham warms you up with a good climb into the trees. Passing above Ape Canyon, the Plains starkly contrast with the surrounding forest that somehow escaped 1980's scorching eruption. Traveling along a rocky, rolling moonscape, the Plains of Abraham Trail will offer a challenge to mountain bikers of intermediate and lower skill levels, but the views are one in a million.

Ride Specs

Start: From the Ape Canyon Trail (Trail 234)
Length: 13.6-mile out-and-back (can extend to 22.5 miles)
Approximate Riding Time: 2–3 hours
Difficulty Rating: Moderate climb, semi-technical singletrack
Terrain: Singletrack, with some rocky sections, through extreme terrain, scattered with rocks and some low foliage in areas recovering from the eruption
Land Status: National monument
Nearest Town: Cougar, WA
Other Trail Users: Hikers
Canine Compatibility: Dogs not permitted
Wheels: Full suspension recommended, but you can squeak by with front suspension

Getting There

From Vancouver: Take I-5 North to Woodland. Take WA 503 (Lewis River Road) east. After 34 miles, turn left on to FS 83 toward Ape Cave and Mount St. Helens viewpoint. Pass FS 8303 to Ape Cave, FS 81 to Climbers Bivouac, Marble Mount, and June Lake. Turn left at Ape Canyon Trailhead—44 miles from Woodland. *DeLorme: Washington Atlas & Gazetteer:* Page 33 C8

O
n May 18, 1980 Mount St. Helens, the smallest of Washington's volcanoes, changed the way she would appear to the world forever. Standing at 9,677 feet prior to the 1980 eruption, Mount St. Helens lost 1,300 feet of her top in just nine hours. The eruption began as steam—enough steam to cast a fiendish 400-degree wind more than 650 miles per hour from the northeastern face of the mountain, killing everything in its path for 150 square miles, including wildlife, plant life, and even human life. She also blew volcanic ash more than 15 miles into the air. Winds carried the ash, consisting of pul-

Ape Canyon.

verized prehistoric rock and solidified lava, eastward across the country, falling most heavily on eastern Washington, but traveling as far away as western Montana.

Molten lava wasn't a problem with the Mount St. Helens eruption in 1980—not like it was two thousand years ago. Mount St. Helens did erupt with lava at one time. The proof can be seen today eight miles south of the Lewis River at Ape Cave. Smooth-flowing lava called *pahoehoe* basalt flowed down the sides of Mount St. Helens for weeks. When the lava began to cool, it formed a crust on the surface, but lava continued to flow beneath it. By the time the lava stopped flowing, a long tunnel had been formed, leaving behind what is called a lava tube.

Ape Cave is almost two-and-a half miles long (12,810 feet), making it the longest intact lava tube in the United States, and the second longest in the world. Ape Cave was named in honor of a local youth group called the Mount St. Helens Apes who hiked and explored the mountain and discovered the tube in the 1950s. It is definitely worth a visit. With the help of a

MilesDirections

0.0 START on the Ape Canyon Trail (Trail 234) from the parking lot at the base of Mount St. Helens. The sign also reads: "Loowit Trail #216, 5.5 miles, and Windy Ridge Road 99, 11.25 miles."

2.1 Switchback view of Mount St. Helens.

4.5 Viewpoint of the peak and washouts.

5.5 Intersection of Loowit Trail (Trail 216). Follow to the right to the Plains of Abraham and head toward the south/southeast side of Mount St. Helens. Up ahead the next sign reads: "Loowit Trail #216, Plains of Abraham Trail #216D, 1.75 miles, Windy Pass 2 miles, Windy Ridge Road 99, 5.75 miles."

6.5 Follow the rock cairns and see the depths of Ape Canyon and the heights of mounts Rainier, Adams, and even Hood at times.

6.8 Pass Trail 216 on the left. Stay straight on the Planes of Abraham Trail (Trail 216D) toward Windy Ridge Road (FS 99). This is the turnaround point. Head back the way you came. *[Option. For a longer ride, continue on Trail 216D for 4.5 miles to FS 99. At 11.25 miles, turn around and retrace your tracks back to the start for a 22.5-mile trip.]*

13.6 Arrive back at your vehicle.

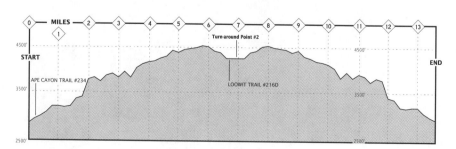

bright lantern and jacket, there are two routes to explore. The Information Station at Ape Cave has additional details.

Within the boundaries of the Mount St. Helens National Volcanic Monument there are over 500 miles of trail to discover. We've charted only three in this book, but the territory is so inviting you may want to explore on your own. The Plains of Abraham ride takes you through fertile forest and mudflow washouts and incredible views of the mountains. The Plains are like a moonscape: dry, crusted remnants of what used to be inside the mountain. This will be a rather warm ride in the heat of summer, yet stunning in the presence of three other active volcanoes: Rainier, Adams, and Hood.

Begin the ride at the trailhead into the forest on steady, mellow grade singletrack. In the fall, the colors are spectacular. Rounding the first bend, Mount St. Helens comes into view for a breathtaking first appearance. Along a narrow ridge, Ape Canyon can be seen below to the right until finally, breaking away from the trees, the trail enters the area of deadfall

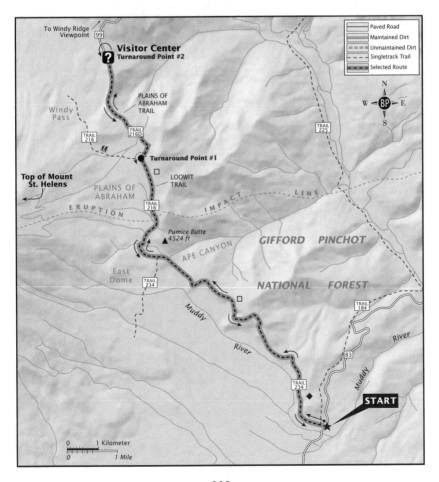

from the 1980 blast. The trail is well marked as it winds its way up the hill-sides. The Plains of Abraham trail is dusty and rolling and intersects with trails heading up to the crater that are not open to mountain bikes. We've marked a turnaround point within the directions, but the trail goes as far as Windy Ridge Road (Forest Service Road 99) before connecting with the Loowit Trail and traveling along the perimeter of the mountain.

Ride Information

❶ Trail Contacts:

Mount St. Helens National Volcanic Monument office: (360) 247–5473 • Mount St. Helen's National Volcanic Monument, Amboy, WA (360) 247–3900

🕘 Schedule:

Year round, weather permitting

❺ Fees/Permits:

$5 per car, per day ($30 for an annual pass); campground fees

❓ Local Information:

Visitor Centers around Mount St. Helens from WA 504 are: **The Mount St. Helens Visitor Center:** (360) 274–2100 • **The Cowlitz County Hoffstadt Bluffs Rest Area and Visitor Center** at milepost 27: (360) 274–7750 • **The Forest Learning Center,** May through October only: (360) 414–3439 • **The Coldwater Ridge Visitor Center:** (360) 274–2114 • **The Johnston Ridge Observatory,** five miles from the crater: (360) 274–2143

🚲 Local Bike Shops:

Jack's Restaurant and Sporting Goods, Ariel, WA (360) 231–4276 – limited bike supplies, mostly backpacking gear • **Chelatchie Store,** Amboy, WA (360) 247–5529

Ⓝ Maps:

USGS maps: Mount St. Helens, WA; Smith Creek Butte, WA

Service Trail/ Surprise Lakes

Ride Summary

A great way to start your day at Mount Adams, the Service Trail near Surprise Lakes offers a wonderful singletrack trip in a relatively short amount of time. There is a mellow road climb along fragrant berry fields, and a winding trail around a couple of lakes before the singletrack races down into the woods on a very dusty trail frequently shared with motorcyclists. This trail doesn't gain much elevation, but climbs in and out of creek drainages, which is almost more tiring because there are few sections of straightaway. It's a quick trip, though, and it makes an invigorating prelude to your day at Mount Adams.

Ride Specs

Start: From the Cultus Creek Campground
Length: 12.9-mile loop (with option for nine additional miles)
Approximate Riding Time: 2–3 hours
Difficulty Rating: Easy road climb and intermediate singletrack
Terrain: Singletrack and forest road climb through thick berry fields into the woods around Mount Adams
Land Status: National forest
Nearest Town: Trout Lake, WA
Other Trail Users: Hikers, equestrians, and motorcyclists
Canine Compatibility: Dogs permitted
Wheels: Front suspension recommended, and mud-shedding tires can come in handy

Getting There

From White Salmon: Travel north on WA 141. After about 28 miles, turn right onto FS 24. Travel nine miles to the Cultus Campground. *DeLorme: Washington Atlas & Gazetteer:* Page 34 D2

T
he Mount Adams Recreational Area offers some of the most scenic trails and views in the state. With the combination of terrain and weather conditions, southern Washington couldn't be more ideal for summer mountain biking adventures and overnight camping. Though the tourism industry hasn't yet littered the base of the mountain with corporate lodges and bus terminals (thankfully), these lands around Mount Adams are still well known to locals and to Native American tribes.

MilesDirections

0.0 START from Cultus Creek Campground. Turn right onto FS 24, heading north.

2.1 Cross a bridge over the Middle Fork of Meadow Creek.

2.3 *[FYI. See a sign about the historic handshake agreement of 1932 giving Native Americans the sole right to pick huckleberries on the east side of the road.]*

2.8 Pass FS 210 on the right, which goes to other camping areas.

3.4 Pass a dirt road on the right. *[FYI. See one of the Surprise Lakes on your right.]*

3.7 Pass FS 221 on the left. At the Middle Trail (Trail 26), turn right and follow a sandy doubletrack into Deadhorse Meadows. Keep to the right-hand trails as you encounter intersections.

4.1 At the T-intersection, turn right onto the Service Trail (also called the Middle Trail or Trail 26, as indicated on the sign here). Sign also points out that this is a "most difficult" trail. Agreed.

4.2 Pass another of the Surprise Lakes, keeping right at the intersection.

4.7 Another sign says you'll come to two road crossings in the next five miles— these are not on the Forest Service map.

6.1 Well into a white-knuckle descent, cross a couple of creeks and head into the forest.

6.4 Cross a wooden bridge and another creek.

6.6 Cross FS 100. Continue climbing.

7.4 Cross Cultus Creek.

7.9 Trail empties onto a road (also not on the Forest Service map). Turn left and catch the trail on the left at the bend in the road. See the diamond marker on the tree. The trail crosses the road again and continues on through the woods.

8.4 Cross a fork of Little Goose Creek.

9.0 Cross the other fork of Little Goose Creek on a wooden bridge.

9.4 Cross another creek.

10.3 Reach a Y-intersection with Trail 35 and Trail 26. *[Option. To add to your loop you can go left into the clearcut and come out farther down the road.]* For this loop, stay to the right.

10.6 Turn right on FS 24 and head back to Cultus Creek Campground.

10.7 Pass Little Goose Campground.

11.9 Pass Hidden Lakes Trail (Trail 106).

12.9 Arrive at Cultus Creek Campground.

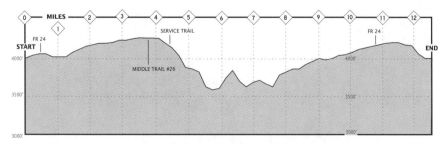

One mile north of Red Mountain Road is a straightaway across an open meadow called the Indian Racetrack. Local tribes once held foot races here, and during the summer harvest, huckleberries were dried here. The area is now preserved and managed by the National Forest Service within the Indian Heaven Wilderness Area. No longer a field for spectator sports, hikers and equestrians come through the Racetrack just to visit and to share in its beauty.

Even though they don't use the Racetrack anymore, Native Americans still frequent the hillsides of Mount Adams to harvest huckleberries. This ride passes by the Sawtooth Berryfields, well known for their sweet, juicy fruit. Certain portions of these fields are open only to Native American

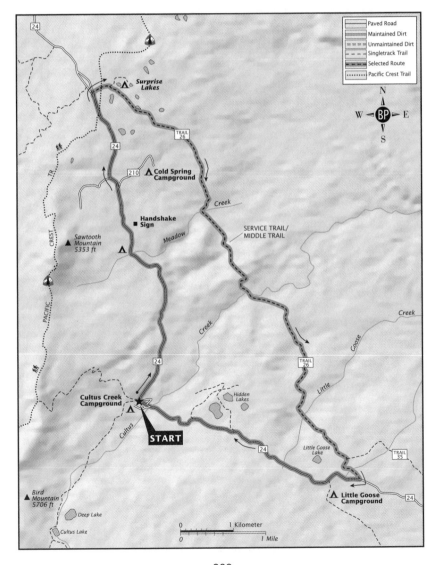

tribes. Other fields are open to the public by permit only. The Forest Service has maps and permits for designated public huckleberry fields. If you are interested in eating but not picking berries, just check out any of the local diners; huckleberry shakes and pies are sure to be on the menu.

The Indian Heaven Wilderness covers 20,690 acres within the Gifford Pinchot National Forest—land that used to be inhabited by the Klickitat and Yakima tribes. This area includes three rather impressive peaks, though somewhat dwarfed by Mount Adams: Sawtooth (5,873 feet), Bird (5,706 feet), and Berry (5,050 feet). The Forest Service in Trout Lake has all sorts of information about the Indian Heaven Wilderness and neighboring

Mount Adams in the background.

Mount Adams Recreational areas. From the best trails to hike to recommendations on where to fish, the forest rangers know how to help you. They can tell you where to find the most picturesque waterfalls to photograph or even where to find choice singletrack. In fact, the Service Trail was one of their recommendations.

This trail runs around a few of the Surprise Lakes in a challenging and dusty singletrack adventure. A few erosion problems, combined with sharply banked turns, make for a thrilling downhill experience. It's a fairly fast ride and can easily be done in a couple of hours. There are several creek crossings that churn the dust under your wheels into thick, pasty mud, which can make snapping into your clipless pedals difficult, and getting out of them even harder. Mountain bikers with toe clips will enjoy worry-free mud pedaling—just make sure you don't ever stop and put your feet down.

There are a couple of forest roads to be crossed along the route, and it seems like every one has a steeper out-take than the crossing before it. It gets tougher and tougher to ride away from the roads, and the embankments seem to get steeper and steeper. Only when you crest the climb and the trail gives you a switchback does your breath catch up with your heart rate. After completing the singletrack, the ride takes you back to camp on the well-graded forest road.

Ride Information

● Trail Contacts:
Gifford Pinchot National Forest, Randle Ranger District: (360) 497–1100 • **Gifford Pinchot National Forest Headquarters,** Vancouver, WA (360) 891–5000 • **Mount Adams Ranger District,** Trout Lake, WA (509) 395–2501

● Schedule:
Open in the summer and fall months before and after snowfall

● Fees/Permits:
$5 per car, per day ($30 for an annual pass); appropriate camping fees at the campgrounds

● Local Information:
Weather Radio: AM 1340

● Local Events/Attractions:
Arts Festival & Volkssport Walk, in July, Trout Lake, WA (509) 395–2294 • **Community Fair and Dairy Show,** in August, Trout Lake, WA (509) 395–2241 (or 395–2289) • **Huckleberry picking,** in August all over the Mount Adams area. Ask at the Ranger Station for a permit and map of the legal areas in which to pick.

● Local Bike Shops:
Dick's Bicycle Center, Vancouver, WA (360) 696–9234 • **Excel Fitness,** Vancouver, WA (360) 834–8506 • **Discovery Bicycles,** Hood River, OR (541) 386–4820 • **Mountain View Cycles & Fitness,** Hood River, OR (541) 386–2888

● Maps:
USGS maps: Mount Adams West, WA

Gotchen Creek Loop

Ride Summary

Another intermediate ride with a memorable road climb, the route up to Gotchen Creek and down Mount Adams is neither too long, nor too technical. Hiking and biking trails fill the peaceful forest, and the singletrack down the mountain is sandy, steep, and as fast as you care to make it. Zipping around the creek toward the bottom, the trail completes its loop with some high whoop-de-doos and brings you back around to the start before you know it.

Ride Specs

Start: From the Wicky Creek Horse Shelter
Length: 15.7-mile loop
Approximate Riding Time: 4 hours
Difficulty Rating: Moderate to Difficult due to steep, sandy, descending single-track
Terrain: Forest roads and singletrack. Roll along tree-covered hillsides with glimpses of the geological history written in stone around Mount Adams.
Land Status: National forest
Nearest Town: Trout Lake, WA
Other Trail Users: Hikers and equestrians
Canine Compatibility: Dogs permitted
Wheels: Front suspension recommended, but not required

Getting There

From White Salmon: Take WA 141 north to Trout Lake. At the road split, follow the Mount Adams Recreational Area Road (FS 80). At the fork, stay straight. Follow FS 80 toward South Climb Trail (Trail 183). You'll see signs for the county and forest boundary lines. Pass Buck Creek Trail (Trail 154). Follow the right fork onto a gravel road heading straight for Mount Adams. Pass two dirt spurs, following ahead as the road turns sharply right. Wicky Creek Horse Shelter is on the left.
DeLorme: Washington Atlas & Gazetteer: Page 34 D4

The Gotchen Creek ride is a National Forest Service ranger's recommendation. Strung along the slopes of Mount Adams, the trail's name may throw you a bit since the ride doesn't exactly hit Gotchen Creek until the very end. But that aside, this is only one of the many exciting trails on and around Mount Adams—whatever they're named for. There are also some super cool geologic sites to witness on Mount Adams. To experience *super cool* quite literally, you must visit the Ice Cave, 10 miles west of Trout Lake off of Washington 141. Discovered more than 100 years ago, the Ice Cave is filled with icy stalactites, stalag-

mites, and huge ice blocks. In the pioneer days, settlers from Hood River and The Dalles, Oregon, harvested ice from this cave. The ice cave is actually an ancient lava tube that retains heavy, cold air from the winter. Because there is no real air circulation, the cave remains frozen year-round. Small amounts of snowmelt in the summer, followed by winter re-

MilesDirections

0.0 START from the Wicky Creek Horse Shelter and head left up FS 80/8040.

1.3 Pass FS 782 on the right.

2.1 Pass FS 792.

3.1 Climb the road and run into Gotchen Creek Trail (Trail 40) on the right. Stay on FS 80/8040, continuing up.

3.7 Pass the Crofton Ridge Trail (Trail 73) trailhead on the left at Morrison Creek. *[**FYI.** This heads into Indian Heaven Wilderness (open to hikers and equestrians only). Parking and camping are available.]* Continue straight.

3.9 Pass Short Horn Trail (Trail 16) on the left. FS 80/8040 turns into FS 500. Continue along FS 8040.

6.7 The climb ends at the South Climb Trail (Trail 183) trailhead parking lot.

6.8 Follow the road through the parking area to Cold Springs Trail (Trail 72). The trail starts out as doubletrack, climbing slightly until it levels out and becomes singletrack.

7.0 Follow the Trail 72.

8.2 Arrive at a small clearing. Catch the trail on the other side. *[**Note.** Be prepared for a short, extremely difficult section to ride. Your descent averages 500 feet per mile.]*

10.3 Travel over a small, exposed arm of a lava bed—somewhat technical.

10.7 Intersect with Trail 40. FS 80/8040 is two miles to the right and FS 8020 is to the left. Turn left on the trail.

11.7 Arrive at the trailhead for the Trail 40. Go about 50 feet past the trailhead, beyond a fenced area, and turn right onto FS 8020.

12.0 Turn right onto FS 020.

12.6 Pass FS 125. Switchback right and left.

13.6 Pass FS 31 on the right.

14.2 Pass the last spur on the right, coming up to FS 80/8040.

14.5 Arrive at FS 80/8040. Turn right and head to Wicky Creek Horse Shelter.

15.7 Arrive at the horse shelter.

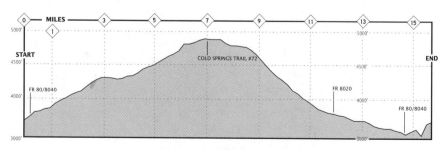

freezing, create the intricate ice formations that grow along the floor and ceiling. To check it out, you'll want a lantern or a good flashlight, boots, warm clothing...and a helmet wouldn't hurt. The Forest Service Ranger Station in Trout Lake has information on the Ice Cave available. Be sure to pick up a pamphlet and learn what *pahoehoe* is and what is meant by *natural bridge*.

> Only 15 percent of the Pacific Northwest's old-growth forests remain—only 5 percent throughout the United States.

After breathing the frosty air from the depths of the Ice Cave, resurface to enjoy the sweet perfumed air of Mount Adams' forests. This ride begins at the Wicky Creek Horse Camp, on the south side of the mountain, with a gradual climb up a shaded forest road. The tree-filled hillsides of Mount Adams have an ethereal feel, especially the higher you climb along the

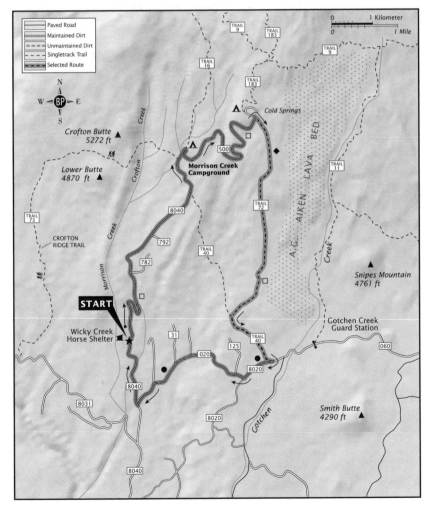

Inside the Ice Cave.

road—it's as if you've entered an enchanted place. The forest has an open-ness to it far different from the rain forests of the Olympic Peninsula. The trees come in every size, but it's the way shafts of afternoon summer sun filter through them that gives the forest a warm, cozy feeling. When the gravel road finally gives way to packed dirt, the climb becomes easier, but because you're riding up the interior of this special place, you hardly feel as if you're climb-ing. Then of course, Mount Adams can be seen through the trees, watching silently as you traverse its sides in the name of that sacred word—FUN.

After seven miles of climbing, you may be greeted by climbers, skiers, and snow boarders coming and going from the peaks above. Judging by the size of the parking area and the number of portable toilets, there's a lot of traffic headed for the base of the snowline. Catch the trail at the end of the parking lot, and your descent begins quickly. As with other rides in the area, if there hasn't been a lot of rain, the trails will be dusty. You'll fly down the Cold Creek Trail and intersect with the Gotchen Creek Trail, which then launches you through the woods. The singletrack ends near a horse corral area, for a rolling ride back, complete with whoop-de-doos and a short climb along low-use forest roads to Wicky Creek Horse Shelter.

Ride Information

● Trail Contacts:
Gifford Pinchot National Forest, Randle Ranger District: (360) 497-1100 • **Gifford Pinchot National Forest Headquarters,** Vancouver, WA (360) 891-5000 • **Mount Adams Ranger District,** Trout Lake, WA (509) 395-2501

● Schedule:
Open when free of snow; best between Memorial Day and mid October

● Fees/Permits:
$5 per car, per day ($30 for an annual pass); appropriate camping fees

● Local Information:
Weather Radio: AM 1340

● Local Events/Attractions:
Arts Festival & Volkssport Walk, in July, Trout Lake, WA (509) 395-2294 •

Community Fair and Dairy Show, in August, Trout Lake, WA (509) 395-2241 (or 395-2289) • **Huckleberry picking,** in August, all over the Mount Adams area. – Ask at the Ranger Station for a permit and map of the legal areas in which to pick.

● Local Bike Shops:
Dick's Bicycle Center, Vancouver, WA (360) 696-9234 • **Excel Fitness,** Vancouver, WA (360) 834-8506 • **Discovery Bicycles,** Hood River, OR (541) 386-4820 • **Mountain View Cycles & Fitness,** Hood River, OR (541) 386-2888

● Maps:
USGS maps: Mount Adams East, WA; Mount Adams West, WA • **USFS maps:** Mount Adams Ranger District Map (Pacific Northwest Region)

Siouxon Creek Out-and-Back

Ride Summary

If you like smooth singletrack, lush forests, and little elevation gain, this ride will easily become one of your favorites. In fact, the ride begins downhill, so the only gain is in climbing retracing your tracks along Siouxon Creek. Ride as fast as you want or slow down to enjoy the view. This trail is enjoyed by all.

Ride Specs

Start: From the trailhead on FS 5701
Length: 14.0-mile out-and-back
Approximate Riding Time: 2–3 hours
Difficulty Rating: Easy, though long
Terrain: Creek side trees and rolling climbs on beautifully maintained single-track with some technical sections
Land Status: National forest
Nearest Town: Chelatchie, WA
Other Trail Users: Hikers and equestrians
Canine Compatibility: Dogs permitted
Wheels: Front suspension recommended

Getting There

From Woodland: Take WA 503 East (Lewis River Road) toward Cougar. Turn right at the traffic light onto Hayes Road (CR 16), following signs for LaCenter/Amboy. At the fork, turn right onto NE Cedar Road and head up the hill. Follow for about 17 miles. Just north of Amboy, stay straight at the fork. Travel two miles to Chelatchie. Pass the Ranger station on the left. Turn right onto Northeast Healy Road. Follow for seven miles over a one-lane bridge. At the fork, turn right and follow the paved road. Enter the Gifford Pinchot National Forest. Veer left at the fork onto FS 57. Turn left onto FS 5701 at the T-intersection. Follow to the sharp bend in the road and look for the trailhead marker on the left-hand side. If you can't find it, drive two miles to the end of the road and park. Pick up the trail there. **DeLorme: Washington Atlas & Gazetteer:** Page 23 A7

his southern Washington ride is located a little over an hour north of the Oregon border in the Gifford Pinchot National Forest, making it an easy trip to and from the cities of Vancouver and Portland. If you're not coming from these cities, they're definitely worth visiting. Situated opposite one another, with the Columbia River and state line running between, both towns, despite their nearness, have histories distinctly their own.

Occupying the Columbia's north bank is Vancouver, named for British explorer Capt. George Vancouver, whose team landed on what is today Vancouver soil in 1792. Now one of Washington's fastest growing cities, Vancouver began as the British-owned Hudson's Bay Company's Northwest outpost, Fort Vancouver. In less than two years, it was a fully functioning town, with 40 buildings, a sawmill, and 700 grazing cattle. After years of dispute between Britain and America, the Hudson's Bay Company eventually abandoned the fort in the 1840s when America and Britain finally settled on a boundary along the 48th Parallel.

Soon after the Hudson's Bay Company left, the United States took over the fort, using it as a military post. Such notable military leaders as Phillip Sheridan and Ulysses S. Grant were stationed here briefly. In short order, a townsite was plotted. Still on the fringe, the town became a thriving settlement. By the late 1800s to early 1900s shipbuilding was Vancouver's big

MilesDirections

0.0 START at the trailhead marker on the north side of FS 5701.

1.2 Intersect with Huffman Peak Trail (Trail 129) and stay straight on Siouxon Creek Trail. *[FYI. Trail 129 leads down to and across Siouxon Creek and then up to Huffman Peak.]*

3.2 At the T-intersection, turn left toward the river. *[FYI. The right turns take you up to the camping areas at the end of FS 5701.]* Traverse down the ridge.

3.5 Cross a bridge over West Creek. Follow the main trail to Siouxon Creek.

4.4 Intersect with Horseshoe Ridge Trail (Trail 140) and keep straight.

4.9 *[FYI. This wooden bridge makes a good lunch spot over Horseshoe Creek.]*

5.0 Intersect with Trail 130B, a spur to Horseshoe Creek Falls. Keep to the Siouxon Creek Trail.

5.3 Arrive at a bench with a beautiful view of the waterfall on Siouxon Creek.

7.0 Come to the other end of Trail 140, having passed signs for the Siouxon Peak Trail (Trail 156A), Wildcat Trail (Trail 156), and Wildcat Falls. Chinook Trail (Trail 130A) is coming up. This is the turnaround point. Retrace your tracks back to the trailhead at FS 5701. *[FYI. The Siouxon Creek Trail can also be continued on as far up the drainage as you want.]*

14.0 Arrive back at the trailhead.

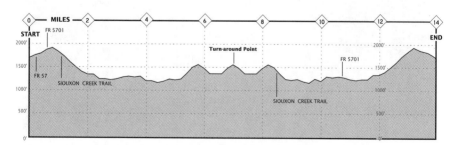

industry. During both World Wars, the city churned out hundreds of ships for the war effort. Woodie Guthrie, the famed folksinger and political activist, contributed to this effort as a laborer for the Kaiser Shipyards. In the years to follow, shipbuilding waned. Today Vancouver's economy depends more heavily on wood products, electronics, and food processing—as well as on the economy of neighboring Portland.

Vancouver has plenty of historic sites to visit. Six of Fort Vancouver's original 27 buildings have been reconstructed and are now managed by the National Park Service. Daily tours are available year-round. Actors in peri-

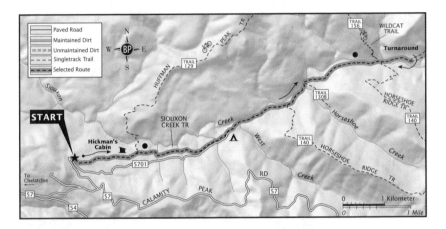

Thankfully, this huge washout was repaired in 1997.

od dress portray what life was like during the Hudson's Bay Company's trading post days. If you'd like to see a real piece of history, stop at the Old Apple Tree Park along the river, east of Interstate 5. In 1826 John McLoughlin, the chief leader of Fort Vancouver, planted the park's centerpiece with seeds he received from London. Many contend that this apple tree, which still produces tiny green apples, is the oldest apple tree in the Northwest.

From Vancouver, the Siouxon Creek ride is about an hour northeast. Starting at the trailhead on Forest Service Road 5701, you head immediately down into the woods. This trail is incredibly smooth. Rip-roaring into some great downhill, your tires hardly make a sound as they whirl across the

needle-covered forest floor in fast pursuit of the river below. Reaching Siouxon Creek, the trail then chases alongside it until you decide to turn around and head back. The gurgling, bubbling water of Siouxon Creek can be heard occasionally over your own breath, urging you to hurry. Cooling waterholes are inviting on hot days, but there is a good portion of the trail that is fairly high above the water.

There are a couple of trail intersections along this ride. Adventurous trails to Siouxon and Huffman peaks make a great loop that will take all day to complete—probably 25 to 30 miles roundtrip. The one trail you must be sure to avoid is the Horseshoe Ridge Trail. Totally overgrown, the Horseshoe Ridge Trail is ridiculously steep; mountain bikers will find themselves carrying their bikes over 75 percent of the trail. There has been little maintenance here, and many fallen trees block the way, making perfect hideouts for communities of bees (a painfully realized fact).

The Siouxon Creek Trail follows the river for a long way though, all the way to Forest Service Road 58, if one is inclined to ride that far—about seven to eight miles. This ride turns around a bit earlier than that. When you're finished, you can camp out at the trailhead and ride it again the next day.

Ride Information

● Trail Contacts:
Gifford Pinchot National Forest, Amboy, WA (360) 247-3900 • **Gifford Pinchot National Forest Headquarters,** Vancouver, WA (360) 891-5000

● Schedule:
Open year round depending on snow levels

● Fees/Permits:
$5 per car, per day ($30 for an annual pass)

● Local Information:
Vancouver/Clark County Visitors Center, Vancouver, WA (360) 694-2588 or 1-800-377-7084 • **Historic Fort Vancouver,** Vancouver, WA (360) 696-7655 or 1-800-832-3599 • **Outdoor Recreational Information:** (206) 470-4060

● Local Events/Attractions:
Vancouver Festival, in mid June, Vancouver, WA (360) 693-1313 • **Vancouver Days,** 4th of July weekend, Vancouver, WA (360) 693-1313 • **Heritage Weekend,** in May, Vancouver, WA (360) 693-1313 • **Victorian Gaming Days and Marshall House Tours,** in July, Vancouver, WA (360) 693-1313

● Local Bike Shops:
Dick's Bicycle Center, Vancouver, WA (360) 696-9234 • **Excel Fitness,** Vancouver, WA (360) 834-8506 • **Discovery Bicycles,** Hood River, OR (541) 386-4820 • **Mountain View Cycles & Fitness,** Hood River, OR (541) 386-2888

● Maps:
USGS maps: Siouxon Peak, WA; Bare Mountain, WA • **Green Trails:** Lookout Mountain No. 396

35 Falls Creek Shuttle

Ride Summary

Water falls, sponge cake-like trail, and lava caves provide this route was all the ingredients for a great mountain bike ride. It's a 16-mile moderate shuttle ride that can be made into a loop by riding back to the sno-park at Oldman Pass (El. 2,788 feet) from the bottom of Falls Creek on a paved forest road. Riding this route in reverse from the river to the pass is quite difficult, and not much fun either.

Ride Specs

Start: From the Oldman Pass Sno-Park
Other Starting Locations: From the Falls Creek Trailhead
Length: 15.8-mile point-to-point
Approximate Riding Time: 2–3 hours
Difficulty Rating: Moderate to difficult because of the technical descents
Terrain: Singletrack, forest roads, and paved roads roll over hill and dale under the cover of typical Pacific Northwest forest
Land Status: National forest
Nearest Town: Carson, WA
Other Trail Users: Hikers, equestrians, and cross-country skiers
Canine Compatibility: Dogs permitted
Wheels: Front suspension is a good idea, but you can ride fine without it.

Getting There

From Woodland: Take WA 503 East (Lewis River Road) past Cougar. WA 503 becomes FS 90 at the Swift Creek Reservoir. Follow FS 90 toward Carson. Turn right on Curly Creek Road. Turn right on Wind River Road (FS 30). Follow to Oldman Pass Sno-Park area and park here. • **Shuttle Point:** Following the directions above, continue down Wind River Road (FS 30) for 8.5 miles to the sharp left up FS 3063. Park here or farther north at the Falls Creek Trailhead.
DeLorme: Washington Atlas & Gazetteer: Page 24 A2

The Falls Creek Shuttle is located in the heart of the Wind River Ranger District within Gifford Pinchot National Forest. Whether you access this ride from the northwest or southwest, the route will be scenic. From the northwest, you'll travel below the edge of the Mount St. Helens National Volcanic Monument. Even from the road, the views are outstanding. Coming from the southwest, follow the Columbia River along Washington 14 and see what caught the attention of early explorers Lewis and Clark. Rising 848 feet above the river is a solid basalt landmark. Beacon Rock is the largest feature of its kind in North America, second only in the world to the Rock of Gibraltar. Just take Washington

Taking a break at Falls Creek Falls.

MilesDirections

0.0 START from the Oldman Pass Sno-Park. Follow the trail running next to Wind River Road to the right. Turn right on Trail 150.

1.2 Look for the blue diamond cross-country ski markers on the trees. Cross a small wooden bridge.

1.8 Turn right on FS 3053.

2.0 Pass a clearcut on the right.

3.0 Pass Snowfoot Trail (Trail 151) on the right. Continue on the road.

3.2 Intersect with Trail 159. Take Trail 157 toward FS 65.

3.3 The road turns into McClellan Meadows Trail (Trail 157).

4.0 Cross a wooden bridge over a creek into Pete's Gulch.

4.5 Cross a dry drainage on a bridge.

5.0 The trail crosses FS 6701. Continue straight.

6.5 Intersect with FS 65. Turn right down the hill on a gravel road.

6.6 Enter Falls Creek Horse Camp at the apex of the hill. Find the trail on the right. Take Trail 157 to the Lava Caves.

8.0 *[FYI. The trail opens to a great view of Mount Hood.]*

8.3 Cross FS 6701. Continue down.

9.4 The singletrack turns into double-track.

9.7 The trail enters a picnic area. Follow FS 6701.

10.0 The doubletrack becomes improved dirt road and the trail is directly across. Follow the trail.

11.0 The trail enters a junction with FS 67 and FS 6701. Follow the sign for Falls Creek Trail (Trail 152), continuing straight.

12.0 Turn left as the singletrack turns onto a gravel road, FS 6053.

13.1 When the doubletrack ends, take the trail to the left.

13.3 Follow the singletrack to the right as the trail widens.

14.8 Arrive at a campsite clearing. *[FYI. Check out Falls Creek Falls on the left.]*

15.0 Arrive at a fork in the trail. The left is to an overlook. Take the trail to the right.

15.8 Turn left to cross a wooden bridge and right after crossing to the parking lot of the Falls Creek Trail trailhead.

*[**Option**. From here, pick up your shuttle or pedal back to Oldman Pass Sno-Park on Wind River Road (FS 30)—8.5 miles.]*

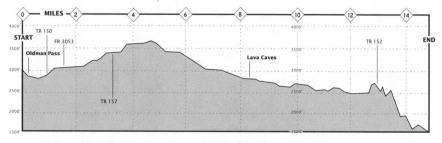

14 (the Lewis and Clark Highway) north of the town of Bonneville—you can't miss it. Beacon Rock is now the center attraction of its own state park; a gift from the family of Henry Biddle who, in 1915, saved it from becoming a rock quarry. Lewis and Clark are reputedly the first white men to have seen it as they journeyed west to the Pacific in 1805. The rock was later seen by a fur trader named Alexander Ross, who, in 1811, called it *Inshoach Castle*, which may explain why the rock was referred to as *Castle Rock* until 1916—the year the U.S. Board of Geographic Names officially proclaimed it Beacon Rock.

Continuing east on Washington 14, you'll come to the Columbia River Gorge Interpretive Center, a mile west of Stevenson. After peering through

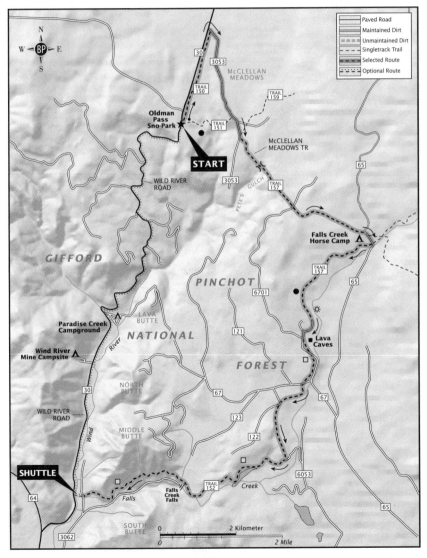

the museum's 40-foot tall picture window at the Columbia River, you can tour their amazing exhibits (like an interior basalt cliff, a waterfall, a 37-foot fishwheel, etc.—not to mention the world's largest collection of Rosary beads). To round out your educational experience, stop off at the Skamania County Historical Museum in Stevenson. If you enjoy history, especially about Washington and the Columbia River, you'll love their collection.

The town of Carson is the end of the line before stepping off into the Gifford Pinchot National Forest (named after the founder of the U.S. Forest Service). Depending on how you feel after the ride, you may opt to return to this quaint little town, complete with old-fashioned false storefronts. This quiet destination is slow-paced and relaxed. Should you need to sooth your mountain bike aches and pains, the historic Carson Hot Springs Resort has some 126°F mineral baths that might do the trick. Discovered in 1876, these springs have long been considered the cure for whatever ails you.

If you need more than one night of pampering, you can stay at the St. Martin Hotel, built in 1897. This bathhouse resort was the vision of Isadore St. Martin. The three-story hotel quickly became a well-known stop for visitors seeking the healing waters of the hot springs. Patrons arrived mostly by steamboat, up the Columbia River. But you can get there via Wind River Road from Washington 14, or follow Hot Springs Road toward Carson. You might also try the Government Mineral Springs, 15 miles north of Carson on Wind River Road.

After you've completed your brief site-seeing tour, travel to Oldman Pass, just south of Mount St. Helens and Mount Adams. The terrain is similar to high desert—dry and warm with low relative humidity. The forest is thick but the ground below its canopy is hardly lush. Ferns and saplings push through long, brown, spiny needles on the forest's floor. The air is crisp,

View of Mt. St. Helens.

making your skin feel dry and your body thirsty. This is the type of climate where even after a heavy workout, your clothes will feel instantly dry.

The trail starts near a sno-park along the paved road. It's used by cross-country skiers in the winter and is well marked as it meanders through meadows and singletrack. There are lava caves about halfway down, which you'll want to check out if you have time. Eventually, the trail leads a winding descent along Falls Creek to Falls Creek Falls. Below the falls, the singletrack is as smooth as silk and as fast as lightning. About two miles from the end, the trail becomes steep and has surprising, sharp turns. Cross the beautiful, sturdy wooden bridge over Falls Creek. The trail stops at the trailhead parking area where welcoming picnic tables and cool river pools await.

After the ride, especially if you've traveled a ways, you'll want a quiet place to camp—that is, unless you head back to the Carson Hot Springs Resort. You'll find a couple of pay-to-camp places between Oldman Pass and the trailhead where the ride ends—Paradise Camp, Little Soda Springs, and Beaver Camp—along Wind River Road. There are always pull-offs from the main road, if you prefer. These sites, usually logging roads, are often quieter than designated campsites. But, they may not always be legal, so make sure you read any postings on trees or telephone poles to make sure you're not trespassing.

Ride Information

● Trail Contacts:
Gifford Pinchot National Forest, Wind River Ranger Station, Carson, WA (509) 427–5645 • **Gifford Pinchot National Forest Headquarters,** Vancouver, WA (360) 891–5000

◐ Schedule:
Open year round depending on seasonal snow levels

⑤ Fees/Permits:
$5 per car, per day ($30 for an annual pass)

❓ Local Information:
Stevenson Chamber of Commerce and Visitor Information Center, Stevenson, WA (509) 427–8911

◉ Local Events/Attractions:
Beacon Rock State Park: (509) 427–8265 • **Columbia Gorge**

Interpretive Center, Stevenson, WA (509) 427–8211 • **Skamania County Historical Museum,** Stevenson, WA (509) 427–9435 • **Columbia Gorge Bluegrass Festival,** Stevenson, WA (509) 427–8928 • **Carson Hot Springs Resort,** Carson, WA (509) 427–8292 or 1–800–607–3678

◉ Local Bike Shops:
Discovery Bicycles, Hood River, OR (541) 386–4820 • **Mountain View Cycles & Fitness,** Hood River, OR (541) 386–2888

Ⓝ Maps:
USGS maps: Termination Point, WA • **USFS maps:** Gifford Pinchot National Forest, Windriver Ranger District Map • **Green Trails:** Lookout No. 396 and Wind River No. 397

Yacolt's Larch Mountain

Ride Summary

This trail is a favorite among local mountain bikers. In an area that is hot and dry in the summer, the cool shade of the initial singletrack climb along Cold Creek is inviting (though it can get a bit humid). It's not an easy climb along the river. There are roots and rocks and slippery surfaces. But once it moves up and away from the water, the trail conditions improve all the way to the top. Up there, the terrain is more like a rock quarry than a mountain biking trail—it's challenging to ride but spectacular for its views.

Ride Specs

Start: From the Rock Creek Campground
Other starting locations: From the Cold Creek Campground
Length: 13.4-mile out-and-back
Approximate Riding Time: 3–4 hours
Difficulty Rating: Difficult due to steep climbing and technical trails
Terrain: Pass majestic old-growth trees interspersed with second-growth native forest on rolling singletrack (muddy in some places, extremely rooty and rocky in others) and Forest Service road
Land Status: Department of Natural Resources land
Nearest Town: Cougar, WA
Other Trail Users: Hikers and equestrians
Canine Compatibility: Dogs permitted
Wheels: Front suspension recommended

Getting There

From Woodland: Take WA 503 East (Lewis River Road) to Cougar. Turn right at the traffic light onto Hayes Road (CR 16), following signs for LaCenter/Amboy. At the fork, turn right onto NE Cedar Road. Travel 17 miles (from Cougar) to a stop sign. Follow the signs to the right for Amboy on CR 16. Travel through Amboy to Moulton Falls County Park. Continue 1.5 miles to Dole Valley Road. After approximately four miles, the pavement turns to gravel and the road becomes L-1000. Rock Creek Campground is within one mile on the left. Cold Creek Campground is another half-mile ahead on L-1000. The trail starts from either place. *DeLorme: Washington Atlas & Gazetteer:* Page 23 C6

L arch Mountain is located within the Yacolt Burn State Forest, bordering the Gifford Pinchot National Forest. There are several mountain biking trails within this Department of Natural Resources operated tract, some connecting with national forest trails. One such trail is an oasis within this fire-torn forest called the Rock Creek/Larch Mountain Trail.

Sheltered from the burning rays of the sun, the Rock Creek/Larch Mountain Trail offers a thick wooded climb along Cold Creek. Riding to

the peak of Larch Mountain is a great way to get a lot of exercise in a rather short amount of time; but there are longer loop options as well. Considerably more comfortable (and more interesting) than riding under the open-sky of a road climb, the singletrack up this trail offers a moderate-to-technical ascent and a powerful return descent. Pedaling by forest ferns

and families of mushroom garlands, the climb grows steeper as the trail pulls away from the creek. Narrow sections of exposed roots and rocks offer a challenge to advanced riders. Less advanced riders might be inclined to walk through these more difficult places. The climb tops out just past an exposed boulder field at a picnic area. At this point, you can do an about-face and head back or take the trail farther up to a radio tower on the peak.

The ride begins at Rock Creek Campground, a first-come/first-serve facility, regulated by the Department of Natural Resources. The camp

MilesDirections

0.0 START from the Rock Creek Campground. Turn left onto L-1000.

0.4 Stay right at the fork on L-1000.

1.0 Pass the entrance for Cold Creek Campground to the right (day-use only.) Stay on L-1000.

1.4 As the road crosses Cold Creek, see the trailhead on the south side to the left. The sign reads: "Larch Mountain/Grouse Mountain Vista Junction: 5.5 miles; Larch Mountain: 6 miles; Grouse Creek: 7.25 miles; Grouse Vista: 8.5 miles." This ride follows the Rock Creek/Larch Mountain Trail (also called the Tarbell Trail).

1.8 Cross a wooden bridge over the creek.

2.0 Cross another wooden bridge over a marshy area.

2.9 Pass a trail turnout that dead-ends.

3.2 Cross a wooden bridge and begin some serious climbing to the summit of Larch Mountain (3,496 feet).

3.8 Cross another bridge over Cold Creek.

3.9 Encounter more switchbacks, still heading up.

4.2 At the five-way intersection, take the trail heading up—the third trail if you count left to right.

5.6 Reach the boulder field for views of Mount Rainier and Mount St. Helens. Enjoy a moment at the Flintstone Picnic Area.

6.2 Arrive at the intersection with Tarbell Trail. Continue straight to Larch Mountain and the radio tower, a half mile ahead. *[**Option.** To ride to Grouse Vista, follow the Tarbell Trail up and left for 2.5 miles. This also leads to L-1200 for an optional road descent.]*

6.7 Reach the top. Turn around and head back the way you came.

13.4 Arrive back at your vehicle.

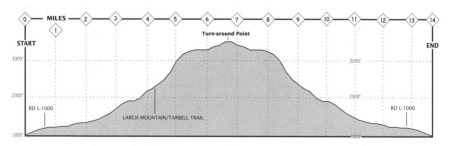

232

host/grounds-keeper is a lovely fellow who lives right at the campground. He has maps if you need them and advice on which trails are best to ride. The trail described here is one of his recommendations.

Depending on trail conditions, you could begin at the Rock Creek Campground up the Tarbell Trail, but it's often muddy and chopped up from horses' hooves. Especially after a rain, the trail can have thick, tire-sucking muck. To avoid the muck, ride L-1000 about a mile up to the Rock Creek/Larch Mountain Trailhead, crossing at Cold Creek. There are a few sticky sections in the beginning of this trail, down by the river, but conditions improve quickly as you climb.

Toward the top, after a climb that never seems to end, the trail crosses a cluster of huge boulders imbedded in the forest floor. The surface of the trail is rounded like lumpy, air-hardened Play-Doh. Moss grows in the shady crevices, which can make the surface treacherously slick. Trees grow next

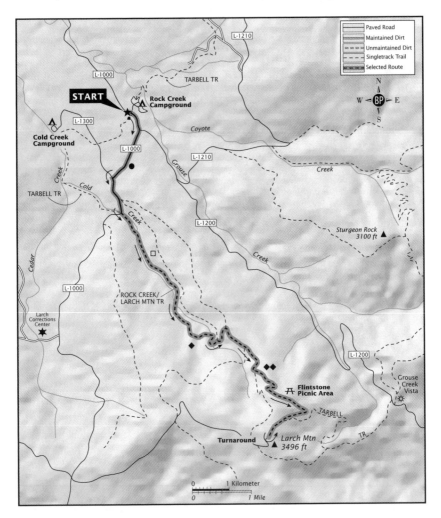

to, on top of, and in-between the boulders, making it a curious site—and a highly technical place to ride.

Closer to the top of Larch Mountain, after passing through the *embouldered forest*, the trail crosses over a field of talus. Huge chunks of sharp, black-gray granite are piled on top of each other. As the rock peaks weaken from lack of forest cover, large sections simply break off and fall to level ground, leaving a sloped pile of debris—what geologists call *talus*. A picnic table has been set up in the center of the talus field. A sign alongside reads: "The Flintstone Picnic Area." The technically skilled rider may be able to negotiate wheels-over-rock through here. Anyone else will recognize his or her limits in short order. The trail, at this point, is nothing more than a faint dusty line made by the dirty bottoms of hikers' boots and a few dirty knobbies.

The top of the mountain is a short ride from a crossroad of trails. This is the turn-around point. From here you can take the trail back the way you

The 1902 Yacolt Burn

On September 12, 1902, sparks from a cut-over being cleared for farmland ignited the nearby forest. On the wings of the fierce autumn winds, the fire blossomed into an inferno and went on to kill 38 people and destroy 238,000 acres of forest before it was through. So big and destructive was the fire that it earned a name: the Yacolt Burn. It lasted only 36 hours but managed to travel 30 miles, between the towns of Carson and Yacolt. It was something that no one at the time was prepared to handle.

People say the fire was so hot that paint blistered on houses in the small town of Yacolt. And the skies were so blackened that chickens went to roost at midday. It's estimated that the amount of wood that burned would have been enough to build every third Washington resident a three-bedroom home—that's 12 billion board feet of lumber, valued in 1902 at $30 million. An informational sign in the area says that it took 20 years for loggers to "clean up" the forests and salvage what they could of the burned timber.

In this arid part of the state, fire is fed easily and can spread quickly when fanned by gusty winds. Although fire is Mother Nature's way of rejuvenating a forest, the lack of forest fire prevention methods are blamed for the 1902 Yacolt fire burning out of control for so long. Despite the state's efforts to reforest the Yacolt area, warm summer winds continue to blow and have fed several fires over the years since 1902. Where fire usually activates new growth in a forest, the fires in the Yacolt have left the soil badly damaged and unable to sustain much plant life.

In recent years, modern methods of reforestation have been employed to bring the forests back. Combined with advanced fire control action, these new methods have allowed a new, green look to come to the Yacolt Burn State Forest. Barren areas are once again beginning to see life return. In the years to come, maybe historians will have to really wonder about why this forest has such a name.

Photo courtesy of DNR.

came—which takes about half the time it did to climb up, or you could continue a little less than one mile further along steep doubletrack to a radio tower and an open field. The views from here are not as rewarding as you'd expect. In fact, they're pretty uninspiring. The trees and the tower tend to obstruct a good view. The talus field actually offers the best views.

There are a few other options to get to the top of Larch Mountain. For a road climb, take L-1200 up the Grouse Creek drainage to the Grouse Creek Vista. At the vista, turn right on the Tarbell Trail and ride two miles to the top of Larch Mountain. From the top, ride down the Rock Creek/Larch Mountain Trail. The total mileage will be about the same as if riding the singletrack up and back. Keep in mind that the road is very gravelly and steep and fully exposed. In the heat of summer, this can be a very hot way to climb.

Another option is to follow the trail as explained in the directions to the top of Larch Mountain. From there, take the Tarbell Trail left for two miles to Grouse Vista. Just past L-1200, the trail forks. Stay left for the Tarbell Trail, (the right heads onto Trail 172 to Silver Star Mountain). Follow the Tarbell Trail through some amazing switchbacks, around Sturgeon Rock, past some falls, and around Squaw Butte for a total of nine miles to the Tarbell Campground. Continue on the Tarbell Trail three miles to complete the loop at Rock Creek Campground. This loop can, of course, be ridden in reverse order, making it about a 21-mile ride.

Ride Information

❶ Trail Contacts:
Department of Natural Resources Southwest Region: (509) 925–6131 or 1–800–527–3305

◔ Schedule:
Open year round depending on snow levels

❓ Local Information:
Vancouver/Clark County Visitors Services: (360) 694–2588 or 1–800–377–7084 • **Historic Fort Vancouver,** Vancouver, WA (360) 696–7655 or 1–800–832–3599 • **Gifford Pinchot National Forest,** Amboy, WA (360) 247–3900

◊ Local Events/Attractions:
Yacolt Herb Festival, in May, Yacolt, WA (360) 686–3537 • **Vancouver**

Festival, in mid June, Vancouver, WA (360) 693–1313 • **Vancouver Days,** 4th of July weekend, Vancouver, WA (360) 693–1313 • **Heritage Weekend,** in May, Vancouver, WA (360) 693–1313 • **Victorian Gaming Days and Marshall House Tours,** in July, Vancouver, WA (360) 693–1313

⚙ Local Bike Shops:
Dick's Bicycle Center, Vancouver, WA (360) 696–9234 • **Excel Fitness,** Vancouver, WA (360) 834–8506

❽ Maps:
USGS maps: Dole, WA; Larch Mountain, WA • **DNR maps:** Tarbell & Jones Creek Trail Systems

Honorable Mentions

Southwest Washington

Compiled here is an index of great rides in the Southwest region that didn't make the A-list this time around but deserve recognition. Check them out and let us know what you think. You may decide that one or more of these rides deserves higher status in future editions or, perhaps, you may have a ride of your own that merits some attention.

(K) Oak Creek Trail

A feeding station for elk just outside of Naches, this desert ride is also a popular place for rattlesnakes. The 10 miles out and back are well maintained and begin moderately but become more advanced. Start from the bridge and pass through the elk gate. After that, the directions are simple: follow the trail west about five miles to the canal and turn around. The canal route continues for a couple of miles with many side trails to explore.

Take U.S. 12 north from Yakima. Shortly after Naches the road splits. Stay to the left on U.S. 12 (WA 410 goes right). Continue to the Oak Creek Elk Feeding Station. Park immediately before the bridge. For more information, contact the Naches Ranger Station at (509) 653–2205. See *DeLorme: Washington Atlas & Gazetteer:* Page 50, C2.

(L) Cowiche Canyon Conservancy Trails

Ideal for all mountain bikers, this ride is situated just outside of Yakima's city limits in a locally-maintained conservancy area. Cowiche Canyon's main trail is an old railroad grade. Follow the well-kept gravel course over nine bridges along the Cowiche Creek east to the Scenic Trail. It's possible to take the Overlook Trail between bridges eight and nine and climb from the canyon floor to the uplands area for a gorgeous view. There is a trailhead and parking on the plateau, also offering great mountain biking trails. Explore the area's miles of rideable trails and create various loops. But do this with care. The Cowiche Canyon Conservancy is a designated shrub-steppe ecosystem. It's very fragile and home to many rare plants. Stay on existing trails and avoid heading in and out of the canyon when the trails are wet to prevent further problems with erosion. Park at the main trailhead at the west end of Summitview at Weikel Road.

From Yakima, head west on Summitview. Pass 96th Avenue. Turn right at Weikel Road (at the log-built veterinary clinic). Travel a quarter of a mile to a green marker sign for the Cowiche Canyon Trail and turn right into the parking lot. Contact the Cowiche Canyon Conservancy in Yakima at (509) 577–9585. See *DeLorme: Washington Atlas & Gazetteer:* Page 50, C3.

(M) Juniper Ridge Loop

One of the state's most beautiful yet demanding rides, the Juniper Ridge Loop covers 18 miles of pavement and approximately 17 miles of single-

track. Not far from Randle, this course encounters about 4,000 feet of elevation change through a variety of mountain and lowland zones. However, there are several alternate routes along this ridge, allowing cyclists to tailor the ride to their own fitness level.

Ride over the Cispus River, then turn right onto FS 23 and again at the North Fork Campground, following FS 23. Climb FS 23 past several spur roads. Turn right on Trail 263 toward Dark Mountain and Jumbo Peak. Turn right at the T-intersection onto Trail 261 heading into some steep switchbacks. Follow the trail around Jumbo, Sunrise, and Juniper peaks, which becomes Trail 294—the Tongue Mountain Trail. Continue down to FS 2801. Turn left on FS 2801 to get back to your car.

From I-5 south of Chehalis, exit onto WA 12 east. Follow 12 to Randle. Turn right onto Woods Creek Road. Turn right onto Cispus Road, following it to the Cispus River. Park along FS 2801. For more information, contact the Randle Ranger District at (360) 497–1100. See *DeLorme: Washington Atlas & Gazetteer*: Page 50, D3–4.

(N) Lewis River

A fast and furious loop along the Lewis River in the southern part of the state, this moderate trail is just about as good as a trail can get. Start at the southern end of the Lewis River Trail 31 from FS 9039. Follow the trail for almost 10 miles, passing Trail 24 on the left, until it reaches FS 90. Turn right on FS 90 and ride back to FS 9039 to your car. You can also arrange for a shuttle at both ends of the trail to make the ride easier.

From I-5 north, take the Woodland exit heading toward Cougar and FS 90. Or, from I-5 south, take WA 503 east to FS 90. Follow FS 90 to FS 9039. Turn left on 9039, and the trailhead is just over the Lewis River after the bridge. For more information, contact Mount Saint Helens Ranger Station at (360) 247–3900. See *DeLorme: Washington Atlas & Gazetteer*: Page 34, D1.

O Siouxon Peak/Huffman Peak Loop

The Siouxon Peak/ Huffman Peak Loop has 25 to 30 miles of advanced singletrack. Toward the top of each mountain, the trail encounters forest roads. Riding in early spring or late autumn months may mean pushing through snow at the highest elevations. Follow the Siouxon Creek Trail Ride about seven or eight miles to the Chinook Trail 130A, the entrance for this ride. Follow the path up and around Siouxon Peak and then over to Huffman Peak before descending the Huffman Peak Trail 129 down to the Siouxon Creek trailhead.

From I-5, take exit 21. Follow WA 503 east toward Cougar. Turn right on CR 16 (also called Hayes Road), toward La Center/Amboy. Turn right up the hill onto Northeast Cedar Road. Follow for about 19 miles to Chelatchie. Pass the Ranger Station on the left. Turn right onto Northwest Healy Road. Follow it to a one-lane bridge. Keep right at the Y-intersection. Pass the Gifford Pinchot National Forest boundary. Come to a Y-intersection in the road and veer left onto FS 57. Turn left at the T-intersection onto FS 5701. Follow to the sharp bend in the road and look for the trail-

head marker on the left-hand side about 50 yards past the bend. For more information, contact the Ranger District in Amboy at (360) 247–3900. See *DeLorme: Washington Atlas & Gazetteer:* Page 23, A1.

(P) Buck Creek Trail System

Located between Mount Hood and Mount Adams in the southern end of the Gifford Pinchot National Forest, the Buck Creek Trail System is open to all non-motorized recreational users and offers two picturesque rides. Whistling Ridge Trail's 26-mile loop traverses thick forest up to Oklahoma Campground and back. The entire route is well marked. The other option, the Buck Creek Falls Loop Trail, is only two-and-a-half miles and runs along a creekside route to a view of the waterfall. Both trails can be accessed from the same trailhead.

From WA 14, turn north on WA 141 through White Salmon. Turn left on Northwestern Lake (B-1000) Road. Turn left on N-1000 Road. The trailhead is two miles ahead. For more information, contact the Department of Natural Resources at (360) 577–2025 or 1–800–527–3305. See *DeLorme: Washington Atlas & Gazetteer:* Page 24, B4.

Eastern
WASHINGTON

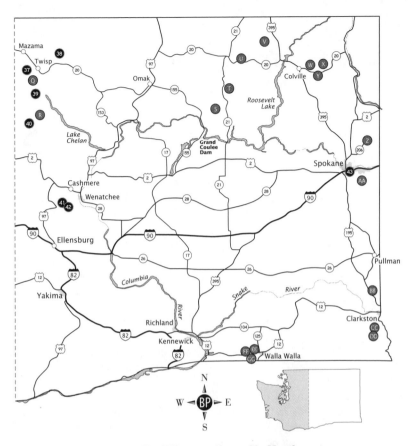

The Rides	Honorable Mentions

The Rides

Sun Mountain **37.**
Lightning Creek to Starvation Mountain **38.**
Foggy Dew Creek/Merchants Basin **39.**
Pot Peak **40.**
Mission Ridge **41.**
Devils Gulch **42.**
Centennial Trail to Riverside Park **43.**

Honorable Mentions

Q. Sawtooth Backcountry
R. Echo Valley
S. Steamboat Rock State Park
T. Down River Trail
U. 13-Mile ORV Area
V. Taylor Ridge Trail
W. Narcisse Block of the Pend Oreille
Area
X. Batey/Bould Trails
Y. 49-Degrees North Alpine Ski Area
Z. Mount Spokane State Park
AA. Liberty Lake Regional Park
BB. The Bill Chipman Palouse Trail
CC. The Snake River Bikeway
DD. Asotin Creek Trail
EE. North Fork Trail/Table Springs Loop
FF. South Fork Trail Out and Back
GG. Elbow Creek—Walla Walla

Eastern Washington

The land of milk and honey—well, almost. Actually, it's more like the land of wheat, wine, and apples—and, of course, mountain biking. The town of Wenatchee, positioned in the dead center of the state, is perhaps the most central location to reach both foothill and desert-like trails. From there you can roll through the Apple Capital of the country, the Wenatchee Mountains, or along the Columbia River.

Trails in the upper northwest quadrant wander through the striking forests of Okanogan and Colville, where the last of Washington's grizzlies still roam (the estimated population in Washington is about 30). Bordering British Columbia to the north, these picturesque groves of ponderosa and fir offer enchanting company while experiencing some fabulous mountain biking.

Eastern Washington's largest city, Spokane, is a recreational hub on the Idaho border. From the popular in-city Riverside State Park to the heights of Mount Spokane, mountain bikers from this far-east destination often wander farther east to "pick their line" on Idaho soil. The city itself is quite biker-friendly and supports a sensational inter-urban trail with authorized off-road singletrack access. Along these paths cyclists can combine recreation with history and exercise—or hop off the bike and do a little rock climbing or horseback riding.

The southeast corner of the state, stretching from Yakima to Pullman, is filled with both hills and valleys, landscapes splashed in hues of brown, beige, and green, and acres of trails throughout DNR, BLM, and state park lands anxiously awaiting the attention of mountain bikers.

A back porch to the rest of the Wild West, eastern Washington is vast and dry plain hemmed in by both mountains and the Columbia River. Weather-wise, the land east of the Cascade Range is another world from that of the western Washington, particularly the rainforests of the Olympic Peninsula. The Wenatchee Valley, the highlands of Lake Chelan, the Selkirk Mountains, and the Columbia River Valley are all protected from Pacific Ocean tradewinds, so the climate is arid. The prevailing dry weather and less demanding topography make eastern Washington ideal for mountain biking spring, summer, and fall.

Sun Mountain

Ride Summary

The cross-country skiing trails on Sun Mountain make incredible mountain biking routes for every skill level. Ride the lower trails to warm up and then ride to the upper trails for a good workout and some fast descents. You'll likely be sharing the mountain with a few others out here, especially in the summer, so come with your best face on.

Ride Specs

Start: From the Chickadee Trail trailhead
Length: 12.5-mile loop
Approximate Riding Time: 2 hours
Difficulty Rating: Moderate due to the climb
Terrain: Tree-lined terrain and smooth singletrack and dirt road
Land Status: National forest
Nearest Town: Winthrop, WA
Other Trail Users: Hikers, equestrians, and cross-country skiers
Canine Compatibility: Dogs permitted (but not recommended, due to the number of trail users)
Wheels: Front suspension recommended

Getting There

From Winthrop: Head west on Twin Lakes Road just south of the Methow River Bridge. This turns into Patterson Lake Road at the intersection of Wolf Ridge Road. Follow the signs for Patterson Lake Road and Sun Mountain Lodge. Patterson Road turns right—follow the signs for the lodge. Continue around the east side of Patterson Lake. Turn left at the Chickadee Trail trailhead.
DeLorme: Washington Atlas & Gazetteer: Page 99 A7

Riding along the eastern edges of the Cascades, it's easy to get swept away in the beauty of it all and forget that fire is a real threat to this region. Much drier than the western portion of the Cascades, in the summer this area can get quite hot and dusty, making it susceptible to Mother Nature's forest rejuvenation plan (i.e. forest fires). About five miles east of Winthrop is the North Cascades Smoke Jumpers Base. Established in the 1930s, the base has served the U.S. Forest Service as the center for developing the technique of smoke-jumping.

Sending fire fighters by regular roads into a forest deluged with fire can take time—maybe too much time, especially if the wind is cranking. So, first attacks on fires usually involve hotshot helicopter crews who drop smoke-jumpers to set up fire breaks which keep the fire from spreading, allowing it to burn out naturally. Parachuting men into fires may seem a lit-

The Methow Valley from Sun Mountain.

tle crazy—and it is incredibly dangerous—but it is a quick means of getting firefighters on the scene.

Since nothing was known in the 1930s about parachuting into hot coals, the Forest Service had to design and test the necessary equipment. They constructed suits made of heavy cotton canvas for the firefighters to wear. Long pockets were sewn into the pants to hold ropes that could be used in climbing out of trees, should the chute become ensnared in branches. These early smoke-jumpers also wore retrofitted football helmets with wire masks to protect their heads. After a test with a stunt dummy and 60 successful live

MilesDirections

With Sun Mountain Lodge's detailed map, you can see that the network of ski trails offers multiple riding opportunities. Every trail can be ridden at least once in a full day. Try testing out the warm-up loops on the lower trails and then advance to the upper trails for some elevation work and fast descents.

A good Warm-up Loop (approximately 6 miles)

Riding from the Chickadee Trail trailhead, cross the Thompson Ridge Road to the Beaver Pond Trail. At the Hough Homestead, follow any of the other trails, like the Fox Loop Trail to the Aqualoop, which circles back to the Hough Homestead. There is also the Rodeo Trail just past the Beaver Pond Trail—which heads back to the Chickadee Trail trailhead.

0.0 START from the Chickadee Trail trailhead climbing up the Thompson Ridge Road.

5.5 Pass Pete's Dragon Trail.

6.1 Reach the Goshawk Trail. Turn left and follow the Goshawk to the Meadowlark Trail.

6.5 Take the Meadowlark Trail and fly down the mountain.

7.9 Arrive at the Lower Inside Passage on the right, and follow it to the Rader Creek Trail.

8.5 Turn right on the Rader Creek Trail, continuing down toward Patterson Lake.

10.0 Arrive at the intersection for Elbow Coulee and Patterson Lake—turn left for Patterson Lake. Ride along the narrow, cliff-like Patterson Lake Trail...carefully.

11.8 At the intersection, continue straight for the Chickadee Trail trailhead. The trail to the right heads to the Patterson Lake Cabins.

12.5 Arrive back at the trailhead.

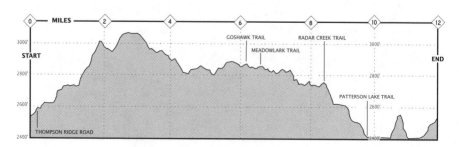

jumps, the smoke-jumping method became common practice for fighting forest fires. Today, it is still the standard for advanced suppression of wildfires in the West.

There is one thing forest fires share with mountain bikers, and that's a love of the forest. And the Methow Valley caters to both. When you arrive in Winthrop with a mountain bike on your car, the first place most people will recommend is the Sun Mountain Lodge. Because this is a cross-coun-

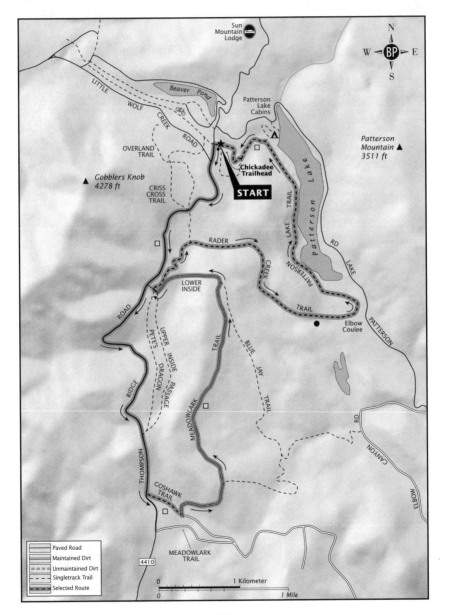

try ski resort, the trails are incredibly smooth, and they're great for the first or the last ride of a long, fat-tire weekend. There are several loops to be made here and the trails are very well marked, making it difficult to get lost.

Moderate climbs and good descents begin with the Thompson Ridge Road. This road takes you to the top of Sun Mountain's property and leads

you to some rip-roaring singletrack descents. One beautiful reason for climbing the Thompson Ridge Road (as if you needed another) is Patterson Lake. Its cobalt-blue water stands out in sharp contrast to the dusty hues of the landscape surrounding its banks.

The lower trails around Beaver Pond are wonderful warm-up or beginner trails. Smooth and wide, there's room to ride side-by-side. There are even welcoming benches along the way for weary legs to rest. And when the day's riding is done, Sun Mountain Lodge is close by with food and facilities. You can even get a room for the night.

Ride Information

● Trail Contacts:

Sun Mountain Lodge: (509) 996–2211 or 1–800–572–0493 *www.sunmountainlodge.com* • **U.S. Forest Service:** (509) 996–4000 or *www.fs.fed.us* • **Okanogan Nation Forest:** (509) 826–3275 • **Winthrop Ranger District:** (509) 997–2131

● Schedule:

April until it snows (about November)

● Fees/Permits:

No fees or permits required

● Local Information:

Winthrop Chamber of Commerce Information Station, Winthrop, WA (509) 996–2125 or 1–888–463–8469 or *www.winthropwashington.com* • **Methow Valley Visitor Center:** (509) 996–4000

● Local Events/Attractions:

The Bone Shaker Mountain Bike Bash (a NORBA-sanctioned race), in May, Winthrop, WA (509) 535–4757 • **Winthrop Rodeo Days,** in May and Labor Day weekend, Winthrop, WA (509) 996–2125 • **Mountain**

Triathlon, 2nd Sunday in September, Winthrop, WA (509) 996–3287 • **Methow Valley Mountain Bike Festival,** in early October, Winthrop, WA (509) 996–3287 • **"October-West"** 2nd weekend in October, Winthrop, WA (509) 996–2125 • **MVSTA Ski & Sports Swap,** in November, Winthrop, WA (509) 996–3287 • **North Cascades Smokejumper Base,** between Winthrop and Twisp along WA 20, WA (509) 997–2031 • **Sun Mountain Lodge,** Winthrop, WA (509) 996–2211 or 1–800–572–0493

● Local Bike Shops:

Winthrop Mountain Sports, Winthrop, WA (509) 996–2886

● Organizations:

Methow Valley Sport Trails Association, Winthrop, WA (509) 996–3287 or 1–800–682–5787 or *www.mvsta.com*

● Maps:

USGS maps: Thompson Ridge, WA; Winthrop, WA

38 Lightning Creek to Starvation Mountain

Ride Summary

Following the trail along the banks of beautiful Lightning Creek is simultaneously heart thumping and peaceful. This is one of the more popular routes in the Winthrop/Twisp area; we've even encountered gun-toting hunters on mountain bikes. The road ride that leads to the top of Starvation Mountain offers river and mountain views, and the steep climb makes for a screaming descent. The singletrack back along Lightning Creek takes about half the time it did to ride up, allowing for an exhilarating finish.

Ride Specs

Start: From the Beaver Creek Campground
Other Starting Locations: From along FS 4230
Length: 21.0-mile out-and-back
Approximate Riding Time: 3–4 hours
Difficulty Rating: Moderate due to the elevation gain
Terrain: Roll through a wooded creek bed before climbing to views of the Methow Valley along singletrack and forest road.
Land Status: National forest
Nearest Town: Twisp, WA
Other Trail Users: Hikers, equestrians, and hunters (in season)
Canine Compatibility: Dogs not permitted
Wheels: Full suspension recommended, but front suspension is okay

Getting There

From Winthrop: Drive east on WA 20, following the signs for the airport, keeping to the north side of the Methow River (do not cross the bridge). After six miles turn left on Bakke Hill Road (Road 1600). Follow it to Beaver Creek Road (Road 1637). Turn left on Beaver Creek Road and continue three miles to the Beaver Creek Campground. Continue beyond the campground two-tenths of a mile. Pass FS 4225 (the Loup Loup Summit Road) and into the Okanogan National Forest shortly thereafter. Park inside the campground or at the end of the road by the gate. *DeLorme: Washington Atlas & Gazetteer:* Page 100 A1

I nterest in mountain biking and hiking has made the quaint northwestern town of Winthrop a mecca of sorts for adventurers. The North Cascades Highway (Washington 20), which opened in 1972, allows more tourists quicker access to the valley than ever before. Winthrop has responded over the years by building new hotels and stores, while somehow managing to maintain the quiet charm of a small, western town. The number of bed and breakfasts, inns, lodges, and hotels is rising as quickly as is the number of recreational trails in the Methow Valley. One of the most comfortable inns in Winthrop is the Chewuch Inn. Or should we say the "resuscitated" Chewuch Inn.

In 1994, Dan and Sally Kuperberg arrived in Winthrop, this time not as tourists. They came not to escape the hustle of everyday life in the big city but rather to escape their city lives altogether. And so they made Winthrop their new home and bought an inn. The Chewuch Inn.

The Chewuch Inn once stood alone by the river, just an old abandoned fish hatchery, until a local man, Hank Dammann, decided to renovate it. He hoped to one day turn it into a hotel. But first he wanted to move it to a better location. Along the way though, the building fell from its trailer and landed sort of askew on the side of Twin Lakes Road, within walking distance of downtown Winthrop.

Leaving the building where it landed, Mr. Dammann decided to begin renovations there. But renovations were slow, and he grew older. It was clear that he wasn't going to be able to complete the task. That's when the Kuperbergs arrived. Buying it and putting their heart and soul into it, Dan and Sally created something special out of that old fish hatchery. Mountain bikers especially will appreciate the Chewuch Inn for its warm cozy beds,

MilesDirections

0.0 START from FS 200, following the sign for the Lightning Creek Trail 425. Follow the road through the campground and look for the trail leading into the woods toward the river. At the cattle guard, the sign reads: "Lightning Creek 5.5 miles, Blue Buck Creek Trail 1 mile, Beaver Meadows 11 miles."

0.3 Cross Lightning Creek over a wooden bridge.

1.1 Come to a T-intersection with Blue Buck Creek Trail and Buck Creek Meadows. Stay right following Lightning Creek.

1.6 Cross Lightning Creek again and begin a steep climb up and away from the river.

3.1 The trail turns into an old double-track road cut.

3.8 Enter a clearcut area.

4.0 Intersect with Spur Road 4230. Follow the trail to the right down the road just a hundred feet or so. Take the trail on the left side of the road, Trail #100, the continuation of The Lightning Creek Trail.

5.1 Singletrack continues again, climbing steeply. Cross a creek. Head up over the ridge, keeping the creek to your right.

6.0 The Lightning Creek Trail intersects with Spur Road 200 to the left, and FS 4235 just beyond that, running north/south. Follow FS 4235 left up to Starvation Mountain.

6.2 Pass turnout on the right at mile marker #7.

6.7 Pass another turnout.

6.8 Pass Spur Road 255 on the right.

7.2 Pass mile marker #8.

8.1 Passing a burned area about one quarter mile long.

8.2 Pass mile marker #9.

8.9 Cross a wide-open area on the right.

9.3 Pass mile marker #10.

10.5 Check out the summit and then head down for a fast descent.

21.0 Reach the bottom at the campground and the trailhead.

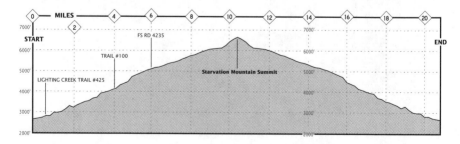

large windows with captivating views, and hearty home-cooked breakfasts. For a more private setting, the Kuperbergs have a few small one-room cabins in the woods a few yards away from the inn. With cathedral ceilings, these cabins combine creature comforts with a slightly rustic touch—a perfect place to crash after a hard mountain bike ride. For information and reservations, call The Chewuch Inn at 1–800–747–3107 or visit *www.chewuchinn.com*.

The word *chewuch* (pronounced chee-WUK, meaning "creek") is a word from the Methow (pronounced MET-how) Indian tribe, who are now affiliated with the Colville Confederation. For 9,000 years Native Americans

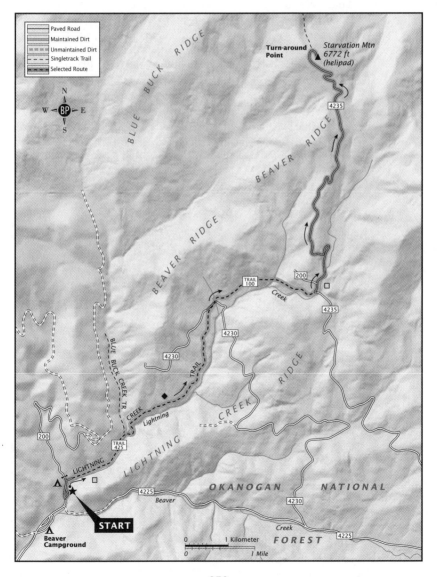

have lived along the banks of this and the other Methow Valley rivers. The government established the Colville Reservation nearby in the 1800s and many tribes continue to live in the Methow Valley.

During the same time period (1800s), trappers came to this area and found gold—the lure of the wild west began to shine. Three of the white settlers who came searching for their fortunes were James Ramsey, Ben Pearygin, and Guy Waring. Waring is considered the founding father of Winthrop, even though the town is named after Theodore Winthrop, an author and graduate of Yale, who was well known for his adventurous spirit.

In 1893 a great fire consumed the town of Winthrop, which at the time was built solely of wood. Waring's original Duck Brand Saloon, built in 1891, survived the fire and is now Winthrop's Town Hall. The novel *The Virginian*, credited with being the first Western novel, is said to have been penned in Winthrop by Owen Wister, Waring's roommate from Harvard.

Located about a half-hour away from Winthrop is the Lightning Creek Trail, above the Methow Valley to the north. The starting point at Beaver Creek Campground is filled with tall ponderosa pines and larch trees. Singletrack leads the way up alongside Lightning Creek where intersections are well marked. After the first mile of level riding, the trail crosses Lightning Creek and begins ascending away, gradually becoming steeper. Although there are a few small technical areas, the trail is very fun to ride.

Clearcut areas, burned forest, sandy trail, and hard-packed earth are all represented along this ride. The forest road to the top of Starvation Mountain may seem like a long five miles after climbing the singletrack. Consider a loop option by riding up the forest road from the campground to the top instead, and descend the singletrack on the way back. The forest road is steep in some sections and becomes a bit of a grind. On cooler days, if you're not properly dressed, the heights of Starvation Mountain can be windy and cold, but the views are great from the top.

Ride Information

🖊 Trail Contacts:
U.S. Forest Service: (509) 996–4000 or *www.fs.fed.us* • **Okanogan Nation Forest:** (509) 826–3275 • **Winthrop Ranger District:** (509) 997–2131

🕐 Schedule:
April until it snows (about November)

💲 Fees/Permits:
No fees or permits required

❓ Local Information:
Winthrop Chamber of Commerce Information Station: (509) 996–2125 or 1–888–463–8469 *www.winthrop-washington.com* • **Methow Valley Visitors Center:** (509) 996–4000

◉ Local Events/Attractions:
The Bone Shaker Mountain Bike Bash (a NORBA-sanctioned race), in May, Winthrop, WA (509) 535–4757 • **Winthrop Rodeo Days,** in May and Labor Day Weekend, Winthrop, WA (509) 996–2125 • **Mountain Triathlon,** second Sunday in September, Winthrop, WA (509)

996–3287 • **Methow Valley Mountain Bike Festival,** in early October, Winthrop, WA (509) 996–3287 • **"October-West,"** second weekend in October, Winthrop, WA (509) 996–2125 • **MVSTA Ski & Sports Swap,** November, Winthrop, WA (509) 996–3287 • **North Cascades Smokejumper Base,** between Winthrop and Twisp along WA 20, WA (509) 997–2031 • **The Chewuck Inn,** Winthrop, WA 1–800–747–3107 *www.chewuchinn. com*

🚲 Local Bike Shops:
Winthrop Mountain Sports, Winthrop, WA (509) 996–2886

👥 Organizations:
Methow Valley Sport Trails Association, Winthrop, WA (509) 996–3287 or 1–800–682–5787 or *www.mvsta.com*

Ⓝ Maps:
USGS maps: Loup Loup Summit, WA; Old Baldy, WA

Foggy Dew Creek/ Merchants Basin

Ride Summary

This hoofer is not for the weak of heart. Consistently steep, the mega-climb begins around 3,600 feet and doesn't quit until it hits almost 8,000 feet—all within only five miles! It's a slightly technical ride as well, as the trail travels over loose rocks from time to time. This is one of the more challenging trails in the state and will take all day to ride, giving real meaning to the word epic.

Ride Specs

Start: From the Foggy Dew Creel Trail trailhead
Length: 16.5-mile loop
Approximate Riding Time: 4–6 hours
Difficulty Rating: Difficult due to steep climbs and technical singletrack descents
Terrain: Technical singletrack and hike-a-bike. Second-growth forest and high-elevation vegetation accompanies extreme up-and-down terrain on this ride.
Land Status: National forest
Nearest Town: Carlton, WA
Other Trail Users: Hikers, equestrians, and motorcyclists
Canine Compatibility: Dogs not permitted
Wheels: Front suspension recommended

Getting There

From Pateros: Head north on WA 153 toward Twisp. At mile marker 16.8, turn left and head west onto Gold Creek Road, which is FS 4340; follow this for almost one mile. Turn left at the T-intersection toward the Foggy Dew Guard Station and Crater Creek Camp. After one mile, continue straight through the intersection for the Foggy Dew Campground. After another four miles, turn left and cross a bridge onto FS 200. Drive past the Foggy Dew Campground on the left after the bridge. The pavement ends here. Continue three and a half miles to the trailhead parking lot.
DeLorme: Washington Atlas & Gazetteer: Page 99 C7

L ake Chelan is a narrow, 55-mile long, natural lake of pure glacial melt. To quote an overzealous *Seattle Times* reporter: "It's deeper than the Grand Canyon!" Well, not quite. It's only 1,484 feet deep (versus the Grand Canyon's 5,816 feet), but you get the point: it's deep. A more accurate superlative would be to say that it's the third deepest lake in the United States (after Crater Lake in Oregon and Lake Tahoe in California). There are two main roads that will take you to the lake, Washington 151 or U.S. Route 97. Otherwise, there are just forest roads, which are few and far between. There are a couple of towns of decent size on the lake as well: Chelan, at

the southeastern tip; Manson a few miles north up the eastern side; Lucerne to the northwest; and Stehekin, to the far north, a completely isolated community accessible only by boat from Chelan. Floatplane is another alternative to getting around the lake, and of course there is your mountain bike.

There are several designated campsites around the lake; the largest is at the Chelan State Park. Located on the southeastern end of the lake, the park covers 127 acres, with 6,545 feet of waterfront. The park has 127 campsites, a bathhouse, 300 linear feet of beach, a boat launch and a dock, water ski floats, a homestead cabin, and a contact station. Everything a traveler could need!

MilesDirections

0.0 START riding up the Foggy Dew Creek Trail (Trail 417).

1.7 Pass a small waterfall on the left.

3.0 Pass Foggy Dew Falls on the left.

5.2 Reach the trail junction with the Martin Creek Trail (Trail 429) on the right. This is where you'll connect on the way down. Continue straight for now up the trail, following signs to Merchants Basin, Sunrise Lake, and Sawtooth Ridge.

5.3 Reach the junction with the Navarre Way Trail (Trail 424). Continue to the right on Trail 417. This is the worst part of the climb.

6.4 Pass the trail junction 417A to Sunrise Lake on the left at the Horse Camp. Continue up the trail to Merchants Basin.

7.6 Reach the top of Merchants Basin and the trail junction with the Angels

Staircase Trail (Trail 1259D)—which heads west to the top of the Sawtooth Ridge. *[**Side-trip.** For a great view, ride or hike up Trail 1259D for 0.4 miles to the top of the ridge, and then to the north, to the top of the 8,321-foot peak. It's worth it.]* Once back at the saddle, head down the other side of the pass toward Cooney Lake.

8.5 Arrive at the Cooney Lake Campsite. Continue along the trail and cross the north fork of Foggy Dew Creek.

8.6 Come to a junction with the Trail 429. Turn right and enjoy the ride.

9.7 Cross a bridge, again over the north fork of Foggy Dew Creek.

11.4 Arrive at the junction with the Trail 417. Turn left. Follow Trail 417 back down to the trailhead.

16.5 Arrive back at the Foggy Dew Creek Trail trailhead parking area.

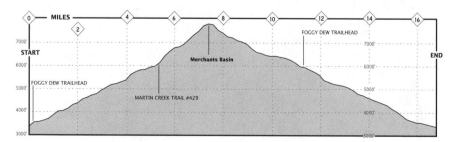

Chelan (pronounced sha-LAN) is the name of an Indian tribe that used to winter at the site where the town now stands. In 1880, Chelan became a military post with civilians arriving a few years later. The town was incorporated in 1902 with mining as the chief means of income. People arrived by steam ship up the Columbia River to stake their mining claims, until 1914 when the railroad finally arrived. Today there are about 3,500 people living in Chelan year round. It has become quite the resort spot. Many of the large Victorian homes from the early days are used today as bed and breakfasts.

Stehekin, to the far north of Lake Chelan, is a quiet, isolated village. There are no cars, no phones, and no televisions in Stehekin—only pristine wilderness, wildlife, and trails to keep you entertained. Mountain bikers can take their choice of summertime boats to get there. By taking the *Lady II* up and the *Lady of the Lake* back, there will be about three hours in between to explore Stehekin. In the summer of 1998, the newest addition to the ferry fleet was added, cutting the travel time down to under two hours from Chelan, allowing for longer visits. There are a few places to rent bikes in Chelan and Stehekin, but it's only a $13 round trip to take your own bike on the ferry. If you'd like to spend the night in Stehekin, there are lodges like the North Cascades Stehekin Lodge and the Stehekin Valley Ranch. Or you can simply camp under the stars.

The climate around Lake Chelan is ideal for mountain biking. With an average of only 24 days a year of sub-32-degree temperatures and 33 days above 90 degrees, you can't go wrong. On average, it rains less than nine days a year, and so you can plan on about 300 perfectly sunny days. And though this area gets its share of snow, the lake never freezes.

For a sun-filled, truly rugged mountain biking experience, try the Foggy Dew Trail, situated inside the Okanogan National Forest, east of the long and slender Lake Chelan. This trail is consistently steep. It begins at rough-

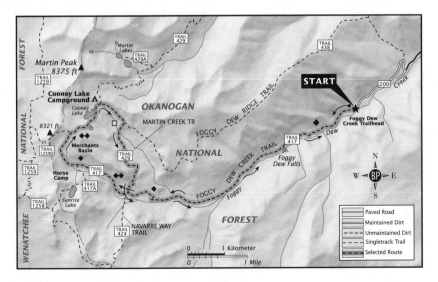

ly 3,600 feet and takes you up to about 8,000 feet in the first five miles. It's moderately technical with a few loose rocky places here and there. Local motorcycle groups maintain the trails, and consequently they stay in fairly good shape. The trails that are closed to motorcycles are typically steep and tough to ride.

After the first six miles of climbing, the trail is transformed into some incredibly steep switchbacks. The hardest part of the climb is toward the top of Merchants Basin. Passing Cooney Lake and heading down, the elevation loss will give you a head rush. Some sections are daringly steep, so don't be embarrassed to walk your bike down. The final downhill back along the Foggy Dew Trail is a sweet reward after the tough climb.

Merchants Basin.

The south side of Cooney Lake.

Ride Information

📞 Trail Contacts:

Okanogan National Forest: (509) 826–3275 • **Twisp Ranger District:** (509) 997–2131 • **Wenatchee National Forest:** Chelan Ranger District: (509) 682–2576

🕐 Schedule:

Open year round, but best between May and October

🕐 Fees/Permits:

No fees or permits required

❓ Local Information:

Lake Chelan Chamber of Commerce: (509) 682–3503 or 1–800–424–3526 • **Lady of the Lake and Lady II ferries,** from Chelan and Stehekin: (509) 682–4584 • **North Cascades Stehekin Lodge,** Stehekin, WA (509) 682–4494 • **Stehekin Valley Ranch,** Stehekin, WA (509) 682–4677

📍 Local Events/Attractions:

Earth Day, in April, Chelan, WA 1–800–424–3526 • **Beachin' Hang Gliding Tournament,** in May, Chelan, WA 1–800–424–3526 • **Cross-Country Hang Gliding Classic,** in July, Chelan, WA 1–800–424–3526 • **North Cascades Stehekin Lodge,** Stehekin, WA (509) 682–4494 • **Stehekin Valley Ranch,** Stehekin, WA (509) 682–4677

🚲 Local Bike Shops:

Der Sportsmann, Leavenworth, WA (509) 548–5623 • **Winthrop Mountain Sports,** Winthrop, WA (509) 996–2886

Ⓝ Maps:

USGS maps: Martin Peak, WA; Hungry Mountain, WA • **Green Trails:** Prince Creek, WA - No. 115

Bicycle Camping

If you consider your mountain bike saddle the most comfortable seat in the house and crave an opportunity to prove your self-sufficiency, try bicycle camping. It does require more planning and preparation than a standard day trip, but the particular satisfaction gained from reaching a campground or a remote outdoor destination on two wheels, knowing you're ready for a cozy night outdoors, makes the extra effort worthwhile.

If you plan on doing a lot of bicycle camping/touring, it's a good idea to invest in quality equipment. Everyone should have a pair of medium-to-large size panniers that can be mounted on a rear rack (if you are planning a long trip, you might consider a front rack). A lightweight backpacking tent, sleeping pad, and sleeping bag can be attached to the rear rack using two or three bungie cords. We all have a tendency to over-pack, but the extra weight of unnecessary equipment may cause you to tire more easily. Here are some tips to help you find the appropriate amount of gear:

- Bring a multi-purpose tool that has a can opener, bottle opener, scissors, knife, and screwdriver.
- Pack only one extra change of clothes, plus any necessary layers such as a polypropylene shirt and tights, polar fleece, wool socks, and rain gear. If you are on a multi-day trip, bring extra shorts and t-shirts, and if it's winter, bring an extra pair of polypropylene tights and shirt, as well as a few extra pairs of wool socks.
- Bring a tin cup and spoon for eating and drinking and one lightweight pot for cooking.
- Invest in a lightweight backpacking stove, tent, and sleeping bag.
- Bring along freeze dried food. You can buy many pre-packaged rice and noodle mixes in the grocery store for half of what you'll pay at backpacking stores.
- Bring the minimum amount of water needed for your intended route. Anticipate if there will be water available. Invest in a water filter that can be used to filter water from water sources along the trail.

Equipment List

Use the checklist of equipment below when you are planning for a single or multi-day trip. You can develop your own equipment list based on the length of your trip, the time of year, weather conditions, and difficulty of the trail.

Essentials

bungie cords
compass
day panniers
duct tape
fenders
pocket knife or multi-purpose tool
rear rack
front rack
trail map
water bottles
water filter
tool kit
patch kit
crescent wrench
tire levers
spoke wrench
extra spokes
chain rivet tool
extra tube
tire pump

Clothing

rain jacket/pants
polar fleece jacket
wool sweater
helmet liner
bicycle tights
t-shirts/shorts
sturdy bicycle shoes/boots
swimsuit
underwear
bike gloves
eye protection
bike helmet/liner

First-Aid Kit

bandages (various sizes)
gauze pads
surgical tape
antibiotic ointment
hydrogen peroxide or iodine
gauze roll

ace bandage
aspirin
moleskin
sunscreen
insect repellent

Personal Items

towel
toothbrush/toothpaste
soap
comb
shampoo

Camping Items

backpacking stove
tent
sleeping bag
foam pad
cooking and eating utensils
can opener
flashlight/batteries
candle lantern
touring panniers
pannier rain covers
Zip-lock bags
large heavy duty plastic garbage bags
citronella candles (to repel insects)
small duffels to organize gear

Miscellaneous Items

camera/film/batteries
notebook/pen
paperback book

Tip:

Zip-lock bags are a great way to waterproof and organize your gear. Large, heavy-duty plastic garbage bags also make excellent waterproof liners for the inside of your panniers.

Pot Peak

Ride Summary

This ride gains 4,300 feet of elevation—it isn't easy. Steady along a ridge top, this singletrack comes with long, painstaking climbs and fast, furious descents. Motorcyclists use this trail too, and contrary to popular stereotypes, the trails are in excellent condition (they are actually maintained by local ORV groups). Mountain bikers rocket down the ridge on banked and occasionally rocky turns. It's a good thing there's a campground at the bottom because, while this ride is exhilarating, it's also totally exhausting.

Ride Specs

Start: From the Ramona Park Campground

Other Starting Locations: From the sno-park at the intersection of FS 5900 (Shady Pass Road) and FS 8410 (to Ramona Park Campground)

Length: 28.7-mile loop

Approximate Riding Time: 7–9 hours

Difficulty Rating: Advanced due to long, steep climbs and technical singletrack descents

Terrain: Singletrack and short gravel road section. Ride under the cover of trees with intermittent fire breaks and more sparse vegetation at higher elevations.

Land Status: National forest

Nearest Town: Chelan, WA

Other Trail Users: Hikers, equestrians, motorcyclists, cross-country skiers, and hunters (in season)

Canine Compatibility: Dogs permitted (but this is an awfully long ride for dogs to trail along)

Wheels: Full suspension recommended, but hardtails will do

Getting There

From Wenatchee: Head north on U.S. 97 (which is on the west side of the Columbia River, not the east). At marker 223, turn left onto WA 971, the Navarre Coulee Road. Travel 30 miles to a T-intersection at the shore of Lake Chelan. Turn left onto South Lakeshore Drive. Follow to just past the Twentyfive Mile Creek State Park. Turn left onto Shady Pass Road, which is FS 5900. Travel three miles to a fork at a sno-park. Park here, or turn left onto FS 8410 and park (or camp) at the Ramona Park Campground. There is a trailhead at the campground where the ride will end; there is no parking at the trailhead where you start.

DeLorme: Washington Atlas & Gazetteer: Page 83 A6

The Pot Peak ride is one serious cardiovascular workout. From the North Fork of the Twentyfive Mile Creek to the top of the ridge, it's a steady, non-technical grinder the entire way up. There are the occasional short, steep sections that you might have to hike, but for the most part, this trail just goes up, up, and up. Starting out at 2,400 feet, don't be alarmed that the high point is 6,881 feet. The good part is that this is a loop, so you're in for some amazingly fast downhill, dropping to 1,900 feet at the finish. How about that! Almost 5,000 feet of elevation work. Are you up to it? Better grab an extra energy bar.

MilesDirections

0.0 START from the sno-park up FS 5900 (it may be marked 5903).

1.0 Arrive at the North Fork of the Twentyfive Mile Creek Trail (Trail 1265). Take this trail, which also leads to the Lone Peak Trail and the Devils Backbone Trail.

3.7 Arrive at a junction with the Lone Peak Trail (Trail 1264). Continue left up Trail 1265.

4.4 Cross a fork of the Twentyfive Mile Creek and head up the ridge.

5.8 Reach the ridge top.

7.2 Hit the ridgeline and ride across it.

7.5 Reach the first false summit on the ridgeline. Continue across for typical ridge top ascents and descents.

11.4 Arrive at the trail junction for the Devil's Backbone Trail (Trail 1448). This is the top of the main ridge. Follow the Trail 1448 left, now heading south to the junction at Angle Peak (6,700 feet). *[Note: For the next three miles (until Angle Peak) this area has been bulldozed as a firebreak. Some sections of the singletrack no longer exist. Option: To bail out, follow the trail to the right to a spur road of FS 5900. Follow it back to the campground.]*

14.4 Pass a trail junction with Trail 1444 on the right. Continue straight to the next intersection, up the ridge to Angle Peak.

14.5 Reach a trail junction with the Four Mile Ridge Trail (Trail 1445). Turn left following the Trail 1448. You're close to the top of Angle Peak at this point.

16.0 Pass a right-hand offshoot trail to a viewpoint overlooking Devil's Backbone. Follow the Trail 1448 to the left, down a very steep, rocky, and technical downhill with tight turns and steep drop-offs.

17.2 Reach the bottom of the downhill. Put your bike on your shoulder and follow the switchbacks up the talus slope.

17.8 Back to the ridge top.

18.3 Arrive at a junction with the Pot Peak Trail (Trail 1266). Follow the Trail 1266 left. (The trail straight leads to Stormy Mountain on Trail 1448.)

23.4 Reach Pot Peak. Follow the trail around the base of the summit.

28.1 Reach the bottom of the trail at Ramona Park trailhead. Turn left up FS 8410.

28.7 Arrive back at the fork and the sno-park.

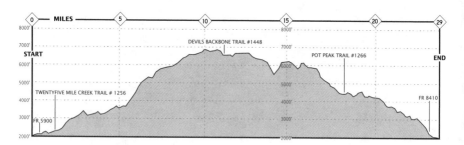

The motocross group in the area is responsible for the marvelous upkeep of these trails. Please do your part to keep the trails in good condition. There are quite a few cinderblock-banked turns that really help with traction, especially when taking tight switchbacks at high speed—they also minimize trail erosion. You can thank the motocross crowd for that, too. In general, the trails are really well maintained and, for the most part, they're pretty smooth. When it's time to head down, just point your bike in the direction you wish to go, and hang on. An optional trip might be to Stormy Mountain and back. It looks fun, but there'll be a road climb on the return.

Just south of Pot Peak is the raging Columbia River, first explored by Anglos in May of 1792. Captain Robert Gray, a fur trader from Boston, decided to name the river he'd found after his ship, the *Columbia Rediviva—redivivus* means to be reborn or restored to life and is also the name of Montana's state flower. The United States government used Gray's exploration as a basis for their claim on the Oregon and Washington territories, which were constantly being disputed by Britain.

A lot has changed along the river. As for the river itself, the Columbia now has 14 dams, 300 miles of main canals, and 2,000 miles of secondary canals that irrigate land stretching as far as 100 miles away from the river's banks. Within 30 years, the Columbia Basin Project of the early 1950s turned a half-million acres of dry, arid land into lush green farmland.

The primary force behind the irrigation restructuring of the west is the Grand Coulee Dam. On December 3, 1933, the pouring of concrete began for the dam. Where most other large dams are filled with soil, the Grand Coulee is solid concrete—the largest all-concrete structure on earth, measuring almost one mile long. That's enough concrete to build a six-foot sidewalk around the Earth's equator. And to further emphasize the dam's enor-

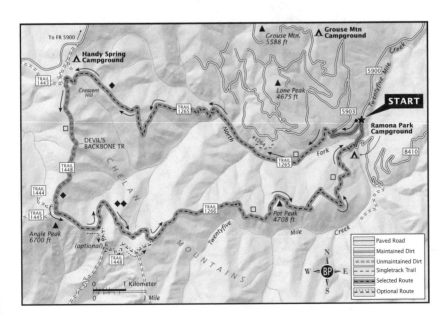

Looking back at the talus slope, Sawtooth Ridge, and Angle Peak.

mity, more wood was used in building the Grand Coulee Dam than in any other structure on the planet. And, only two other dams, the Guri Dam in Venezuela and the Itaipu Dam of Brazil, generate more power than the Grand Coulee. It's only logical, then that the lake behind the Grand Coulee would be large as well. And so it is. Roosevelt Lake is the second largest man-made lake in the world.

The engineers of the 1930s knew surprisingly little about building a dam. Some of the clever quick fixes they came up with as they went along are quite funny. When sliding mud was a problem, they'd freeze it with a refrigeration unit. When the coffer dam sprang a leak, they'd mix together whatever they could with bentonite clay and stuff it into the holes to stop it from leaking—including mattresses and Christmas trees.

The Grand Coulee was finally completed in 1941, three months before the United States entered World War II. The power it generated helped with manufacturing aluminum for the war effort. Over half of the country's aluminum was made in Northwest plants that drew their energy from the dam. If you'd like to visit the 12 million cubic yards of concrete and steel that comprise the Grand Coulee Dam, just stop by the Visitor Center on Washington 155. They offer tours daily.

Ride Information

❶ Trail Contacts:
Twentyfive Mile Creek State Park: (509) 687-3610 • **Wenatchee National Forest,** Chelan Ranger District: (509) 682-2576 • **Entiat Ranger District:** (509) 784-1511

❷ Schedule:
Open year round, but best between May and October

❸ Fees/Permits:
No fees or permits required

❹ Local Information:
Grand Coulee Visitor Arrival Center, Coulee City, WA: (509) 633-9265 • **Lake Chelan Chamber of Commerce:** (509) 682-3503 or 1-800-424-3526

❺ Local Events/Attractions:
Earth Day, in April, Chelan, WA 1-800-424-3526 • **Beachin' Hang Gliding Tournament,** in early May, Chelan, WA 1-800-424-3526 • **Cross-Country Hang Gliding Classic,** in July, Chelan, WA 1-800-424-3526

❻ Local Bike Shops:
Der Sportsmann, Leavenworth, WA (509) 548-5623 • **Leavenworth Ski & Sports,** Leavenworth, WA (509) 548-7864

❼ Maps:
USGS maps: Stormy Mountain, WA • **Green Trails:** Brief, WA – No. 147

Mission Ridge

Ride Summary

This is a true ridge ride: located out in the open, exposed to the views and the sun. The 14-mile ascent is gradual with the occasional steep section. It hooks up with some exceptional ridge-top singletrack that leads to false summits and around tight switchbacks. There is a little bit of everything here. It will be a challenge to intermediate riders, but for the advanced mountain biker it's a true delight.

Ride Specs

Start: From the Mission Ridge Trail trailhead
Length: 26.4-mile loop
Approximate Riding Time: 3–5 hours
Difficulty Rating: Moderate to Difficult
Terrain: Gravel road and singletrack. This quintessential ridge-top ride features exposure to the elements and an epic downhill.
Land Status: National forest
Nearest Town: Cashmere, WA
Other Trail Users: Hikers, equestrians, and motorcyclists
Canine Compatibility: Dogs not permitted
Wheels: Full suspension recommended, but hardtails are okay

Getting There

From Cashmere: Exit onto Division Street from U.S. 2. Follow Division Street right around the Vale School and continue as the Division Street changes names to Pioneer Street. Take the immediate left onto Mission Creek Road, following it to Binder Road. Turn right onto Binder Road. Mission Creek Road picks up again immediately on the left. Turn left on Mission Creek Road. Follow for 10.4 miles to a fork in the road. Turn left on FS 7100 and drive 2.6 miles to the trailhead for Mission Ridge Trail and Devils Gulch Trail. *DeLorme: Washington Atlas & Gazetteer:* Page 67 B5

D uring the summertime, Mission Ridge provides an exceptional opportunity for soaking up the sun along the Wenatchee Mountains. Not far from Mission Ridge is the town of Wenatchee, a moderately sized city nestled between the Wenatchee and Columbia rivers, due-south of Cashmere. Houses almost 3,000 years old were discovered in an orchard here, and ancient buffalo-spearheads and other stone tools have been discovered in and around Wenatchee dating back 11,000 years. Though it's unclear exactly how long people have resided here, we know that "Wenatchee" has only been around since the late 1800s.

It was in those first few years of settlement that the Great Northern Railroad, who owned a considerable chunk of land not far from Wenatchee,

convinced Wenatchee's citizens to move their town closer to the railroad's proposed train depot site. No sweat; the railroad was footing the bill. When trains began running through town in 1892, Wenatchee blossomed like a fertilized field of sun-fed apple trees.

One person responsible for the growth of the orchard business in eastern Wenatchee was Jacob Shotwell. He built an irrigation ditch to bring water from the Wenatchee River to the dry benchlands of Wenatchee. His irrigation channel caused such a boom that land plots which had been going for $25-an-acre, jumped to $400-an-acre. In 1908, Bridge Street was constructed over the Columbia River to carry the water pipelines from the channels to the benchlands. The bridge also allowed wagons, and later cars, to cross the river. In 1951 the bridge closed to all vehicles and is now open only to bicycle and foot traffic. Shotwell's irrigation channels brought to the

MilesDirections

0.0 START from the trailhead parking area for Mission Ridge/Devils Gulch. Ride up FS 7100.

2.5 At the T-intersection with FS 7101, turn right continuing on FS 7100.

9.2 Arrive at the intersection with FS 9712. Turn right on the well-traveled FS 9712.

9.7 Pass a spur road. Continue straight up FS 9712.

10.4 Pass another spur on the right-hand side.

11.7 Pass the Devils Gulch Trail on the right. *[FYI. The Pipeline Trail on the left takes you to the Mission Ridge Ski Area.]*

13.8 Pass the Squilchuck Trail (which goes to the Mission Ridge Ski Area). Arrive at the Mission Ridge Trail trailhead on the right. Take the trail. This is the official beginning of the singletrack.

17.7 Arrive at another junction of the Devils Gulch Trail. Go straight through the four-way intersection and climb. For the next nine miles there are many false summit climbs.

26.2 Arrive at a T-intersection with the Devils Gulch Trail. Turn right. Follow the Devils Gulch Trail from here on out.

26.3 The Red Hill Spur Trail intersects with the Devils Gulch Trail from the left. Stay on the Devils Gulch Trail.

26.4 Arrive back at the trailhead parking area.

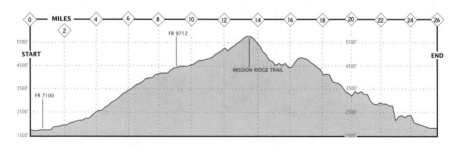

Wenatchee Valley the most crucial element to successful fruit growing. Fruit growing continues, but the channels have since been replaced by underground and drip-method irrigation systems.

If Washington is famous for anything, it's apples. Even though thousands of apple varieties are grown in Washington, Red and Golden Delicious apples are by far the most popular varieties. Hot, dry summer days cooled by crisp, clear nights provide ideal growing conditions for juicy, delicious apples. Apple growing is a year-round process. Pruning trees begins in January. Bees are brought in to assist pollination in the spring. And finally in September and October the apples are harvested. The Washington State

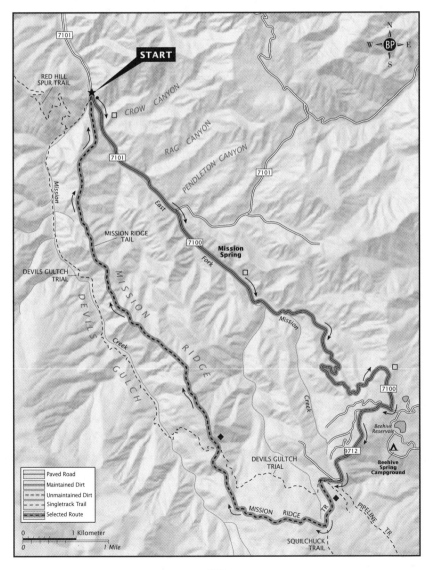

Apple Commission offers a brief video presentation on the apple industry development. Their facility is located south of Wenatchee.

After you've completed your tour of the orchards and learned all you can about Washington's apple growing industry, gather your apple-stuffed fanny-pack and your mountain bike, and get ready to roll. The Mission Ridge ride begins with a 13.8-mile ascent up Forest Service Road 7100. It has moderate-to-steep grades, but is easily ridden. Don't be surprised if you are passed along the way by cars shuttling mountain bikers to the top—just remember, you're earning your descent.

The Mission Ridge ride begins on Forest Service Road 9712, just below Mission Peak. The three-mile climb between the Devils Gulch Trail and the Mission Ridge Trail is the steepest climb of the ride. The singletrack of the Mission Ridge Trail begins in the open woods on the ridge-top. These are fast running trails that alternate with steep downhills and tight switchbacks. Follow the singletrack for about four miles until arriving at a four-way intersection with the Devils Gulch Trail. Continue straight through the intersection—then the good stuff begins. There is a steep nine-tenths-mile climb here, but, just to warn you, there are plenty of false summits on the way down as well. Take in the great views from the ridge-tops and enjoy the ride all the way down. This is as true a ridge-ride as you can get.

The icing to this epic ride is the downhill. A good amount of it is steep—so steep, in fact, that you'll be riding with your belly on the back of your saddle. Some drop-offs here and there may surprise you, and fast-riding sections quickly fall into switchbacks, so stay alert. The Mission Ridge ride offers a great trip with a little bit of everything.

Splashing through Mission Creek.

Mom's Apple Pie

3 cups of peeled apples, cored and sliced (Recommended varieties include: Macintosh, for good pie texture; Granny Smith, tart and sweet; or Golden Delicious, simply sweet.)
¾ cup sugar (+ or - depending on tartness of apples used)
½ Tablespoon lemon juice
2 Tablespoons flour
¼ – ½ teaspoon cinnamon
1 Tablespoon cold butter cubed small

Mix all ingredients, except the butter. Add optional ¼ – ½ cup oatmeal to thicken. Let the apple mixture sit for ½ hour. Pour into pie or pastry shell. Dot butter on top. Secure the top pastry and add decorative slices or cut slits in the top crust and crimp edges. Bake for one hour at 400 degrees. **Hint:** *Pre-cooking the bottom shell for five to seven minutes at 400 degrees will help dry the crust so it doesn't get mushy after baking.*

Ride Information

🍴 Trail Contacts:
Wenatchee National Forest, Leavenworth Ranger District, Leavenworth, WA (509) 782–1413 • **Lake Wenatchee Ranger District:** (509) 763–3103 or 1–800–452–5687

⏱ Schedule:
Open year round, but best between April and November, when there's less snow

💲 Fees/Permits:
$5 per car, per day charge ($30 for an annual pass)

❓ Local Information:
Leavenworth Chamber of Commerce Visitor Center, Leavenworth, WA (509) 548–5807 • **Wenatchee Chamber of Commerce:** (509) 662–2116

💡 Local Events/Attractions:
Washington State Apple Blossom Festival, in April, Wenatchee, WA (509) 662–3616 • **Apple Industry Tour,** in October, Wenatchee, WA (509) 663–9600 • **Founder's Day,** in June, Cashmere, WA (509) 782–7404 • **Apple Days,** in October, Cashmere, WA (509) 782–7404 • *[See Ride 11 for more information.]*

🚲 Local Bike Shops:
Arberg Sports, Wenatchee, WA (509) 663–7401 • **Aspund's Outdoor Recreation 1,** Wenatchee, WA (509) 662–6539 • *[See Ride 11 for more information.]*

🅝 Maps:
USGS maps: Monitor, WA

Devils Gulch

Ride Summary

Reputedly the best mountain bike ride in the state, the Devils Gulch Trail is a great place to escape the damp weather farther west. In the heart of the eastern Cascade foothills, this trail begins with a forest road climb before cutting into the woods and riding along Mission Creek below Mission Ridge. Not too tough, not too technical, this ride is just right for strong climbing legs and the desire for fast singletrack.

Ride Specs

Start: From the Devils Gulch Trail trailhead

Other starting locations: From along FS 7100

Length: 24.4-mile loop

Approximate Riding Time: 2–4 hours

Difficulty Rating: Moderate to difficult due to steep trail climb

Terrain: Ride through second-growth timberland and along a ridge top on singletrack and steep forest road.

Land Status: National forest

Nearest Town: Cashmere, WA

Other Trail Users: Hikers, equestrians, and motorcyclists

Canine Compatibility: Dogs not permitted

Wheels: Full suspension recommended, but hardtail is okay

Getting There

From Cashmere: Exit onto Division Street from U.S. 2. Follow Division Street right around the Vale School and continue as the Division Street changes names to Pioneer Street. Take the immediate left onto Mission Creek Road, following it to Binder Road. Turn right onto Binder Road. Mission Creek Road picks up again immediately on the left. Turn left on Mission Creek Road. Follow for 10.4 miles to a fork in the road. Turn left on FS 7100 and drive 2.6 miles to the trailhead for Mission Ridge Trail and Devils Gulch Trail. *DeLorme: Washington Atlas & Gazetteer* Page 67 B5

The Devils Gulch ride is nestled in the hills east of the Cascade mountain range, an area well regarded for its tasty apples, but also known for its award-winning wines. Just southeast of Yakima, all the way to the Columbia River, and as far north as Spokane, juicy grapes of all varieties grow. Similar to the climes of northern France, the weather in this eastern Washington region is ideal for growing fine wine fruit. Long sunny summer days that aren't too hot produce the best fruit, which in turn make the best wine. Some of the better years for wine in this area were 1985, 1988, 1989, and 1992—all were exceptionally good weather years. But

grapes wouldn't survive here without water. The water issue changed dramatically with the damming of the Columbia River, which turned the once desert-like territory of eastern Washington into fertile farmland. Other crops thrive here now as well (fruits, vegetables, herbs, hops, etc.), making this area the leading source of Washington's produce.

The area is also well known for mountain biking, led by this popular, sun-filled ride on the trail through Devils Gulch. Many Washington mountain bikers agree that Devils Gulch is one of the best rides in the state. It has everything a mountain biker could want: a long climb, ultra-smooth singletrack, more downhill than uphill, beautiful scenery, the soothing sounds of Mission Creek, great views of Mount Stewart, views of Wenatchee, banked turns, creek crossings, wild flowers, open meadows, sneaky switchbacks, and lots of hot sunshine (usually). And during the weekends an increasing number of cars shuttle riders to the trailhead to ride the downhill without working for it. With us as your ride guides, however, you'll be earning your descent.

MilesDirections

0.0 START from the trailhead parking area for Mission Ridge/Devils Gulch. Ride up FS 7100.

2.3 Stay right on FS 7100, following along the East Fork of Mission Creek. This is where the climbing begins. FS 7100 is on the left.

5.5 The gravel road turns to hard packed dirt.

6.0 Enter the National Forest boundary.

9.2 At the intersection, turn right on FS 9712.

9.5 Enter the Beehive Soil and Management Area.

9.7 Pass a spur road. Stay straight on FS 9712.

10.4 Pass a road on the right.

11.5 Turn right on to the Devils Gulch Trail.

14.0 The trail, once rolling, now flattens and straightens somewhat. The trees are open, offering an unobstructed view. This trail is porcelain smooth.

15.8 Encounter some sneaky switchbacks. Prepare to cross Mission Creek and feeder creeks a dozen times or so.

18.0 Continue rolling on the trail as it drops down and across the creek several times.

24.4 Arrive back at the trailhead parking area.

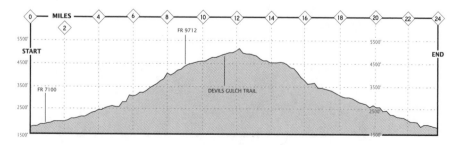

Actually, this ride isn't too horrible on ascents. The first 11.5 miles take you up a not-too-steep gain in elevation. After the initial two-to-three miles of riding on gravel, the road turns into smooth, hard-packed dirt. The climb is surprisingly easy from then on. It winds up through the canyon and crosses Mission Creek several times along the way. As easy as this climb is, it's surprising how many riders still opt for the two-car shuttle.

After six miles, the road crosses into the National Forest boundary. Eventually the views turn toward Wenatchee where you are able to make out the town and the mighty Columbia River. As the road climbs, Glacier

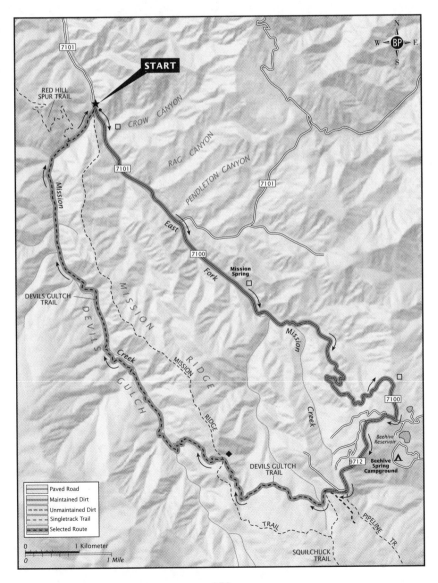

Peak and Mission Ridge come into view. When you hit the trail on the back side of Mission Ridge, the real fun begins. It's all fast, silky-smooth, downhill singletrack. You can't beat it. At first the trail is rolling, then it takes on a different attitude. Sharp switchbacks will surprise you—controlled speed will be more fun than flying over the edge because you missed a turn. And when you arrive at the bottom, you'll be ready to do it all over again, maybe this time on the Mission Ridge Trail.

Ride Information

🕓 Trail Contacts:
Wenatchee National Forest, Leavenworth Ranger District: (509) 548–6977 • **Lake Wenatchee Ranger District:** (509) 763–3103 or 1–800–452–5687

🕓 Schedule:
Open year round, but best between April and November, when there's less snow

💲 Fees/Permits:
$5 per car, per day charge ($30 for an annual pass)

❓ Local Information:
Leavenworth Chamber of Commerce Visitor Center, Leavenworth, WA (509) 548–5807 • **Wenatchee Chamber of Commerce:** (509) 662–2116

💡 Local Events/Attractions:
Washington State Apple Blossom Festival, in April, Wenatchee, WA (509) 662–3616 • **Apple Industry Tour,** in October, Wenatchee, WA (509) 663–9600 • **Founder's Day,** in June, Cashmere, WA (509) 782–7404 • **Apple Days,** in October, Cashmere, WA (509) 782–7404 • *[See Ride 11 for more information.]*

🚲 Local Bike Shops:
Arberg Sports, Wenatchee, WA (509) 663–7401 • **Aspund's Outdoor Recreation 1,** Wenatchee, WA (509) 662–6539 • *[See Ride 11 for more information.]*

🅽 Maps:
USGS maps: Blewett Pass, WA; Mission Peak, WA

Centennial Trail to Riverside Park

Ride Summary

The Centennial Trail begins in Idaho and runs all the way through the bicycle-friendly city of Spokane, smack into Riverside State Park. The trail is popular among more than just mountain bikers, but the singletrack within the park is where the mountain bikers leave the others behind. There are miles and miles of double- and singletrack to explore within the park. Take an hour or take a full day. You won't be able to ride it all in one visit.

Ride Specs

Start: *Riverside State Park:* From the parking lot at Seven Mile Road and Aubrey White Parkway. *Centennial Trail:* From the visitor center at the Idaho border.

Length: *Riverside State Park:* Varies depending on routes chosen. *Centennial Trail:* 37-mile point-to-point.

Difficulty Rating: Easy, mostly paved path. Trails range from easy to difficult depending on elevations.

Terrain: The trail is paved but turns to singletrack, doubletrack, fire roads, washboard, and sand as it runs through the rolling hills of Riverside State Park.

Land Status: State park

Nearest Town: Spokane, WA

Other Trail Users: *Paved path:* pedestrians, joggers, and in-line skaters. *Trails:* hikers, equestrians, and cross-country runners.

Canine Compatibility: Dogs permitted

Wheels: Any bike will work on paved trails, though front suspension is a great idea for the Riverside State Park trail network

Getting There

To the Paved Centennial Path. From I-90: Take the Maple Street exit and head north. Follow it over the City Bike Path to Nora Avenue—turn left. Turn right on Pettet Drive and look for the signs for Riverside Park parking.

To the Riverside State Park Trails. From I-90: Take the Maple Street exit heading north. Follow Maple to Northwest Boulevard—turn left. Follow for a mile or two until it turns into Assembly Road and then Nine Mile Road. Continue on Nine Mile Road about one mile to Seven Mile Road. Follow Seven Mile Road over the bridge. Turn left immediately after the bridge onto Aubrey White Parkway (also called Riverside Park Drive). Follow this to the parking lot. *DeLorme: Washington Atlas & Gazetteer:* Page 88-89 C4-5

The city of Spokane and the Spokane River, along which the city is situated, were both named after the Spokane Indian tribe. The first Anglo pioneer to be drawn to the roar of Spokane's falls was James N. Glover, who in 1872 began the task of building a township. Glover expected big things from this new town that he called *Spokane Falls*. He waited anxiously for the railroad to arrive, realizing that this would determine the success or failure of his venture. In 1878, Spokane Falls became "official," and its population grew to 100 within a year. The railroad finally came in 1881. By 1883, a Dutch mortgage company began financing the construction of the town, envisioning the potential for waterpower along the mighty river, which meant industry development and future capital.

In 1889, Spokane Falls succumbed to a fate that befell many pioneer towns of the West in those rugged days of isolation. Cause unknown, a devastating fire destroyed 32 blocks of the town's financial district. The townspeople quickly gathered their resources and within a year rebuilt—this time in brick and granite. From the ashes the city of Spokane emerged, dropping "Falls" from its name. This time the city developed quickly; 500 buildings were erected the first year. Due to inflated wages that came with the insistence on quick recovery, workmen flocked to Spokane, and the population escalated to 25,000 in two years' time.

Spokane was probably a relatively easy place to build a town in the 1800s. The weather is sunny and dry most months of the year—which explains the Indian word *spokan* meaning "Sun People." The climate is markedly different from its sister cities to the west. Spokane is protected by the Cascade Range to the west—which keeps precipitation on average below 20 inches a year—and the Rocky Mountains to the east—which keep winters rather mild. This combination of low rainfall and mild winters gives Spokane a longer mountain biking season as well. There are many places to mountain bike on the outskirts of town and within the city limits. Travel to the top of Mount Spokane to ride the singletrack that the National Off-Road Bicycle Association (NORBA) has used for mountain bike races, or stay close to town and follow a self-guided tour along The Centennial Trail.

The Centennial Trail is a 37-mile paved pathway that begins at the Washington/Idaho state line (connecting to the Idaho Centennial Trail) and ends, presently, at the Nine Mile Dam where the Spokane and Little Spokane rivers converge. Some of the most scenic sections of trail run through Riverside State Park—where approximately 10.5 miles of dirt singletrack and doubletrack trail can be found for in-city mountain biking. The trails are accessed easily from several places along The Centennial

Trail. Riverside State Park has at least seven parking lots of its own. The most direct access to the singletrack is from the Seven Mile Road parking area, mid-center of the park. There you'll find an entrance to an area jam-packed with singletrack. While our map attempts to provide a general rendering of the trail system, it should in no way be considered complete. The trail network continues to grow all the time. Its pathways are nonetheless fun to explore even without the most complete map and getting lost shouldn't be of great concern.

MilesDirections

Centennial Trail: START from the Washington/Idaho state line at the Washington State Visitor Information Center. Travel west through downtown Spokane for 37 miles to the trails end at Nine Mile Dam.

Riverside State Park: START from the parking lot at Seven Mile Road and Aubrey White Parkway near Camp Seven Mile to access the park's vast network of off-road bicycling trails. Make up your own rides within the park and have a blast!

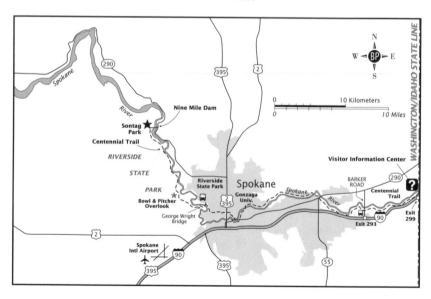

The route along the Centennial Trail is open to everyone: strollers, skaters, bicycle riders, and hikers. If you want to ride the entire Washington portion of the trail, begin at the Washington State Visitor Information Center at the Idaho border. From there, the trail continues west past small parks and river rapids. A dozen or so miles into the trail, you'll pass Boulder Beach and Minnehaha Rocks (a great place to rock climb). Moving into the city, still following the Spokane River, the Centennial

Trail passes the Spokane Community College and Gonzaga University (Bing Crosby's alma mater) before meandering through town a little and heading into Riverside State Park's 7,655 acres. From there you can ride to the current end-point at Nine Mile Dam. Riding the Centennial Trail out-and-back, you can cover almost 80 miles!

Ride Information

❶ Trail Contacts:
Riverside State Park: (509) 456–3964

❷ Schedule:
Year round, open dawn to dusk

❸ Fees/Permits:
No fees or permits required

❹ Local Information:
Spokane Regional Convention and Visitors Bureau, Spokane, WA (509) 747–3230 or 1–800–248–3230 • **Friends of the Centennial Trail,** Spokane, WA (509) 624–7188 • **Spokane Outdoors web site:** *www.spokaneoutdoors.com*

❺ Local Events/Attractions:
Wheelsport Bike Sale, in April, Spokane Interstate Fairgrounds,

Spokane, WA (509) 326–3977 • **The Annual Bloomsday Race,** in early May, Riverfront Park, Spokane, WA (509) 838–1579 • **The Lilac Festival,** for 10 days in May, Spokane, WA (509) 326–3339 • **Walk-in-the-Wild Zoo,** Spokane, WA (509) 924–7220 • **Spokane House Interpretive Center,** 12 miles NW of Spokane on WA 291: (509) 466–4747

❻ Local Bike Shops:
There are a number of quality bike stores and outdoor stores in Spokane, around every turn. Check out the local phone book for the one nearest your point of departure.

❼ Maps:
USGS maps: Nine Mile Falls, WA; Airway Heights, WA

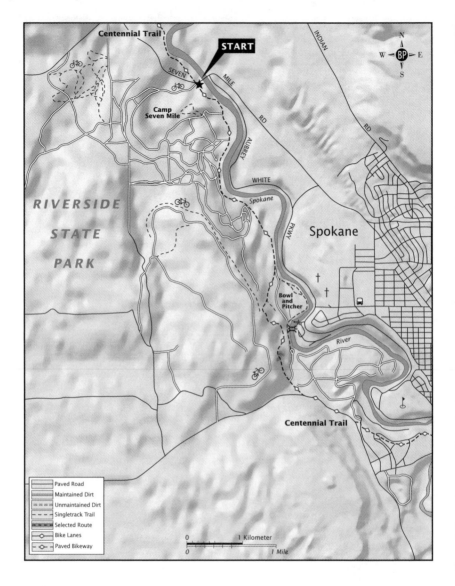

Honorable Mentions

Eastern Washington

Compiled here is an index of great rides in the Eastern region that didn't make the A-list this time around but deserve recognition. Check them out and let us know what you think. You may decide that one or more of these rides deserves higher status in future editions or, perhaps, you may have a ride of your own that merits some attention.

(Q) Sawtooth Backcountry

This region has 28 miles of singletrack and connects to the Foggy Dew area (see chapter 36) for epic mountain biking possibilities. Every trail in the area is open to mountain biking except the Summer Blossom Trail and trails 420, 1254, and 1259 which are in Wilderness Area. From the 4.5-mile Foggy Dew Trail at the Foggy Dew Campground, head north to Cooney Lake, Martha Lakes, and down to the Crater Creek Trailhead for a 12.5-mile shuttle ride. Or, begin at the Crater Creek Trail and take the northwest Trail 431 to Horsehead Pass and Boiling Lake for a 20-mile out-and-back. From WA 97 north to Pateros: Head north on WA 153 toward Twisp. At mile marker 16.8, turn left heading west onto Gold Creek Road, which is FS 4340. Follow for almost one mile. Turn left at the T-intersection toward the Foggy Dew Guard Station and Crater Creek Camp. After one mile, continue straight through the intersection for the Foggy Dew Campground. After four miles, turn left and cross a bridge onto FS 200. Drive past the Foggy Dew Campground on the left after the bridge. The pavement ends here. Continue three-and-a-half miles to the trailhead parking lot.

From Pateros: Head north on WA 153 toward Twisp. At mile marker 16.8, turn left heading west onto Gold Creek Road, which is FS 4340. Follow for almost one mile. Turn left at the T-intersection toward the Foggy Dew Guard Station and Crater Creek Camp. After one mile, continue straight through the intersection for the Foggy Dew Campground. After four miles, turn left and cross a bridge onto FS 200. Drive past the Foggy Dew Campground on the left after the bridge. The pavement ends here. Continue three and a half miles to the trailhead parking lot. For more information, call the Chelan Ranger District at (509) 682–2576. See *DeLorme: Washington Atlas & Gazetteer:* Page 99 C-7.

(R) Echo Valley

North of Chelan on Cooper Mountain Road, this snow park area has great trails for mountain biking. At least 30 kilometers of trail run through this valley, making this a great area to explore while hanging out at Lake Chelan.

From U.S. 2, head north on U.S. 97 to Lake Chelan. Follow WA 150 up the east side of the lake. Turn right on Boyd Road and left on Copper

Mountain Road. For more information, call the Chelan Visitors Information at 1–800–424–3526. See *DeLorme: Washington Atlas & Gazetteer*: Page 83 B8.

(S) Steamboat Rock State Park

Sitting out in the middle of Banks Lake, there are 25 miles of paths and trails on, around and over Steamboat Rock—a massive basalt bluff. The 3,500-acre park is well maintained and has lots of camping available. This area is also a popular water sport destination.

From U.S. 2 east, travel on WA 155 north toward Grand Coulee, following the signs for the park to the west. For more information, call the State Park at 1–800–233–0321. See *DeLorme: Washington Atlas & Gazetteer*: Page 85 B7.

(T) Down River Trail

Follow the Columbia River downstream for about seven miles from the Grand Coulee Dam and turn around. A great family trail, just pick up the path at the Mason City Park.

From U.S. 2 and Coulee City, head north on WA 155, or WA 174 farther east, to Grand Coulee. Follow WA 155 to the dam. For more information, call the Grand Coulee Visitor Center at (509) 633–9265. See *DeLorme: Washington Atlas & Gazetteer*: Page 86 A1.

(U) 13-Mile ORV Area

This trail system lies within the peaks of Cougar, Granite, Fire, and Seventeenmile Mountains. Alternate trails to the peaks of Fire Mountain (5,890 feet) and Thirteen Mile Mountain (4,885 feet) make great side trips. Lower trails weave around the rock cliffs of the Sanpoil River Canyon. Check out the eagles here in late April and early May.

From the town of Republic, head south on WA 21. Take Hall Creek Road 99 south to the trailhead for Trail 23, or take WA 21 south 13 miles to the Thirteen Mile Trailhead. For more information, call the Colville National Forest Republic Ranger District at (509) 775–3305. See *DeLorme: Washington Atlas & Gazetteer*: Page 116 D-3.

(V) Taylor Ridge Trail #74

This trail begins at the Taylor Ridge Trailhead and ends at the Indian Creek Road 430. Almost 10 miles long one-way, this trail is steep and moderately difficult. It can be ridden as a shuttle or as an out-and-back. Located within an area that has over 20 miles of mountain bike and ORV trails, this system offers incredible views of the Kettle Range. Climbing from the valley floor, this trail crosses several creeks before topping-out after a 3,550 foot climb between the two trailheads.

From Spokane, travel north on I-395, 22 miles past Kettle Falls to the Boulder-Deer Creek Road 6100. Head west on Boulder-Deer Creek Road 6100 to South Boulder Road 6110, turning left. The trailhead is two miles ahead. For more information, call the Colville National Forest Republic Ranger District at (509) 775–3305. See *DeLorme: Washington Atlas & Gazetteer:* Page 117 B-7.

(W) Narcisse Block of the Pend Oreille Area

This is a large area consisting of 68 miles of multi-purpose trails, great views of Thomas and Green Mountain, as well as fields full of huckleberries in late summer. Access the system from either of three places. Although there are several loops to make, consider making one big 30-mile shuttle trip between Frater Lake and Clark Creek Trailhead. This trail is west of WA 20, so park at both ends and ride the Radar Dome Trail in between. On the east side of WA 20 is the 6.5 mile Tacoma Divide Trail that leads to Lake Sherry or to the 8.3-mile Rufus Trail and up to Frater Lake.

From Colville. A.) The Clark Creek Trailhead, 3.1 miles south of the Radar Dome Vista: Travel on WA 20 twenty miles east of Colville to FS 2389 continuing to the trailhead. B.) The Mill Creek Trailhead: Take WA 20 26 miles east of Colville to County Road 4954 and the trailhead. And C.) The Frater Lake Trailhead: Follow WA 20 29 miles east of Colville finding the trailhead adjacent to the highway.

For more information, call the Northeast Region of the Department of Natural Resources at (509) 684–7474 or the Colville Ranger District at (509) 684–7010. See *DeLorme: Washington Atlas & Gazetteer:* Page 118 D3–4.

(X) Batey/Bould Trails

Just west of the Idaho border, along the Oreille River, are 38 miles of trail ranging from easy to most difficult. The Alpha and Lone Wolf trails are the easiest. The Arctic, Howter, and Scapegoat trails are the toughest, ranging in elevation from 2,500 feet to 4,400 feet.

From Spokane, head north on U.S. 2 to WA 211 to WA 20 north. Turn west on to Kapps Lane. Head north on West Calispell (CR 9205) to CR 2341, following the signs to the trailhead. For more information, call the Colville Ranger District at (509) 684–7010. See *DeLorme: Washington Atlas & Gazetteer:* Page 105 A-6.

(Y) 49-Degrees North Alpine Ski Area

Open for mountain biking during the year, this resort actually supports a World Cup dual slalom race in the snow on Valentine's Day every year. There is also an annual WIM (Washington, Idaho, Montana) Series race offering both cross-country and downhill divisions for novice to expert racers. Singletrack and logging roads are accessed either from the base area or a mile from the ski area opposite Crest Drive.

From Spokane, travel 42 miles north on I-395. Turn right at the light onto Flowery Trail Road, and continue 10 miles more to the resort. For more information, call the ski area at (509) 935–6649 or 458–9208. See *DeLorme: Washington Atlas & Gazetteer*: Page 104 B-4.

(Z) Mount Spokane State Park

Mount Spokane State Park surrounds the highest peak around for miles: Mount Spokane, which stands at 5,883 feet. The cross-country ski trails weaving throughout the park make ideal mountain biking routes in the summer. There are several trails on the mountain to try, including the Spirit Lake Trail, Valley View Trail, and the Larch Trail. Just about every level of rider can find an appropriate route here. Park at the sno-park for most rides on Mount Spokane. Maps are available at the resort or on the outdoor board at the trailhead.

Take U.S. 2 to WA 206. Follow WA 206 for 15 miles to the State Park entrance, continuing on to the sno-park parking area. The trailhead has an outdoor board map. Call Mount Spokane State Park for more information at (509) 238–4258. See *DeLorme: Washington Atlas & Gazetteer*: Page 89 A-7&8.

(AA) Liberty Lake Regional Park

Part of the Spokane County Parks and Recreation system, equi-distant from both Spokane and Coeur d'Alene, ID, this ORV area has miles of trail between its 3,000 acres, spanning into both Washington and Idaho soil.

From Spokane, take I-90 to Idaho Road heading south, just west of the Idaho border in Washington. For more information, call Spokane Country Parks and Recreation at (509) 456–4730. See *DeLorme: Washington Atlas & Gazetteer*: Page 89 C-8.

(BB) The Bill Chipman Palouse Trail

Part of the Rails-to-Trails Program, this easy-grade, eight-mile paved trail opened in April of 1998, in a cooperative effort between active citizens and several government agencies. This trail was named in the memory of Bill Chipman, a local businessman, civic leader, family man, and friend, who was admired in Pullman and Moscow. Running between Washington State University in Pullman and the University of Idaho in Moscow, this all-purpose recreational trail crosses 12 old railroad tresses along scenic Paradise Creek. Access the path at Bishop Boulevard in Pullman near Bishop and WA 270. For more information, contact Whitman County Parks at (509) 397–6238. See *DeLorme: Washington Atlas & Gazetteer*: Page 57 C-7.

ⓒⓒ The Snake River Bikeway

Along the Snake River, which marks the boundary line between Washington and Idaho, there is a wonderful paved path running from Clarkston to Asotin, past several parks and scenic stops, including Swallow's Nest Rock, a one-million-year-old slab of basalt that hosts thousands of nesting swallows each spring.

The trail begins at Beachview Park in Clarkston at the corner of Beachview and Chestnut Streets. For more information, contact the Clarkston Chamber of Commerce at (509) 758–7712. See **DeLorme: Washington Atlas & Gazetteer:** Page 43 A-8.

ⒹⒹ Asotin Creek Trail

The route along Asotin Creek is an easy-grade, scenic, and popular trail. Just follow the trail along the creek for about eight miles and then turn around. For a more moderate loop option, ride the trail eight miles, and instead of turning around, follow the trail up and away from Asotin Creek. The trail will loop around and end at the parking area, completing a 15-mile loop.

From Clarkston, head south on WA 129 to Hells Canyon. Turn right onto Asotin Creek Road. Drive four miles to the split and the parking area. For more information, contact the Washington State Parks and Recreation Department at 1–800–233–0321. See **DeLorme: Washington Atlas & Gazetteer:** Page 43 B-8.

ⒺⒺ North Fork Trail/Table Springs Loop

This advanced ride requires technical skill and endurance. At one point, a three-mile climb gains over 2,300 feet. Begin on the FS 65. Follow a mile or so to U.S. 040 and turn right. Turn right onto the North Fork Trail. Follow the trail over FS 6512 after half a mile. Out of the woods, a Jeep trail heads right; follow the trail left across the meadow. Ride over eight miles up and down to Cub Saddle at Bear Creek. Turn left on the Table Springs Trail. At the end of the trail turn left onto FS 6512. Stay left at the junction with FS 090, and to the right at the junctions of FS 080 and 060. Follow FS 6512 back to your car.

From Walla Walla, take Isaacs Avenue east to Mill Creek Road. Turn right on Mill Creek and continue 13 miles, turning right on Tiger Canyon Road. Park here to add to the climb, or drive up seven and a half miles to the top of the canyon. For more information, contact the U.S. Forest Service at (509) 522–6290. See **DeLorme: Washington Atlas & Gazetteer:** Page 41 D-7.

(FF) South Fork Trail Out-and-Back

This 13-mile, easy-grade ride is by far the busiest trail in the area. There are a creek or two to cross and some rocky singletrack, but the climb is minimal, unless you decide to hoof it all the way up to the Burnt Cabin Bridge. From the BLM parking area, follow the South Fork Walla Walla Road up the river. Turn right in one mile, just before the third bridge, onto the South Fork Walla Walla Trail. Follow this singletrack/doubletrack trail up the north side of the river. Pass the Table Springs Trail after five miles and turn around when you get to the Burnt Cabin Bridge Trail, a mile or so farther.

From Walla Walla, head south on Park Street to Howard Street. Follow Howard south a mile-and-a-half where it becomes Cottonwood Road. Follow Cottonwood straight to Powerline Road, continuing straight. Cross the North Fork of the Walla Walla after almost nine miles. Turn left and climb the valley of the South Fork. Drive seven miles to Harris Park. The parking area is half a mile ahead. For more information, contact the U.S. Forest Service at (509) 522–6290, or the Bureau of Land Management in Baker City, OR, at (541) 523–1256. See *DeLorme: Washington Atlas & Gazetteer:* Page 41 D-7.

(GG) Elbow Creek—Walla Walla

Heralded as one of the best rides in Walla Walla, this 26-mile loop features 3,000 feet of climbing, tight switchbacks, and rocky singletrack. The best part of the ride is the refueling stop at the half-way mark, offering a welcome opportunity to restock your water or food. Start at the BLM parking area, above Harris County Park. Follow the South Fork of the Walla Walla River on a dirt road for one mile. Branching left, cross a bridge and begin following Elbow Creek. Climb about 2,000 feet in six miles to Lincton Mountain Road. Bear right at the fork on top of the ridge toward Lincton Mountain Road. Turn left onto the road. The Tollgate Mountain Chalet is just up the road. Turn left at the Chalet onto paved Oregon State Highway 204 and ride for 4.6 miles to the Tollgate store, past Langdon Lake. Turn left on FS 64 following the sign for Jubilee Lake. Turn left onto FS 6401 to Target Meadows and right into Target Meadows Campground. Find the Burnt Cabin Trail on the left fork just after the campground. Take this singletrack to the South Fork of the Walla Walla River. Crossing a bridge, turn left onto the South Fork Walla Walla Trail. Descend another five miles to South Fork Walla Walla Road and turn right. One mile down is the BLM parking area.

From Walla Walla, head south on Park Street to Howard Street. Follow Howard south a mile-and-a-half where it becomes Cottonwood Road. Follow Cottonwood straight to Powerline Road, continuing straight. Cross the North Fork of the Walla Walla after almost nine miles, turn left and climb the valley of the South Fork. Drive seven miles to Harris Park and the parking area half a mile ahead. For more information, contact the U.S. Forest Service at (509) 522–6290, or the Bureau of Land Management in Baker City, OR, at (541) 523–1256. See *DeLorme: Washington Atlas & Gazetteer:* Page 41 D-7.

BONUS HONORABLE MENTIONS—Western Idaho

Canfield Mountain Trail System

A popular mountain biking area for Spokane bicyclists, the area along the Buttes is central to many activities and has 46 miles of old roads and trails open to mountain bikers.

From Spokane, take I-90 east into Idaho, then head north up FS 268 to the Canfield Buttes and the Cannfield Mountain Trail System. The Coeur d'Alene National Forest has trail information at (208) 752–1221.

The Coeur d'Alene River Trail

Twenty-one miles long, this beautiful trail is easy to ride. You can access it from several locations, including Jordan Camp at Cathedral Peak on FS 412.

From Spokane, head east on I-90 through Coeur d'Alene and Kellogg to Wallace. Turn left on FS 465 to Bunn. Continue north on FS 456. Turn right on FS 208. Follow 208 past FS 442, turning right on FS 412. Stay on 412 all the way to the trailhead at Cathedral Peak. The Coeur d'Alene National Forest has trail information at (208) 752–1221.

Fourth of July Pass

This cross-country ski area has extensive forest roads and ski trail roads to explore. Have a map and a compass—it is easy to get turned around.

From Spokane, head east on I-90 through Coeur d'Alene, ID, to exit 28 north. The Coeur d'Alene National Forest has trail information at (208) 752–1221.

Silver Mountain Alpine Ski Area

Near the town of Kellogg, ID, this ski resort opens to mountain bikers only on weekends and holidays from the first weekend in July to Labor Day weekend. Take the gondola up (the world's longest!) and experience their 12-mile long runs for some super sweet descents.

From Spokane, head east on I-90 to exit 49. Head south on County Road 90 to Silver Mountain just west of Kellogg. For more information, call the resort at (208) 783–1111 or visit their web site, *www.silvermt.com.*

Farragut State Park

The park has 4,000 acres and is one of Idaho's largest and most popular parks on the shores of Lake Pend Oreille. There is a nine-mile designated mountain biking trail here and over 20 miles of hiker only paths.

From Spokane, head east on I-90 in to Coeur d'Alene to I-95. Follow I-95 north to WA 54 northeast to Lake Pend Oreille and the park. For more information, call Farragut State Park at (208) 683–2425.

Elsie Lake Trail #106

Within the Coeur d'Alene National Forest, follow this 1.7-mile trail from the lake into the Saint Joe Divide area. Connect with Trail #16, which heads east and west, for some fabulous mountain biking. Take the trail as far east as Montana or back into the Silver Mountain mountain biking trail system. There are several trail accesses to the St. Joe district: from the Dot Creek Trail, the Striped Peak Trail up to Moon Pass, or to the Silver Hills Trail on the way up to Lake Elsie along the Coeur d'Alene Divide. Give yourself a week and you may be able to explore a good portion of this trail system.

From Spokane, travel east on I-90. Turn south on Big Creek Road between Kellogg and Wallace, or south on Placer Creek Road from Wallace to FS 389. For more information, call the Coeur d'Alene National Forest at (208) 765-7223.

Schweitzer Basin Ski Resort

Close to Sandpoint, ID, this ski resort is a great mountain biking destination. Hosting one of the National Off-Road Bicycle Association (NORBA) series races in August (1998), this ski resort is open for mountain biking July 1 to Labor Day weekend. The chair lift is open Fridays, Saturdays, and Sundays in the summer for easy access to the upper trails, but lower trails are great fun, too.

From Spokane, travel east on I-90 to Coeur d'Alene. Head north on U.S. 2/95 for 11 miles to Sandpoint and follow the signs for the resort. For more information, call the resort at 1–800–831–8810.

The Great Escape

John Wayne Pioneer Trail
Two Wheels and Seven Days

Day 1

North Bend to Lake Easton

Ride Summary

Expect to see riders of all age and skill levels on this westernmost and very popular section of the cross-state John Wayne Pioneer Trail. The former Milwaukee Road railroad grade offers an easy route up and through Snoqualmie Pass, and with the unique attraction of the 2.3-mile Snoqualmie Tunnel in the middle of the ride, it's a major draw for bikers and hikers. A climbing area along the route draws rock climbers to the trail as well.

Ride Specs

Start: From Rattlesnake Lake Park
Length: 38.9-mile point-to-point
Approximate Riding Time: 4–6 hours
Difficulty Rating: Beginner to intermediate
Terrain: Using a gravel doubletrack and an old railroad grade, gradually climb to a pass and then descend.
Land Status: State park
Nearest Town: North Bend, WA
Other Trail Users: Hikers and equestrians
Canine Compatibility: Dogs permitted (but be aware of other riders, as the trail can be quite busy on weekends)
Wheels: Any mountain bike will work, but front suspension is recommended for dealing with the shock of riding on hard-pack railroad bed.

Getting There

From Seattle: Take I-90 East across Lake Washington, past Bellevue and farther east to Exit 32. Turn right at the end of the off-ramp and go 3.5 miles south, just past the entrance to the Rattlesnake Lake Recreation Area and left to the Iron Horse State Park parking lot. A short spur trail links to the west end of the John Wayne Pioneer Trail. **DeLorme: Washington Atlas & Gazetteer:** Page 64 A2

Who would have thought that the demise of a railroad company would lead to the creation of one of the most unique mountain bike routes in Washington. When the Milwaukee Road ceased operating from Chicago to Seattle and Tacoma in 1980, it left a cross-state railroad grade open to hikers and other recreational users—which has since become the John Wayne Pioneer Trail. The Washington State Parks Department has taken over this portion of the trail (from Rattlesnake Lake to the Columbia River) and turned it into a long, winding park known as Iron Horse State Park. So don't get confused if you hear "Iron Horse" and "John Wayne" thrown around; the two are interchangeable for this western-most section of the trail.

Ride Information

📞 Trail Contacts:
Washington State Parks and Recreation Commission, Olympia, WA (360) 902–8500 or *www.parks.wa.gov/ ironhors.htm* • **John Wayne Pioneer Trail Hotline:** 1–800–233–0321

🕐 Schedule:
Open May 1 through October 31

💲 Fees/Permits:
No fees or permits required

❓ Local Information:
Milwaukee Road Historical Association: *www.mrha.com* • **The Upper Snoqualmie Valley Chamber of Commerce:** (425) 888–4440 or *www.snovalley.org*

💡 Local Events/Attractions:
Alpine Days, September 12–13, North Bend, WA • **The Northwest Railroad Museum,** Snoqualmie, WA

🚌 Bus Service:
To North Bend: King County Metro offers service to North Bend where you can start your ride via the Snoqualmie Valley Trail to the Rattlesnake Lake trailhead: (206) 553–3000 or *www.transit.metrokc.gov* • **To Snoqualmie Pass:** Greyhound stops at Bob's Summit Deli, 521 WA 906: *www.greyhound.com*

🚲 Local Bike Shops:
Valley Bike Rack, Snoqualmie, WA (425) 888–4886

🛏 Accommodations:
Public campgrounds near the trail: **Tinkham Campground** (Exit 42); **Denny Creek Campground** (Exit 47); **Lake Kachess Campground** (Exit 62); **Crystal Springs Campground** (Exit 62) **Lake Easton State Park** campsite reservations: 1–800–452–5687

🗺 Maps:
USGS maps: North Bend, WA

Although this trail starts on one side of the Cascade Mountains and ends on another, it's still an easy spin for cyclists because of the gradual nature of railroad grades—the route never climbs or falls at greater than a two percent grade over this section of the trail. The doubletrack trail is so wide in spots that it resembles a fire road. Since the riding is so easy, riders can expect to encounter more traffic on this ride than on most mountain bike excursions in the state. At times the ride can feel more like a mountain bike version of the Seattle-to-Portland bike ride (the wildly popular 200-mile road ride that brings out 8,000 riders each year).

This portion of the John Wayne Pioneer Trail is highlighted by sweeping views from some of the highest former railroad trestles in the state. You'll also encounter the second-longest railroad tunnel in the Cascades: the 2.3-mile Snoqualmie Tunnel. Built in 1915 to help improve the grade up and over the pass, the tunnel is long enough and bends just enough at the east end to block all light for a rider or walker going west-to-east. Since it's dark, a headlight or helmet light is necessary to help guide the way through the tunnel. And bring warm clothes, because even in the hottest part of the summer the temperature inside the tunnel won't top 58°F.

MilesDirections

0.0 START at the Rattlesnake Lake Recreation Area.

4.7 Pass the Twin Falls Trail trailhead on left and notice I-90 just north of the trail below.

5.9 *[FYI. Pass the Deception Crags Climbing Area, a popular destination for rock climbers.]*

7.7 Cross the impressive Mine Creek Bridge.

10.2 Pass the McCellan Butte Trail and the trail to Annette Lake.

19.2 The western entrance to the Snoqualmie Tunnel. *[Note. Turn on your headlight and guard against the dripping ceiling.]*

36.9 Go straight off the gravel road and back onto the John Wayne Pioneer Trail.

37.0 Cross the scenic Yakima River on a fairly new bridge built just for the trail.

37.9 Veer off the railroad grade and follow the signs into Lake Easton State Park. *[Note. A trestle was out over the Yakima River here in 2000, but it's expected to be replaced soon.]*

38.9 Finish at Lake Easton State Park

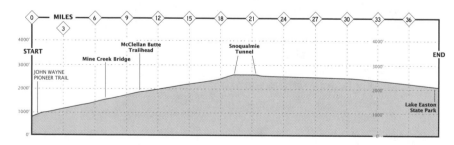

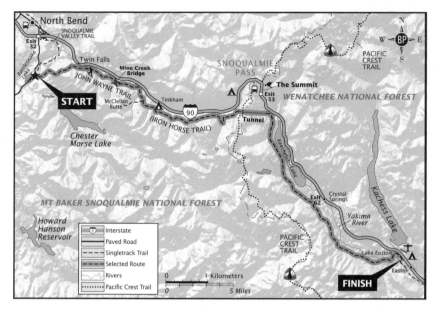

Shortly after the tunnel was built, workers on the Milwaukee Road used to close the tunnel doors in winter and run heaters inside to help prevent dripping water from freezing on the tracks. And although the tunnel is too warm to allow freezing in the summer months, riders still have to beware of drips and downright streams that pour from the tunnel ceilings in sections.

The Snoqualmie Tunnel is at the midpoint in the first section of the John Wayne Pioneer Trail. And although it also marks the high elevation point in the ride, the rest of the trail leading down to the finish at Lake Easton State Park doesn't really feel like a downhill grade at all. The roughness of the trail and the slight grade of less than two percent makes this section feel more flat than downhill. The trail skirts the edge of Keechelus Lake—a lake that dams up waters from the upper Yakima River for irrigation uses downstream. The Yakima River then flows east from the lake toward Lake Easton.

The ride concludes at Lake Easton State Park, which offers camping and a host of watersport activities such as swimming and fishing.

Day 2

Lake Easton to Ellensburg

Ride Summary

This mostly flat section of the John Wayne Pioneer Trail offers outstanding views as it winds across prairie lands near Easton, then eastward through South Cle Elum before moving into the sagebrush-dotted lands along the Yakima River, near the farming town of Thorp. The ride concludes in the college town of Ellensburg, home to Central Washington University.

Ride Specs

Start: From Lake Easton State Park
Length: 38.4-mile point-to-point
Approximate Riding Time: 4–5 hours
Difficulty Rating: Beginner to intermediate, due to the distance covered
Terrain: Using gravel doubletrack and an old railroad grade, cross prairie farmlands and then travel the Yakima River Valley through rock outcroppings before entering the fertile farm valleys near Ellensburg.
Land Status: State park
Nearest Town: Easton, WA
Other Trail Users: Hikers and equestrians
Canine Compatibility: Dogs permitted (but dogs aren't a good idea, as it's a long ride, over rough gravel)
Wheels: Any mountain bike will work, but front suspension is recommended for dealing with the shock of riding on a hard-pack railroad bed.

Getting There

From Seattle: Take I-90 East across Lake Washington and through Bellevue, then continue east over Snoqualmie Pass and down along Keechelus Lake until you reach the exit for Lake Easton State Park (Exit 70). *DeLorme: Washington Atlas & Gazetteer:* Page 65 B7

The history of the Milwaukee Road railroad line comes to life on this scenic and nearly flat section of the John Wayne Pioneer Trail. Rejoining the trail in the tiny town of Easton, the route flattens out for a 12-mile pedal into the former railway stop of South Cle Elum. Coming into town—which is a bit of an exaggeration, since this is really not a major part of the main town of Cle Elum—riders pass the old train depot, which has fallen into disrepair since the railroad ceased operating in 1980. Just to the north of the trail is the electrical substation that helped power this part of

the railway, which ran on electricity from Othello in the east to Tacoma in the west. (The railroad switched to electricity to speed up the train and to cut down on smoke problems within the Snoqualmie Tunnel.)

For a real treat, railroad buffs can stop just 100 yards or so down the trail from the South Cle Elum Trail trailhead, where, on the other side of the trail, the 1909 bunkhouse that housed railroad workers now operates as the Iron Horse Inn, a local bed and breakfast. The building is listed on the National Register of Historic Places and includes an impressive collection of memorabilia from the Milwaukee Road. The popular bed and breakfast can also serve as a stopover for riders looking to do an alternate ride and complete the trail from North Bend all the way to the Columbia River in just two days, since it is located conveniently midway along the 115-mile route.

The Milwaukee Road railroad company started in the early 1900s as the Chicago, Milwaukee, & St. Paul Railway, and began serving this part

of eastern Washington in 1909. At its peak, the Milwaukee Road ran from Minneapolis, Minnesota, all the way to Seattle and Tacoma; it also had spur lines that continued on to the Grays Harbor region and the Olympic Peninsula.

Besides the run-down depots and electrical substations, riders will encounter a countless number of rusted railroad spikes and peculiarly numbered markers along every mile of the trail. The markers count down the distance to Chicago. From here, it's just over 2,000 miles to go.

Heading east from Cle Elum, the trail goes under Interstate 90 and crosses a short plain to border the Yakima River as it heads toward the Thorp Tunnels. These tunnels mark a passage from riding along a barren, rock-strewn riverside to irrigated fields near the grain town of Thorp—known for Thorp Mill, a 1883 structure that's now a museum and listed on the National Register of Historic Places.

The ride culminates in Ellensburg—home to Central Washington University, not to mention one of the biggest rodeos in Washington.

MilesDirections

0.0 START from Easton State Park and take a right out of the park onto Cabin Creek Road. Go through town before turning to cross the railroad tracks.

0.2 Turn left onto the John Wayne Memorial Trail once again.

12.3 Pedal into South Cle Elum. *[FYI. Note the former railroad station to the left. Off in the distance, on the other side of the tracks, is the old boarding house that's now the Iron Horse Inn.]*

25.2 The trail follows the Yakima River into a canyon and bends before entering the Thorp Tunnels.

30.9 Reach the Thorp trailhead.

37.7 After riding past some new trailside housing developments, reach the Ellensburg West trailhead. From here go right onto Water Street, and then left on 14th Avenue, through the Central Washington University campus.

38.2 Turn right onto Alder Street. Proceed across a major thoroughfare.

38.4 Finish at the Ellensburg East trailhead.

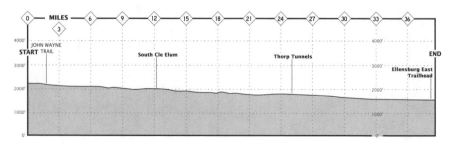

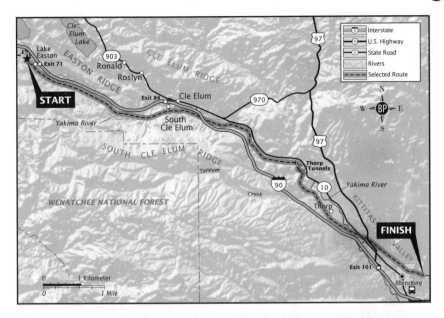

Ride Information

📞 Trail Contacts:
Washington State Parks and Recreation Commission, Olympia, WA (360) 902–8500 or *www.parks.wa.gov/ ironhors.htm* • **John Wayne Pioneer Trail Hotline:** 1–800–233–0321

🕐 Schedule:
Open year round, but best between May and October

💲 Fees/Permits:
No fees or permits required

❓ Local Information:
Milwaukee Road Historical Association: *www.mrha.com* • **Ellensburg Chamber of Commerce,** Ellensburg, WA (509) 925–3138 or *www.ellensburg-chamber.com*

📍 Local Events/Attractions:
Thorp Mill, Thorp, WA (509) 964–9640 • **Olmstead Place State Park,** Ellensburg, WA (509) 925–1943

🚌 Bus Service:
Greyhound Terminal, Ellensburg, WA (509) 925–1177: *www.greyhound.com*

🛏 Accommodations:
Iron Horse Inn, South Cle Elum, WA 1–800–22–TWAIN or (509) 674–5939

🚲 Local Bike Shops:
Cle Elum Bike & Hike, Cle Elum, WA (509) 674–4567 • **Recycle Bicycle Shop,** Ellensburg, WA (509) 925–3326

🅽 Maps:
USGS maps: Easton, WA; Ronald, WA; Cle Elum, WA; Teanaway, WA; Thorp, WA; Ellensburg North, WA; Ellensburg South, WA

Day 3

Ellensburg to the Columbia River

Ride Summary

Leave the green Kittitas Valley behind and climb into the Boylston and Saddle mountains before dropping down the other side of the ridge to the Columbia River south of Vantage. Don't let the earlier flat sections of the John Wayne Pioneer Trail lull you into complacency, though. This ride offers climbing as well as a soft, hard-to-ride trail surface.

Ride Specs

Start: From Ellensburg
Length: 31.5-mile point-to-point
Approximate Riding Time: 4–6 hours
Difficulty Rating: Beginner to intermediate, due to the trail condition, exposure to the desert elements, and remoteness
Terrain: Using gravel doubletrack and an old railroad grade, it's a gradual climb into the desolate Boylston Mountains and Saddle Mountains, then a long sloping downhill to the Columbia River.
Land Status: State park and U.S. Army property
Nearest Town: Ellensburg, WA
Other Trail Users: Hikers and equestrians
Canine Compatibility: Dogs permitted (however, this is not friendly terrain for dog friends)
Wheels: Front suspension recommended and come ready for sandy conditions

Getting There

From Ellensburg: Heading east on I-90, take either Exit 106 or Exit 109 and follow the signs toward Central Washington University. The East Ellensburg trailhead is located on the east end of the Central Washington University campus, at the Kittitas County Fairgrounds. ***DeLorme: Washington Atlas & Gazetteer:*** Page 66 4D

For mountain bikers who are used to riding hills and toiling through difficult terrain, this section of the John Wayne Pioneer Trail will make you feel right at home. The former two- to three-percent grade takes a break during these 31.5 miles, thanks to a detour on the road over Interstate 90 and some serious climbing on the route up and over the Boylston Mountains.

The interesting geology of the Columbia Basin is ever-present along this ride. After a short pedal past Kittitas Valley farmlands, the trail leaves the irrigated grounds and moves into sagebrush country. Once on the south side of Interstate 90 and after a short road detour caused by an out-of-service

trestle over the highway, riders climb a steep hillside to rejoin the trail in all of its sandy glory at the check-in station called Army West. The trail starts its climb through the Boylston Mountains. The old railroad grade slices through rolling sections of flood basalts that form the basin. The rock was left by one of the largest volcanic eruptions in the Earth's history. More than 15 million years ago, one volcanic center, in the southeastern section of Washington, sent more than 200 cubic miles of lava over tens of thousands of square miles.

The John Wayne Pioneer Trail cuts through some of the last of the flood basalts that originated in the nearby Saddle Mountains. Railroad builders had to blast through the basalt to create the flat surface for the tracks. And today the sides of these rough cuts through the basalt are caving in to form obstacle courses on the trail. It can be challenging to keep up speed while rolling through and over the rough rock, but a good motivation for rolling through the cuts is that this is rattlesnake country, and during the hot summer months, snakes can hang out in the relative cool of the railroad cuts.

Just when toiling through the sandy soils along the steady uphill is about to be too much, you reach the Boylston Tunnel. This tunnel marks a passage into an even more remote area, but more significantly, it marks the highest elevation on the ride. The trail emerges on the east side of the tunnel and drops steadily over the next 12 miles toward the Columbia River. This downhill can be a screaming fun ride, especially if you happen to be heading downhill with a tailwind. The biggest challenge over these last few miles is staying on the bike. Be careful when choosing your lines through the soft sandy sections. Be alert; a wrong move in the sand could end in an epic crash at high speeds.

The trail ends at the intersection with Huntzinger Road, a few miles south of the Wanapum Dam, near the Columbia River. The trail picks up on the east side of the river, but no one is allowed to cross the river on the old railroad bridge. The best way to bike over to the east side of the river is to ride north on Huntzinger Road, toward the town of Vantage, and then take the Interstate-90 bridge over the river. Turn south on Washington 26 and then take Washington 243 en-route to the trailhead near the tiny town of Beverly.

MilesDirections

0.0 START from East Ellensburg.

4.9 Pass the Kittitas trailhead and the old train depot.

7.5 Reach a detour at the intersection with Prater Road. Turn right onto Prater Road and cross an overpass over I-90.

7.6 Take a left onto Boylston Road that parallels I-90 on the south side of the freeway.

11.0 Take a right at the intersection with Stevens Road. A few hundred yards up a steep climb, leave the road and climb up to the check-in station at the Army West trailhead. *[**Note.** Register at the kiosk for a free trail permit that allows passage through this section of the U.S. Army Yakima Training Center grounds.]*

18.8 Reach the Boylston Tunnel. On the other side, start the long downhill toward the Columbia River.

30.8 Reach the Army East trailhead. The trail continues up and over one last ridge before reaching the intersection with Huntzinger Road.

31.5 Finish at Huntzinger Road. *[To cross the river, go north on Huntzinger Road, cross the I-90 bridge, go south on WA 26 and then south on WA 243. Cross under the abandoned railroad bridge and turn left into the town of Beverly. The next leg starts from the DNR lot along Crab Creek Road.]*

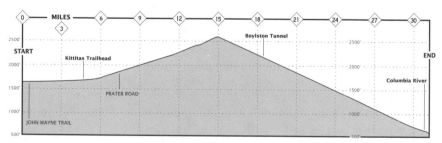

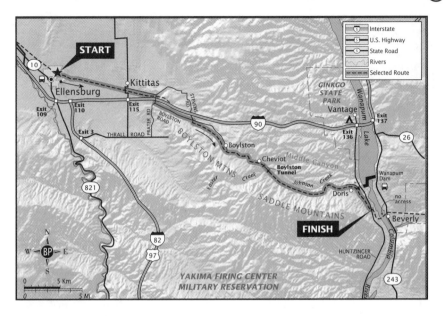

Ride Information

📞 Trail Contacts:
Washington State Parks and Recreation Commission, Olympia, WA (360) 902–8500 or *www.parks.wa.gov/ ironhors.htm* • **John Wayne Pioneer Trail hotline:** 1–800–233–0321

🕐 Schedule:
Open May through October

💲 Fees/Permits:
No fees required but you must register for a free permit at the U.S. Army Yakima Training Center kiosk.

❓ Local Information:
Milwaukee Road Historical Association: *www.mrha.com* • **Ellensburg Chamber of Commerce,** Ellensburg, WA (509) 925–3138 or *www.ellensburg-chamber.com*

📍 Local Events/Attractions:
Olmstead Place State Park, Ellensburg (509) 925–1943

🚌 Bus Service:
Greyhound Terminal, Ellensburg, WA (509) 925–1177: *www.greyhound.com*

🚲 Local Bike Shops:
Recycle Bicycle Shop, Ellensburg (509) 925–3326

🅽 Maps:
USGS maps: Kititas, WA; East Kititas, WA; Boylston, WA; Gingko, WA; Doris, WA; Beverly, WA

Day 4

Columbia River to Warden

Ride Summary

Get ready for sand, extreme desert riding conditions, and a long road detour to complete this section of the John Wayne Pioneer Trail. Starting at the Columbia River, the trail winds through the Crab Creek Wildlife Area before hitting the road for the towns of Othello and Warden, where the trail once again opens to the public.

Ride Specs

Start: From the DNR lot along Crab Creek Road in Beverly
Length: 60.3-mile point to point
Approximate Riding Time: 5–6 hours
Difficulty Rating: Beginner to Intermediate, due to sandy terrain, heat, and remoteness of the trail
Terrain: Take in the sights of the Saddle Mountains to the south and the soft sand trail under your wheels in desert sage country. Travel over sand and gravel doubletrack and an old railroad grade, followed by a road detour.
Land Status: Department of Natural Resources land
Nearest Town: Beverly, WA
Other Trail Users: Hikers and equestrians
Canine Compatibility: Dogs permitted (however, this is not friendly terrain for dog friends)
Wheels: Front suspension recommended

Getting There

From Vantage: Take I-90 East across the Columbia River and turn right onto WA 26 heading south along the river. Merge onto WA 243 and continue south toward Beverly. Cross under the abandoned railroad bridge and turn left into Beverly. Find parking in a DNR lot along Crab Creek Road. *DeLorme: Washington Atlas & Gazetteer:* Page 52 B1

Day four of The John Wayne Pioneer Trail brings mountain bikers to the remote eastern portion of this route—entering an area where permits are required and amenities along the trail are sparse. Other than in the small towns through which the route passes, you'll find no food, water, or restrooms along the way. So trail users have to be self-sufficient. But with remoteness comes many rewards, including passage through the scenic Crab Creek Wildlife Area and the Columbia National Wildlife Refuge. The scenery can make passage along the desert trail enjoyable, but summer passage rouses a very real concern. In short, beware of fire.

Eastern Washington is not a stranger to the effects of fire. The entire Columbia Basin is built on a foundation of fires of unimaginable intensity, caused more than 15 million years ago when huge pools of lava covered and formed the basin floor. Since those early fires, blazes ignited by lightning and humans have swept across the sagebrush country. In the summer of 2000, when fires dominated the West, I was surprised a few miles to find smoldering areas where fire had just swept across the trail. Fire crews worked to clean up the hot spots and make sure that the fire was out as my riding partner and I aborted the ride to explore sand dunes along Crab Creek. But the situation serves as a great reminder to keep an eye on the dangers of bik-

Ride Information

Trail Contacts:
Department of Natural Resources: (509) 925-8510 • John Wayne Pioneer Trail Hotline: 1-800-233-0321

Schedule:
Open May through October

Fees/Permits:
$25 permits are required, and riders should allow up to two weeks for permit approval.

Local Information:
Warden City Offices, Warden, WA (509) 349-2033 or www.cityof warden.org • Grant County website: www.grantcounty-wa.com • Othello Chamber of Commerce, Othello, WA (509) 488-2683 or www.othello-wa.com

Local Events/Attractions:
Sandhill Crane Festival, third week of March, Othello, WA – This celebrates the migration of nearly 25,000 sand-

hill cranes through the Othello area each spring and fall.

Bus Service:
Grant Transit Authority (GTA) offers limited bus service to Wanapum Dam, Royal City, and Beverly from the Amtrak station in Ephrata. There is more frequent bus service between Warden City Hall and Moses Lake. All GTA buses are equipped with bike racks. For more information, call 1-800-406-9177 or visit www.gta-ride.com

Local Bike Shops:
Northwest Sports Inc., Moses Lake, WA (509) 766-8226

Maps:
USGS maps: Beverly, WA; Beverly SE, WA; Smyrna, WA; Wahatis Peak, WA; Corfu, WA; Taunton, WA; Othello, WA; Bruce, WA; Warden, WA

ing in open country where all of the elements—fire, water, earth, and air—can play a role in the outcome of the ride.

The rugged trail from Beverly to Smyrna is a preview for the rest of the uncivilized John Wayne Pioneer Trail through eastern Washington to the Idaho border. The trail is managed by the Department of Natural Resources, but sections of the trail are privately owned and passage is regulated to minimize the effects of trail use on land owners. If you're trying to make the connection between the 14 miles of open trail from Beverly to Smyrna and the next open trail section near Warden, you'll need to arrange either a shuttle over the 46-mile road detour or buckle down and ride the roads to finish a long day of riding. A benefit of the riding the road is passing through part of the Columbia National Wildlife Refuge, a 23,000-acre area marked by small lakes and creeks that serve as a stopover for migrating birds. More than 25,000 sandhill cranes gather in the refuge during the spring months, and more than 100,000 ducks and Canadian geese gather to stay over the winter.

The town of Othello, which sits midway along the route, dates back to 1910. The old Milwaukee Road helped put the town on the map as a farming center. The same can be said of the town of Warden, which sits at the end of this route. Both Othello and Warden offer some amenities, and lodging is available in either town.

MilesDirections

0.0 START at any of the DNR lots along Lower Crab Creek Road.

2.2 Pass the sand dunes along Crab Creek on the left

13.0 Pass through the old byway of Smyrna.

14.0 Reach the end of the trail corridor for this section. *[**Option.** Either pick up a shuttle or bike the 46-mile road detour to Warden, we're you'll pick up the next leg of the Great Escape.]* Turn onto Lower Crab Creek Road and continue east.

24.3 Leave Lower Crab Creek Road and merge onto WA 26 and continue into the city of Othello.

40.2 After entering Othello, take a left onto Main Street, then turn right onto Cunningham Road.

48.6 Turn left onto Booker Road, which will head north into Warden.

60.3 Finish in Warden.

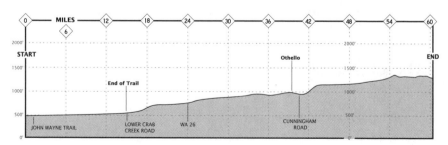

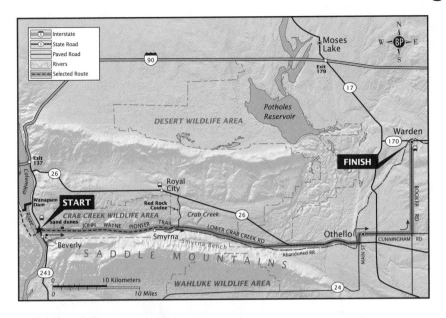

Deep sand may keep your speed in check.

In Addition

Rails-to-Trails

The mission of the Rails-to-Trails Conservancy is to "enhance America's communities and countryside by converting thousands of miles of abandoned rail corridors and connecting open spaces into a nationwide network of public trails."

Every large city and small town in America, by the early 20th Century, was connected by steel and railroad ties. In 1916, the United States had laid nearly 300,000 miles of track across the country, giving it the distinction as having the world's largest rail system. Since then, other forms of transportation, such as cars, trucks, and airplanes, have diminished the importance of the railroad and that impressive network of rail lines has shrunk to less than 150,000 miles. Railroad companies abandon more than 2,000 miles of track each year, leaving unused rail corridors overgrown and idle.

It wasn't until the mid 1960s that the idea to refurbish these abandoned rail corridors into useable footpaths and trails was introduced. And in 1963, work began in Chicago and its suburbs on a 55-mile stretch of abandoned right-of-way to create the Illinois Prairie Path.

It took nearly two decades for the idea of converting old railways into useable footpaths to catch on. Then in 1986 the Rails-to-Trails Conservancy was founded, its mission specifically to help communities see their dreams of having a useable rail corridor for recreation and non-motorized travel a reality. At the time the Conservancy began operations, only 100 open rail-trails existed. Today, more than 500 trails are open to the public, totaling more than 5,000 miles of converted pathways. The Rails-to-Trails Conservancy is currently working on more than 500 additional rails-to-trails projects.

Ultimately, their goal is to see a completely interconnected system of trails throughout the entire United States. If you're interested in learning more about rails-to-trails and wish to support the Conservancy, please write to:

Rails-to-Trails Conservancy
1400 16th Street, NW, Suite 300
Washington, DC 20036-2222
or call (202) 797–5400

Day 5

Warden to Lind

Ride Summary

Wheat fields and desert scablands invite riders on this section of the John Wayne Pioneer Trail. But come prepared, because once you leave Warden, you won't find services, bathrooms, or water until you reach Lind.

Ride Specs

Start: From Warden
Length: 23.8-mile point-to-point
Approximate Riding Time: 4–5 hours
Difficulty Rating: Intermediate, due to remoteness of the trail and difficult desert riding conditions
Terrain: Traverse desert scablands with some rough rock sections on sand and gravel doubletrack and an old railroad grade.
Land Status: Department of Natural Resources land
Nearest Town: Warden, WA
Other Trail Users: Hikers and equestrians
Canine Compatibility: Dogs permitted (however, this is not friendly terrain for dogs)
Wheels: Front suspension recommended

Getting There

From Warden: Take WA 170 East through town to the point where the abandoned railroad surface departs the road at the northeast corner of town.

Public Transportation: From Moses Lake, take Grant Transit Authority bus No. #10 to Warden City Hall at 2nd Avenue and Ash Avenue. Now on your bike, head north one block to 1st Avenue (WA 170) and turn right. Head east on 1st Avenue to the point where the abandoned railroad surface departs the road at the northeast corner of town. *DeLorme: Washington Atlas & Gazetteer:* Page 53 A8

I t is hard to imagine when setting out from the northeastern corner of Warden that the section of Washington you're about to ride through is an area that was repeatedly inundated by some of the largest floods in Earth's history. Travel back in time some 15,000 years, and rather than bike across rough desert terrain, you could be swept away by a wall of water 500 feet high and moving up to 65 mph across the land. Toward the end of the last ice age, a series of floods washed across this region, forming well-known land features such as Grand Coulee and Dry Falls, as well as lesser-known features like Lind Coulee, which this trail winds through. The floods originated in northern Montana and Idaho near Missoula, where a lake larger than Lake Ontario and Lake Erie, combined, formed behind a huge ice dam. Referred to as Glacial Lake Missoula, the lake rose to a depth of about 2,000 feet before it floated the ice dam off its

Ride Information

Trail Contacts:
Department of Natural Resources: (509) 925–8510 • John Wayne Pioneer Trail Hotline: 1–800–233–0321

Schedule:
Open May through October

Fees/Permits:
$25 permits are required, and riders should allow up to two weeks for permit approval.

Local Information:
Milwaukee Road Historical Association: www.mrha.com • Warden City Offices, Warden, WA (509) 349–2033 or www.cityof warden.org • Grant County website: www.grantcounty-wa.com • Adams County website: www.co.adams.wa.us • Lind website: www.lindwa.com

Local Events/Attractions:
Lind's Weekend, first weekend in June, Lind, WA – a celebration combining a demolition derby and rodeo

Bus Service:
Grant Transit Authority (GTA): 1–800–406–9177 or www.gta-ride.com

Maps:
USGS maps: Warden, WA; Hatton NW, WA; Roxboro, WA; Providence, WA; Lind, WA

MilesDirections

0.0 START where the trail begins at the northeastern corner of Warden, off East 1ˢᵗ Street.

8.1 Roll past the settlement of Roxboro and into the Lind Coulee.

20.1 Cross WA 21 and continue toward Lind.

21.0 Start the detour around a removed railroad trestle by turning left onto WA 21.

23.8 Turn right onto Van Marter Avenue in Lind. *[FYI. In short order you'll pick up the rail-trail again, on the left. Start the next day's leg here.]*

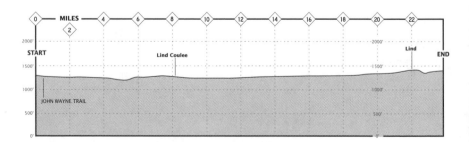

hold, unleashing a flood estimated by geologists to have contained 10 times the flow of all the rivers in the world combined. All of that water poured from north of Spokane and across what today is an arid desert, pockmarked with intermittent farm fields where irrigation has helped transform the land into fertile fields.

Evidence of the ancient floods that occurred repeatedly over hundreds of years is easy to see on the way to Lind. After the former railroad grade leaves the town of Warden, it parallels roads through farms and small settlements before veering south into Lind Coulee. This coulee is one of the many washouts formed by the glacial floods. Waters from the floods emptied out of the glacial lake within about 48 hours, drenching and destroying everything in their path as the waters worked there way toward the Columbia River. The water slowed near the Wallula Gap on the Columbia, where the water was forced through a narrow gap between mountains. It then rushed down the Columbia River Gorge, carrying chunks of ice and rocks and debris into the Willamette Valley in Oregon, and ultimately to the Pacific Ocean.

Once the rail-trail departs from Lind Coulee and climbs toward the town on Lind, the only detour looms ahead. Due to the removal of an old railroad trestle, trail users have to use Washington 21 and Van Marter Avenue to bypass the trestle and complete the ride to Lind. Pick up the trail at the intersection with Van Marter Avenue if you're continuing east. But the next section of trail is even more remote, so Lind is the last logical town to spend a night along the route before heading east.

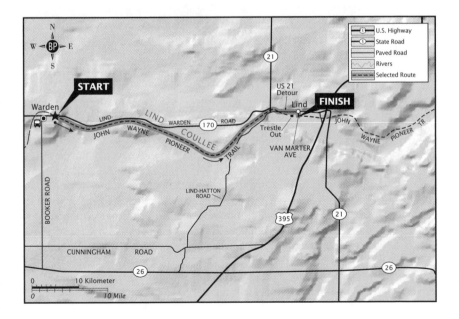

Day 6

Lind to Ewan

Ride Summary

If you're looking for desert adventure, this section of the John Wayne Pioneer Trail is a good bet. Venture into more desert scablands and ride among the sagebrush before taking a long road detour from Ralston to Marengo. This long ride wraps up in the tiny town of Ewan, a town with very little to offer outside of a name on the map.

Ride Specs

Start: From the rail-trail intersection with Van Marter Avenue in Lind
Length: 61.8-mile point-to-point
Approximate Riding Time: 6–7 hours
Difficulty Rating: Intermediate, due to desert conditions and rough trail
Terrain: Pass through sagebrush country and desert scablands interspersed with farm fields utilizing sand and gravel doubletrack and an old railroad grade.
Land Status: Department of Natural Resources land
Nearest Town: Lind, WA
Other Trail Users: Hikers and equestrians
Canine Compatibility: Dogs permitted (however, this is not friendly terrain for dogs)
Wheels: Front suspension recommended

Getting There

From Lind: Take Van Marter Avenue south to the intersection with the rail-trail, and then head east to start the ride.
DeLorme: Washington Atlas & Gazetteer: Page 54 A3

There is hot weather mountain biking, and then there is this ride. Eastern Washington never felt so hot as on a sunny summer day riding through Lind Coulee or taking the road detour into Ritzville with the sun's rays beating down on the pavement.

I learned this lesson the hard way, riding in 90°F temperatures. To avoid facing either heat exhaustion or heat stroke, doctors recommend that you acclimatize yourself to the conditions you intend to encounter. And when you face the heat, be sure to take frequent breaks and drink lots of water, even if you aren't thirsty. Just keep drinking.

Symptoms of heat stroke commonly include the halt of perspiration, especially when you would most expect to be sweating. If you start to feel

dizzy, confused, or nauseated, stop riding and seek immediate medical help. Sufferers from heat stroke can have their body temperatures soar to more than 106°F. Prolonged periods with that high of a body temperature can lead to brain damage. The recommended treatment for someone dealing with heat stroke is to call an ambulance and then take steps to cool down the victim by moving to a cooler area or soaking the victim in a cool bath. Still, the best advice is to avoid being in this situation. Take breaks and drink lots of water.

This section of the trail sets out from the east side of Lind and heads eastward inside the Lind Coulee. After 13 miles on the trail, riders are forced to take a long road detour to get around a closed section of the trail ahead at Cow Creek. The road detour veers north to Ritzville, and then east before turning south again to rejoin the trail in the small town of Marengo.

The trail follows a small creek the rest of the way into the town of Ewan. It's the first taste of riding along a water source in quite a while, and you can make the most of it by taking a short detour near the end of the ride. Just outside Ewan, a trail leads north from the rail-trail toward Rock Creek Falls. If you have the time and energy, it's well worth the one-mile detour to take in the falls.

After covering a little more than 60 miles, this ride rolls into Ewan. There are no services or lodging options in this town, so be prepared to make alternate lodging plans. If you plan to sleep along the trailside, be sure to clear your plan with the Department of Natural Resources when you apply for your trail use permit.

This trailside water trough is great for horses—bikes on the other hand...

MilesDirections

0.0 START by heading east on the rail-trail from its intersection with Van Marter Avenue.

1.3 Cross U.S. 395 and continue straight down the trail toward the tiny town of Ralston.

13.2 Reach the town of Ralston. Turn left onto WA 261. *[**Note.** You're turning off the rail-trail to detour around a break in the trail a little farther at Cow Creek.]*

23.7 Pass over I-90 and enter the town of Ritzville. Turn right onto Wellsandt Road.

28.7 Turn right onto McCall Road.

34.0 Turn right onto Marengo Road.

37.5 Veer left back onto the rail-trail in the tiny town of Marengo.

42.5 Cross the railroad crossing at Benge-Ritzville Road. Continue straight on the trail.

53.0 Reach the small town of Revere. Continue straight down the rail-trail.

61.8 Finish in the town of Ewan

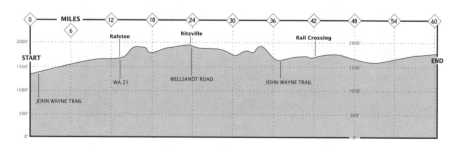

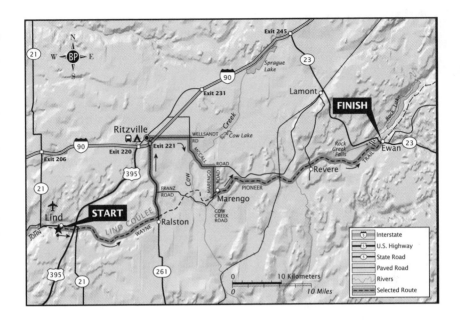

Ride Information

📞 Trail Contacts:
Department of Natural Resources: (509) 925–8510 • **John Wayne Pioneer Trail Hotline:** 1–800–233–0321

🕐 Schedule:
Open May through October

💲 Fees/Permits:
$25 permits are required, and riders should allow up to two weeks for permit approval.

❓ Local Information:
Milwaukee Road Historical Association: www.mrha.com • **Adams County website:** www.co.adams.wa.us • **Lind website:** www.lindwa.com • **Ritzville Area Chamber of Commerce,** Ritzville, WA: www.ritzville.com/chamber

📍 Local Events/Attractions:
Lind's Weekend, first weekend in June, Lind, WA – a celebration combining a demolition derby and rodeo • **Ritzville Rodeo & Wheatland Communities Fair,** Labor Day weekend, Ritzville, WA • **Ritzville Blues Festival,** second Saturday in July, Ritzville, WA

🚌 Bus Service:
Greyhound, Ritzville, WA (509) 659–0815 or www.greyhound.com

🅝 Maps:
USGS maps: Lind, WA; Pizarro, WA; Ralston, WA; Marengo, WA; Macall, WA; Revere, WA; Texas Lake, WA; Ewan, WA

Day 7

Ewan to Tekoa

Ride Summary

Move from the scablands and desert terrain into the rolling Palouse hills in this ride that concludes the cross-state John Wayne Pioneer Trail. This ride concludes in the town of Tekoa, but for a real sense of completion, you can continue on to the Idaho border by adding another seven miles to the ride.

Ride Specs

Start: From the rail-trail intersection with WA 23 just north of Ewan
Length: 57.7-mile point-to-point
Approximate Riding Time: 4–5 hours
Difficulty Rating: Intermediate, due to desert conditions and remoteness of the trail
Terrain: Sand and gravel doubletrack and an old railroad grade take you out of the desert scablands and into the hills of the Palouse country.
Land Status: Department of Natural Resources land
Nearest Town: Ewan, WA
Other Trail Users: Hikers and equestrians
Canine Compatibility: Dogs permitted (however, this is not friendly terrain for dogs)
Wheels: Front suspension recommended

Getting There

From Ewan: Take WA 23 North to its intersection with the rail-trail, a short distance north of town. *DeLorme: Washington Atlas & Gazetteer:* Page 72 D3

To the Endpoint: To reach the end point of the John Wayne Pioneer Trail, drive Highway 2 into Tekoa and find a parking spot in town. Since the trail detours around a missing railroad trestle to the north of town, you can arrange to be picked up at any point along the highway, from Lone Pine Road to Washington Street. *DeLorme: Washington Atlas & Gazetteer:* Page 72–73 C8

The John Wayne Pioneer Trail culminates in the rolling hills of the Palouse country, just southeast of Spokane. It's fitting that the trail, which started west of the Cascade Mountains, ends in the rolling hills of the Palouse, seeing as these hills are the result of years of erosion depositing topsoil from the Cascades some 200 miles east to gather and form the Palouse Hills. The soil deposits that constitute the Palouse Hills are known as loess, a light yellowish silt. Thousands of years ago, these rolling hills were sand dunes, slowly marching across eastern Washington on the winds to bury the underlying rocks. In some areas along this section of the trail, you can see

hilltops covered with trees poking up from the top of the grass-covered hills. Those hilltops are native ground that wasn't buried when the Palouse sands blanketed the northeast.

Riding through the Palouse Hills, it's easy to imagine what drew pioneers to the tiny towns along the route, including Rosalia and the eastern terminus of the trail in Tekoa. After setting out from Ewan, trail users are forced to make a long road detour due to a break in the trail along Rock Lake. Rejoin the trail at the east end of the lake and roll onward toward the towns of Malden and Rosalia. History buffs riding through Rosalia may want to check out the Rosalia Museum (on Fifth Street off Whitman) to view information about local Indian wars and Whitman County history. Read about how in 1858, before the first settlers moved to the immediate area, a 156-man calvary unit fought against Native Americans from the Spokane, Palouse, and Coeur D'Alene tribes and suffered a major loss in a battle called Te-Hots-Nim-Me. The Steptoe Battle Historical Marker, half a mile south of town on WA 195, commemorates the battle.

The ride departs Rosalia, with its population of 552 people, and heads east toward Tekoa. The trail winds between Palouse hills en-route to Tekoa and its 900 residents. A small farm community nestled against the base of Tekoa Mountain, it's one of the many towns that was put on the map when the railroad came to town. Two railroad lines ran through Tekoa—the Washington & Idaho Railroad run by Northern Pacific and the Oregon & Washington Railroad. The town even attracted a visit from President Theodore Roosevelt and his election entourage in 1903. Details of Tekoa's history are revealed in the Tekoa Museum, which is open by appointment only.

From Tekoa, the John Wayne Pioneer Trail continues east for another seven miles or so before reaching the Idaho border. Whether you opt to finish the trail in Tekoa or at the border, there is bound to be a feeling of accomplishment after traveling across much of Washington on bike. If you still haven't had enough of rail-trail riding, you can drive north to Spokane and check out the trails branching toward Idaho from there (see the Centennial Trail, Ride 43), and work is underway to make more of the former Milwaukee Road right-of-way a trail through Idaho, Montana, and onward.

MilesDirections

0.0 START just north of Ewan off WA 23, heading east on the rail-trail.

2.0 Turn right onto Rock Lake Road. This begins a road detour around Rock Lake.

4.7 Turn left onto Stephen Road and follow it for the next 11 miles.

15.7 Take a left onto Hole in the Ground Road.

16.1 Turn right onto the rail-trail near the settlement of Kenova.

27.1 Reach the small town of Malden. Continue straight down the trail.

34.6 *[Note. Two trestles are missing so you'll need to detour through Rosalia.]* Turn left off the trail onto 1ˢᵗ Street. Then turn right onto Whitman Street and go a couple of blocks to 7ᵗʰ Street. Turn right onto 7ᵗʰ Street, then left onto Pine Street.

35.0 Turn left, back onto the trail.

50.5 Reach the small town of Lone Pine. *[Note. After crossing the Seabury Trestle, get ready in 1.6 miles to turn right off the trail for another quick detour.]*

52.1 Turn left off the trail, then right onto Lone Pine Road.

54.2 Turn right onto Chase Road, and then rejoin the rail-trail.

57.7 Reach the town of Tekoa and the end of the ride. *[Option. You can continue on to the Idaho border from here by riding another seven miles down the trail.]*

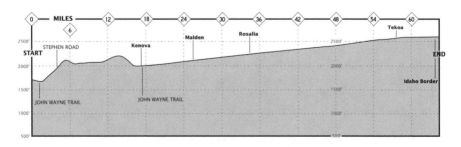

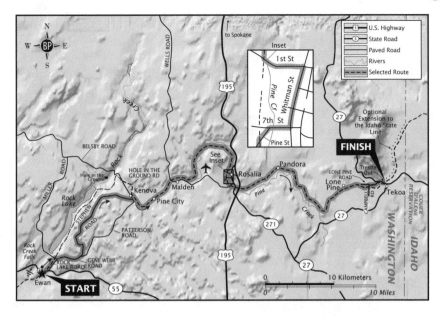

Ride Information

🟢 Trail Contacts:
Department of Natural Resources: (509) 925–8510 • **John Wayne Pioneer Trail Hotline:** 1–800–233–0321

🕐 Schedule:
Open May through October

💲 Fees/Permits:
$25 permits are required, and riders should allow up to two weeks for permit approval.

❓ Local Information:
Milwaukee Road Historical Association: *www.mrha.com* • **Rosalia Chamber of Commerce,** Rosalia, WA (509) 523–5991 • **City of Tekoa website:** *www.tekoa-wa.com*

⊖ Bus Service:
Northwestern Stage Lines stops at Ace Hardware in Colfax (25 miles south of Rosalia). Additional bus, air, and rail services are located in Spokane (40 miles northwest of Tekoa).

📍 Local Events/Attractions:
Tekoa Museum, Tekoa, WA (509) 284–2753 – *open by appointment only*

🅝 Maps:
USGS maps: Ewan, WA; Rock Lake, WA; Pine City, WA; Malden, WA; Rosalia, WA; Oaksdale, WA; Tekoa, WA

The Art of MOUNTAIN BIKING

The Art of Mountain Biking

Welcome to the new generation of bicycling! Indeed, the sport has evolved dramatically from the thin-tired, featherweight-frame days of old. The sleek geometry and lightweight frames of racing bicycles, still the heart and soul of bicycling worldwide, have lost much ground in recent years, unpaving the way for the mountain bike, which now accounts for the majority of all bicycle sales in the U.S. And with this change comes a new breed of cyclist, less concerned with smooth roads and long rides, who thrives in places once inaccessible to the mortal road bike.

The mountain bike, with its knobby tread and reinforced frame, takes cyclists to places once unheard of—down rugged mountain trails, through streams of rushing water, across the frozen Alaskan tundra, and even to work in the city. There seem to be few limits on what this fat-tired beast can do and where it can take us. Few obstacles stand in its way, few boundaries slow its progress. Except for one—its own success. If trail closure means little to you now, read on and discover how a trail can be here today and gone tomorrow. With so many new off-road cyclists taking to the trails each year, it's no wonder trail access hinges precariously between universal acceptance and complete termi-

nation. But a little work on your part can go a long way to preserving trail access for future use. Nothing is more crucial to the survival of mountain biking itself than to read the examples set forth in the following pages and practice their message. Then turn to the maps, pick out your favorite ride, and hit the dirt!

WHAT THIS BOOK IS ABOUT

Within these pages you will find everything you need to know about off-road bicycling in Washington. This guidebook begins by exploring the fascinating history of the mountain bike itself, then goes on to discuss everything from the health benefits of off-road cycling to tips and techniques for bicycling over logs and up hills. Also included are the types of clothing to keep you comfortable and in style, essential equipment ideas to keep your rides smooth and trouble-free, and descriptions of off-road terrain to prepare you for the kinds of bumps and bounces you can expect to encounter. The major provisions of this book, though, are its unique perspectives on each ride, it detailed maps, and its relentless dedication to trail preservation.

Without open trails, the maps in this book are virtually useless. Cyclists must learn to be responsible for the trails they use and to share these trails with others. This guidebook addresses such issues as why trail use has become so controversial, what can be done to improve the image of mountain biking, how to have fun and ride responsibly, on-the-spot trail repair techniques, trail maintenance hotlines for each trail, and the worldwide-standard Rules of the Trail.

Each of the 50 rides is complete with maps, photos, trail descriptions and directions, local history, and a quick-reference ride information guide including such items as trail contact information, park schedules, fees/permits, local bike stores, dining, lodging, entertainment, alternative map resources and more. Also included at the end of each regional section is an "Honorable Mentions" list of alternative off-road rides (89 rides total).

It's important to note that mountain bike rides tend to take longer than road rides because the average speed is often much slower. Average speeds can vary from a climbing pace of three to four miles per hour to 12 to 13 miles per hour on flatter roads and trails. Keep this in mind when planning your trip.

MOUNTAIN BIKE BEGINNINGS

It seems the mountain bike, originally designed for lunatic adventurists bored with straight lines, clean clothes, and smooth tires, has become globally popular in as short a time as it would take to race down a mountain trail.

Like many things of a revolutionary nature, the mountain bike was born on the west coast. But unlike Rollerblades, purple hair, and the peace sign, the concept of the off-road bike cannot be credited solely to the imaginative Californians—they were just the first to make waves.

The design of the first off-road specific bike was based on the geometry of the old Schwinn Excelsior, a one-speed, camel-back cruiser with balloon tires. Joe Breeze was the creator behind it, and in 1977 he built 10 of these "Breezers" for himself and his Marin County, California, friends at $750 apiece—a bargain.

Breeze was a serious competitor in bicycle racing, placing 13th in the 1977 U.S. Road Racing National Championships. After races, he and friends would scour local bike shops hoping to find old bikes they could then restore.

It was the 1941 Schwinn Excelsior, for which Breeze paid just five dollars, that began to shape and change bicycling history forever. After taking the bike home, removing the fenders, oiling the chain, and pumping up the tires, Breeze hit the dirt. He loved it.

His inspiration, while forerunning, was not altogether unique. On the opposite end of the country, nearly 2,500 miles from Marin County, east coast bike bums were also growing restless. More and more old, beat-up clunkers were being restored and modified. These behemoths often weighed as much as 80 pounds and were so reinforced they seemed virtually indestructible. But rides that take just 40 minutes on today's 25-pound featherweights took the steel-toed-boot- and-blue-jean-clad bikers of the late 1970s and early 1980s nearly four hours to complete.

Not until 1981 was it possible to purchase a production mountain bike, but local retailers found these ungainly bicycles difficult to sell and rarely kept them in stock. By 1983, however, mountain bikes were no longer such a fringe item, and large bike manufacturers quickly jumped into the action, producing their own versions of the off-road bike. By the 1990s, the mountain bike had firmly established its place with bicyclists of nearly all ages and abilities, and now command nearly 90 percent of the U.S. bike market.

There are many reasons for the mountain bike's success in becoming the hottest two-wheeled vehicle in the nation. They are much friendlier to the cyclist than traditional road bikes because of their comfortable upright position and shock-absorbing fat tires. And because of the health-conscious, environmentalist movement of the late 1980s and 1990s, people are more activity minded and seek nature on a closer front than paved roads can allow. The mountain bike gives you these things and takes you far away from the daily grind—even if you're only minutes from the city.

MOUNTAIN BIKING INTO SHAPE

If your objective is to get in shape and lose weight, then you're on the right track, because mountain biking is one of the best ways to get started.

One way many of us have lost weight in this sport is the crash-and-burn-it-off method. Picture this: you're speeding uncontrollably down a vertical drop that you realize you shouldn't be on—only after it is too late. Your front wheel lodges into a rut and launches you through endless weeds, trees, and pointy rocks before coming to an abrupt halt in a puddle of thick mud. Surveying the damage, you discover, with the layers of skin, body parts, and lost confidence littering the trail above, that those unwanted pounds have been shed—*permanently*. Instant weight loss.

There is, of course, a more conventional (and quite a bit less painful) approach to losing weight and gaining fitness on a mountain bike. It's called the workout, and bicycles provide an ideal way to get physical. Take a look at some of the benefits associated with cycling.

Cycling helps you shed pounds without gimmicky diet fads or weight-loss programs. You can explore the countryside and burn nearly 10 to 16 calories per minute or close to 600 to 1,000 calories per hour. Moreover, it's a great way to spend an afternoon.

No less significant than the external and cosmetic changes of your body from riding are the internal changes taking place. Over time, cycling regularly will strengthen your heart as your body grows vast networks of new capillaries to carry blood to all those working muscles. This will, in turn, give your skin a healthier glow. The capacity of your lungs may increase up to 20 percent, and your resting heart rate will drop significantly. The Stanford University School of Medicine reports to the American Heart Association that people can reduce their risk of heart attack by nearly 64 percent if they can burn up to 2,000 calories per week. This is only two to three hours of bike riding!

Recommended for insomnia, hypertension, indigestion, anxiety, and even for recuperation from major heart attacks, bicycling can be an excellent cure-all as well as a great preventive. Cycling just a few hours per week can improve your figure and sleeping habits, give you greater resistance to illness, increase your energy levels, and provide feelings of accomplishment and heightened self-esteem.

BE SAFE—KNOW THE LAW

Occasionally, even the hard-core off-road cyclists will find they have no choice but to ride the pavement. When you are forced to hit the road, it's important for you to know and understand the rules.

Outlined below are a few of the common laws found in Washington's Vehicle Code book.

- **Bicycles are legally classified as vehicles in Washington.** This means that as a bicyclist, you are responsible for obeying the same rules of the road as a driver of a motor vehicle.

- **Bicyclists must ride with the traffic—NOT AGAINST IT!** Because bicycles are considered vehicles, you must ride your bicycle just as you would drive a car—with traffic. Only pedestrians should travel against the flow of traffic.

- **You must obey all traffic signs.** This includes stop signs and stoplights.

- **Always signal your turns.** Most drivers aren't expecting bicyclists to be on the roads, and many drivers would prefer that cyclists stay off the roads altogether. It's important, therefore, to clearly signal your intentions to motorists both in front and behind you.

- **Bicyclists are entitled to the same roads as cars (except controlled-access highways).** Unfortunately, cyclists are rarely given this consideration.

- **Be a responsible cyclist.** Do not abuse your rights to ride on open roads. Follow the rules and set a good example for all of us as you roll along.

THE MOUNTAIN BIKE CONTROVERSY

Are Off-Road Bicyclists Environmental Outlaws? Do We have the Right to Use Public Trails?

Mountain bikers have long endured the animosity of folks in the back-country who complain about the consequences of off-road bicycling. Many people believe that the fat tires and knobby tread do unacceptable environmental damage and that our uncontrollable riding habits are a danger to animals and to other trail users. To the contrary, mountain bikes have no more environmental impact than hiking boots or horseshoes. This does not mean, however, that mountain bikes leave no imprint at all. Wherever man treads, there is an impact. By riding responsibly, though, it is possible to leave only a minimum impact—something we all must take care to achieve.

Unfortunately, it is often people of great influence who view the mountain bike as the environment's worst enemy. Consequently, we as mountain bike riders and environmentally concerned citizens must be educators, impressing upon others that we also deserve the right to use these trails. Our responsibilities as bicyclists are no more and no less than any other trail user. We must all take the soft-cycling approach and show that mountain bicyclists are not environmental outlaws.

ETIQUETTE OF MOUNTAIN BIKING

When discussing mountain biking etiquette, we are in essence discussing the soft-cycling approach. This term, as mentioned previously, describes the art of minimum-impact bicycling and should apply to both the physical and social dimensions of the sport. But make no mistake—it is possible to ride fast and furiously while maintaining the balance of soft-cycling. Here first are a few ways to minimize the physical impact of mountain bike riding.

- *Stay on the trail.* Don't ride around fallen trees or mud holes that block your path. Stop and cross over them. When you come to a vista overlooking a deep valley, don't ride off the trail for a better vantage point. Instead, leave the bike and walk to see the view. Riding off the trail may seem inconsequential when done only once, but soon someone else will follow, then others, and the cumulative results can be catastrophic. Each time you wander from the trail you begin creating a new path, adding one more scar to the earth's surface.

- *Do not disturb the soil.* Follow a line within the trail that will not disturb or damage the soil.
- *Do not ride over soft or wet trails.* After a rain shower or during the thawing season, trails will often resemble muddy, oozing swampland.

The best thing to do is stay off the trails altogether. Realistically, however, we're all going to come across some muddy trails we cannot anticipate. Instead of blasting through each section of mud, which may seem both easier and more fun, lift the bike and walk past. Each time a cyclist rides through a soft or muddy section of trail, that part of the trail is permanently damaged. Regardless of the trail's conditions, though, remember always to go over the obstacles across the path, not around them. Stay on the trail.

- *Avoid trails that, for all but God, are considered impassable and impossible.* Don't take a leap of faith down a kamikaze descent on which you will be forced to lock your brakes and skid to the bottom, ripping the ground apart as you go.

Soft-cycling should apply to the social dimensions of the sport as well, since mountain bikers are not the only folks who use the trails. Hikers, equestrians, cross-country skiers, and other outdoors people use many of the same trails and can be easily spooked by a marauding mountain biker tearing through the trees. Be friendly in the forest and give ample warning of your approach.

- *Take out what you bring in.* Don't leave broken bike pieces and banana peels scattered along the trail.
- *Be aware of your surroundings.* Don't use popular hiking trails for race training.
- *Slow down!* Rocketing around blind corners is a sure way to ruin an unsuspecting hiker's day. Consider this—If you fly down a quick single-track descent at 20 mph, then hit the brakes and slow down to only six mph to pass someone, you're still moving twice as fast as they are!

Like the trails we ride on, the social dimension of mountain biking is very fragile and must be cared for responsibly. We should not want to destroy another person's enjoyment of the outdoors. By riding in the backcountry with caution, control, and responsibility, our presence should be felt positively by other trail users. By adhering to these rules, trail riding—a privilege that can quickly be taken away—will continue to be ours to share.

TRAIL MAINTENANCE

Unfortunately, despite all of the preventive measures taken to avoid trail damage, we're still going to run into many trails requiring attention. Simply put, a lot of hikers, equestrians, and cyclists alike use the same trails—some wear and tear is unavoidable. But like your bike, if you want to use these trails for a long time to come, you must also maintain them.

Trail maintenance and restoration can be accomplished in a variety of ways. One way is for mountain bike clubs to combine efforts with other trail users (i.e. hikers and equestrians) and work closely with land managers to cut new trails or repair existing ones. This not only reinforces to others the commitment cyclists have in caring for and maintaining the land, but also breaks the ice that often separates cyclists from their fellow trailmates. Another good way to help out is to show up on a Saturday morning with a few riding buddies at your favorite off-road domain ready to work. With a good attitude, thick gloves, and the local land manager's supervision, trail repair is fun and very rewarding. It's important, of course, that you arrange a trail-repair outing with the local land manager before you start pounding shovels into the dirt. They can lead you to the most needy sections of trail and instruct you on what repairs should be done and how best to accomplish the task. Perhaps the most effective means of trail maintenance, though, can be done by yourself and while you're riding. Read on.

ON–THE–SPOT QUICK FIX

Most of us, when we're riding, have at one time or another come upon muddy trails or fallen trees blocking our path. We notice that over time the mud gets deeper and the trail gets wider as people go through or around the obstacles. We worry that the problem will become so severe and repairs too difficult that the trail's access may be threatened. We also know that our ambition to do anything about it is greatest at that moment, not after a hot shower and a plate of spaghetti. Here are a few on-the-spot quick fixes you can do that will hopefully correct a problem before it gets out of hand and get you back on your bike within minutes.

Muddy Trails. What do you do when trails develop huge mud holes destined for the EPA's Superfund status? The technique is called corduroying, and it works much like building a pontoon over the mud to support bikes, horses, or hikers as they cross. Corduroy (not the pants) is the term for roads made of logs laid down crosswise. Use small-and medium-sized sticks and lay them side by side across the trail until they cover the length of the muddy section (break the sticks to fit the width of the trail). Press them into the mud with your feet, then lay more on top if needed. Keep adding sticks until the trail is firm. Not only will you stay clean as you cross, but the sticks may soak up some of the water and help the puddle dry. This quick fix may last as long as one month before needing to be redone. And as time goes on, with new layers added to the trail, the soil will grow stronger, thicker, and more resistant to erosion. This whole process may take fewer than five minutes, and you can be on your way, knowing the trail behind you is in good repair.

Leaving the Trail. What do you do to keep cyclists from cutting corners and leaving the designated trail? The solution is much simpler than you may think. (No, don't hire an off-road police force.) Notice where people are leaving the trail and throw a pile of thick branches or brush along the path, or place logs across the opening to block the way through. There are probably dozens of subtle tricks like these that will manipulate people into staying on the designated trail. If executed well, no one will even notice that the thick branches scattered along the ground in the woods weren't always there. And most folks would probably rather take a moment to hop a log in the trail than get tangled in a web of branches.

Obstacle in the Way. If there are large obstacles blocking the trail, try and remove them or push them aside. If you cannot do this by yourself, call the trail maintenance hotline to speak with the land manager of that particular trail and see what can be done.

We must be willing to sweat for our trails in order to sweat on them. Police yourself and point out to others the significance of trail maintenance. "Sweat Equity," the rewards of continued land use won with a fair share of sweat, pays off when the trail is "up for review" by the land manager and he or she remembers the efforts made by trail-conscious mountain bikers.

RULES OF THE TRAIL

The International Mountain Bicycling Association (IMBA) has developed these guidelines to trail riding. These "Rules of the Trail" are accepted worldwide and will go a long way in keeping trails open. Please respect and follow these rules for everyone's sake.

1. **Ride only on open trails.** Respect trail and road closures (if you're not sure, ask a park or state official first), do not trespass on private property, and obtain permits or authorization if required. Federal and state wilderness areas are off-limits to cycling. Parks and state forests may also have certain trails closed to cycling.

2. **Leave no trace.** Be sensitive to the dirt beneath you. Even on open trails, you should not ride under conditions by which you will leave evidence of your passing, such as on certain soils or shortly after a rainfall. Be sure to observe the different types of soils and trails you're riding on, practicing minimum-impact cycling. Never ride off the trail, don't skid your tires, and be sure to bring out at least as much as you bring in.

3. **Control your bicycle!** Inattention for even one second can cause disaster for yourself or for others. Excessive speed frightens and can injure people, gives mountain biking a bad name, and can result in trail closures.

4. **Always yield.** Let others know you're coming well in advance (a friendly greeting is always good and often appreciated). Show your respect when passing others by slowing to walking speed or stopping altogether, especially in the presence of horses. Horses can be unpredictable, so be very careful. Anticipate that other trail users may be around corners or in blind spots.

5. **Never spook animals.** All animals are spooked by sudden movements, unannounced approaches, or loud noises. Give the animals extra room and time so they can adjust to you. Move slowly or dismount around animals. Running cattle and disturbing wild animals are serious offenses. Leave gates as you find them, or as marked.

6. **Plan ahead.** Know your equipment, your ability, and the area in which you are riding, and plan your trip accordingly. Be self-sufficient at all times, keep your bike in good repair, and carry necessary supplies for changes in weather or other conditions. You can help keep trails open by setting an example of responsible, courteous, and controlled mountain bike riding.

7. **Always wear a helmet when you ride.** For your own safety and protection, a helmet should be worn whenever you are riding your bike. You never know when a tree root or small rock will throw you the wrong way and send you tumbling.

Thousands of miles of dirt trails have been closed to mountain bicycling because of the irresponsible riding habits of just a few riders. Don't follow the example of these offending riders. Don't take away trail privileges from thousands of others who work hard each year to keep the backcountry avenues open to us all.

THE NECESSITIES OF CYCLING

When discussing the most important items to have on a bike ride, cyclists generally agree on the following four items.

Helmet. The reasons to wear a helmet should be obvious. Helmets are discussed in more detail in the Be Safe—Wear Your Armor section.

Water. Without it, cyclists may face dehydration, which may result in dizziness and fatigue. On a warm day, cyclists should drink at least one full bottle during every hour of riding. Remember, it's always good to drink before you feel thirsty—otherwise, it may be too late.

Cycling Shorts. These are necessary if you plan to ride your bike more than 20 to 30 minutes. Padded cycling shorts may be the only thing preventing your derriere from serious saddle soreness by ride's end. There are two types of cycling shorts you can buy. Touring shorts are good for people who don't want to look like they're wearing anatomically correct cellophane. These look like regular athletic shorts with pockets, but have built-in padding in the crotch area for protection from chafing and saddle sores. The more popular, traditional cycling shorts are made of skin-tight material, also with a padded crotch. Whichever style you find most comfortable, cycling shorts are a necessity for long rides.

Food. This essential item will keep you rolling. Cycling burns up a lot of calories and is among the few sports in which no one is safe from the "Bonk." Bonking feels like it sounds. Without food in your system, your blood sugar level collapses, and there is no longer any energy in your body. This instantly results in total fatigue and light-headedness. So when you're filling your water bottle, remember to bring along some food. Fruit, energy bars, or some other forms of high-energy food are highly recommended. Candy bars are not, however, because they will deliver a sudden burst of high energy, then let you down soon after, causing you to feel worse than before. Energy bars are available at most bike stores and are similar to candy bars, but provide complex carbohydrate energy and high nutrition rather than fast-burning simple sugars.

BE PREPARED OR DIE

Essential equipment that will keep you from dying alone in the woods:

Be Prepared or Die

- Spare Tube
- Tire Irons: *See the Appendix for instructions on fixing flat tires.*
- Patch Kit
- Pump
- Money: *Spare change for emergency calls.*
- Spoke Wrench
- Spare Spokes: *To fit your wheel. Tape these to the chain stay.*
- Chain Tool

- Allen Keys: *Bring appropriate sizes to fit your bike.*
- Compass
- First-Aid Kit
- Rain Gear: *For quick changes in weather.*
- Matches
- Guidebook: *In case all else fails and you must start a fire to survive, this guidebook will serve as excellent fire starter!*

To carry these items, you may need a bike bag. A bag mounted in front of the handlebars provides quick access to your belongings, whereas a saddle bag fitted underneath the saddle keeps things out of your way. If you're carrying lots of equipment, you may want to consider a set of panniers. These are much larger and mount on either side of each wheel on a rack. Many cyclists, though, prefer not to use a bag at all. They just slip all they need into their jersey pockets, and off they go.

BE SAFE—WEAR YOUR ARMOR

While on the subject of jerseys, it's crucial to discuss the clothing you must wear to be safe, practical, and—if you prefer—stylish. The following is a list of items that will save you from disaster, outfit you comfortably, and most important, keep you looking cool.

Helmet. A helmet is an absolute necessity because it protects your head from complete annihilation. It is the only thing that will not disintegrate into a million pieces after a wicked crash on a descent you shouldn't have been on in the first place. A helmet with a solid exterior shell will also protect your head from sharp or protruding objects. Of course, with a hard-shelled helmet, you can paste several stickers of your favorite bicycle manufacturers all over the outer shell, giving companies even more free advertising for your dollar.

Shorts. Let's just say Lycra™ cycling shorts are considered a major safety item if you plan to ride for more than 20 or 30 minutes at a time. As mentioned in The Necessities of Cycling section, cycling shorts are well regarded as the leading cure-all for chafing and saddle sores. The most preventive cycling shorts have padded "chamois" (most chamois is synthetic nowadays) in the crotch area. Of course, if you choose to wear these traditional cycling shorts, it's imperative that they look as if someone spray painted them onto your body.

Gloves. You may find well-padded cycling gloves invaluable when traveling over rocky trails and gravelly roads for hours on end. Long-fingered gloves may also be useful, as branches, trees, assorted hard objects, and, occasionally, small animals will reach out and whack your knuckles.

Glasses. Not only do sunglasses give you an imposing presence and make you look cool (both are extremely important), they also protect your eyes from harmful ultraviolet rays, invisible branches, creepy bugs, dirt, and may prevent you from being caught sneaking glances at riders of the opposite sex also wearing skintight, revealing Lycra™.

Shoes. Mountain bike shoes should have stiff soles to help make pedaling easier and provide better traction when walking your bike up a trail becomes necessary. Virtually any kind of good outdoor hiking footwear will work, but specific mountain bike shoes (especially those with inset cleats) are best. It is vital that these shoes look as ugly as humanly possible. Those closest in style to bowling shoes are, of course, the most popular.

Jersey or Shirt. Bicycling jerseys are popular because of their snug fit and back pockets. When purchasing a jersey, look for ones that are loaded with bright, blinding, neon logos and manufacturers' names. These loudly deco-

First Aid

- band aids
- mole skin
- various sterile gauze and dressings
- white surgical tape
- an ace bandage
- an antihistamine
- aspirin
- Betadine® solution
- a First aid book
- Tums®
- tweezers
- scissors
- anti-bacterial wipes
- triple-antibiotic ointment
- plastic gloves
- sterile cotton tip applicators
- syrup of ipecac (to induce vomiting)
- a thermometer
- a wire splint

rated billboards are also good for drawing unnecessary attention to yourself just before taking a mean spill while trying to hop a curb. A cotton T-shirt is a good alternative in warm weather, but when the weather turns cold, cotton becomes a chilling substitute for the jersey. Cotton retains moisture and sweat against your body, which may cause you to get the chills and ills on those cold-weather rides.

OH, THOSE COLD, WET WASHINGTON DAYS

If the weather chooses not to cooperate on the day you've set aside for a bike ride, it's helpful to be prepared.

Tights or leg warmers. These are best in temperatures below 55 degrees. Knees are sensitive and can develop all kinds of problems if they get cold. Common problems include tendinitis, bursitis, and arthritis.

Plenty of layers on your upper body. When the air has a nip in it, layers of clothing will keep the chill away from your chest and help prevent the development of bronchitis. If the air is cool, a Polypropylene™ or Capilene™ long-sleeved shirt is best to wear against the skin beneath other layers of clothing. Polypropylene or Capilene, like wool, wicks away moisture from your skin to keep your body dry. Try to avoid wearing cotton or baggy clothing when the temperature falls. Cotton, as mentioned before, holds moisture like a sponge, and baggy clothing catches cold air and swirls it around your body. Good cold-weather clothing should fit snugly against your body, but not be restrictive.

Wool socks. Don't pack too many layers under those shoes, though. You may stand the chance of restricting circulation, and your feet will get real cold, real fast.

Thinsulate® or Gortex® gloves. We may all agree that there is nothing worse than frozen feet—unless your hands are frozen. A good pair of Thinsulate™ or Gortex™ gloves should keep your hands toasty and warm.

Hat or helmet on cold days? Sometimes, when the weather gets really cold and you still want to hit the trails, it's tough to stay warm. We all know that 130 percent of the body's heat escapes through the head (overactive brains, I imagine), so it's important to keep the cranium warm. Ventilated helmets are designed to keep heads cool in the summer heat, but they do little to help keep heads warm during rides in sub-zero temperatures. Cyclists should consider wearing a hat on extremely cold days. Capilene® Skullcaps are great head and ear warmers that snugly fit over your head beneath the helmet. Head protection is not lost. Another option is a helmet cover that covers those ventilating gaps and helps keep the body heat in. These do not, however, keep your ears warm. Some cyclists will opt for a simple knit cycling cap sans the helmet, but these have never been shown to be very good cranium protectors.

All of this clothing can be found at your local bike store, where the staff should be happy to help fit you into the seasons of the year.

TO HAVE OR NOT TO HAVE... *(Other Very Useful Items)*

Though mountain biking is relatively new to the cycling scene, there is no shortage of items for you and your bike to make riding better, safer, and easier. We have rummaged through the unending lists and separated the gadgets from the good stuff, coming up with what we believe are items certain to make mountain bike riding easier and more enjoyable.

Tires. Buying yourself a good pair of knobby tires is the quickest way to enhance the off-road handling capabilities of your bike. There are many types of mountain bike tires on the market. Some are made exclusively for very rugged off-road terrain. These big-knobbed, soft rubber tires virtually stick to the ground with unforgiving traction, but tend to deteriorate quickly on pavement. There are other tires made exclusively for the road. These are called "slicks" and have no tread at all. For the average cyclist, though, a good tire somewhere in the middle of these two extremes should do the trick.

Toe Clips or Clipless Pedals. With these, you will ride with more power. Toe clips attach to your pedals and strap your feet firmly in place, allowing you to exert pressure on the pedals on both the downstroke and the upstroke. They will increase your pedaling efficiency by 30 percent to 50 percent. Clipless pedals, which liberate your feet from the traditional straps and clips, have made toe clips virtually obsolete. Like ski bindings, they attach your shoe directly to the pedal. They are, however, much more expensive than toe clips.

Bar Ends. These great clamp-on additions to your original straight bar will provide more leverage, an excellent grip for climbing, and a more natural position for your hands. Be aware, however, of the bar end's propensity for hooking trees on fast descents, sending you, the cyclist, airborne.

Fanny Pack. These bags are ideal for carrying keys, extra food, guidebooks, tools, spare tubes, and a cellular phone, in case you need to call for help.

Suspension Forks. For the more serious off-roaders who want nothing to impede their speed on the trails, investing in a pair of suspension forks is a good idea. Like tires, there are plenty of brands to choose from, and they all do the same thing—absorb the brutal beatings of a rough trail. The cost of these forks, however, is sometimes more brutal than the trail itself.

Bike Computers. These are fun gadgets to own and are much less expensive than in years past. They have such features as trip distance, speedometer, odometer, time of day, altitude, alarm, average speed, maximum speed, heart rate, global satellite positioning, etc. Bike computers will come in handy when following these maps or to know just how far you've ridden in the wrong direction.

Water Pack. This is quickly becomming an essential item for cyclists pedaling for more than a few hours, especially in hot, dry conditions. The most popular brand is, of course, the Camelback™, and these water packs can carry in their bladder bags as much as 100 ounces of water. These packs strap onto your back with a handy hose running over your shoulder so you can be drinking water while still holding onto the bars on a rocky descent with both hands. These packs are a great way to carry a lot of extra liquid on hot rides in the middle of nowhere.

TYPES OF OFF-ROAD TERRAIN

Before roughing it off road, we may first have to ride the pavement to get to our destination. Please, don't be dismayed. Some of the country's best rides are on the road. Once we get past these smooth-surfaced pathways, though, adventures in dirt await us.

Rails-to-Trails. Abandoned rail lines are converted into usable public resources for exercising, commuting, or just enjoying nature. Old rails and ties are torn up and a trail, paved or unpaved, is laid along the existing corridor. This completes the cycle from ancient Indian trading routes to railroad corridors and back again to hiking and cycling trails.

Unpaved Roads are typically found in rural areas and are most often public roads. Be careful when exploring, though, not to ride on someone's unpaved private drive.

Forest Roads. These dirt and gravel roads are used primarily as access to forest land and are generally kept in good condition. They are almost always open to public use.

Singletrack can be the most fun on a mountain bike. These trails, with only one track to follow, are often narrow, challenging pathways through the woods. Remember to make sure these trails are open before zipping into the woods. (At the time of this printing, all trails and roads in this guidebook were open to mountain bikes.)

Open Land. Unless there is a marked trail through a field or open space, you should not plan to ride here. Once one person cuts his or her wheels through a field or meadow, many more are sure to follow, causing irreparable damage to the landscape.

TECHNIQUES TO SHARPEN YOUR SKILLS

Many of us see ourselves as pure athletes—blessed with power, strength, and endless endurance. However, it may be those with finesse, balance, agility, and grace that get around most quickly on a mountain bike. Although power, strength, and endurance do have their places in mountain biking, these elements don't necessarily form the framework for a champion mountain biker.

The bike should become an extension of your body. Slight shifts in your hips or knees can have remarkable results. Experienced bike handlers seem to flash down technical descents, dashing over obstacles in a smooth and graceful effort as if pirouetting in Swan Lake. Here are some tips and techniques to help you connect with your bike and float gracefully over the dirt.

Braking

Using your brakes requires using your head, especially when descending. This doesn't mean using your head as a stopping block, but rather to think intelligently. Use your best judgment in terms of how much or how little to squeeze those brake levers.

The more weight a tire is carrying, the more braking power it has. When you're going downhill, your front wheel carries more weight than the rear. Braking with the front brake will help keep you in control without going into a skid. Be careful, though, not to overdo it with the front brakes and accidentally toss yourself over the handlebars. And don't neglect your rear brake! When descending, shift your weight back over the rear wheel, thus increasing your rear braking power as well. This will balance the power of both brakes and give you maximum control.

Good riders learn just how much of their weight to shift over each wheel and how to apply just enough braking power to each brake, so not to "endo" over the handlebars or skid down a trail.

GOING UPHILL—Climbing Those Treacherous Hills

Shift into a low gear (push the shifter away from you). Before shifting, be sure to ease up on your pedaling so there is not too much pressure on the chain. Find the gear best for you that matches the terrain and steepness of each climb.

Stay seated. Standing out of the saddle is often helpful when climbing steep hills with a road bike, but you may find that on dirt, standing may cause your rear tire to lose its grip and spin out. Climbing requires traction. Stay seated as long as you can, and keep the rear tire digging into the ground. Ascending skyward may prove to be much easier in the saddle.

Lean forward. On very steep hills, the front end may feel unweighted and suddenly pop up. Slide forward on the saddle and lean over the handlebars. This will add more weight to the front wheel and should keep you grounded.

Keep pedaling. On rocky climbs, be sure to keep the pressure on, and don't let up on those pedals! The slower you go through rough trail sections, the harder you will work.

GOING DOWNHILL—The Real Reason We Get Up in the Morning

Shifting into the big chainring before a bumpy descent will help keep the chain from bouncing off. And should you crash or disengage your leg from the pedal, the chain will cover the teeth of the big ring so they don't bite into your leg.

Relax. Stay loose on the bike, and don't lock your elbows or clench your grip. Your elbows need to bend with the bumps and absorb the shock, while your hands should have a firm but controlled grip on the bars to keep things steady. Steer with your body, allowing your shoulders to guide you through each turn and around each obstacle.

Don't oversteer or lose control. Mountain biking is much like downhill skiing, since you must shift your weight from side to side down narrow, bumpy descents. Your bike will have the tendency to track in the direction you look and follow the slight shifts and leans of your body. You should not think so much about steering, but rather in what direction you wish to go.

Rise above the saddle. When racing down bumpy, technical descents, you should not be sitting on the saddle, but standing on the pedals, allowing your legs and knees to absorb the rocky trail instead of your rear.

Drop your saddle. For steep, technical descents, you may want to drop your saddle three or four inches. This lowers your center of gravity, giving you much more room to bounce around.

Keep your pedals parallel to the ground. The front pedal should be slightly higher so that it doesn't catch on small rocks or logs.

Stay focused. Many descents require your utmost concentration and focus just to reach the bottom. You must notice every groove, every root, every rock, every hole, every bump. You, the bike, and the trail should all become one as you seek singletrack nirvana on your way down the mountain. But if your thoughts wander, however, then so may your bike, and you may instead become one with the trees!

WATCH OUT!
Back-road Obstacles

Logs. When you want to hop a log, throw your body back, yank up on the handlebars, and pedal forward in one swift motion. This clears the front end of the bike. Then quickly scoot forward and pedal the rear wheel up and over. Keep the forward momentum until you've cleared the log, and by all means, don't hit the brakes, or you may do some interesting acrobatic maneuvers!

Rocks and Roots. Worse than highway potholes! Stay relaxed, let your elbows and knees absorb the shock, and always continue applying power to your pedals. Staying seated will keep the rear wheel weighted to prevent slipping, and a light front end will help you to respond quickly to each new obstacle. The slower you go, the more time your tires will have to get caught between the grooves.

Water. Before crossing a stream or puddle, be sure to first check the depth and bottom surface. There may be an unseen hole or large rock hidden under the water that could wash you up if you're not careful. After you're sure all is safe, hit the water at a good speed, pedal steadily, and allow the bike to steer you through. Once you're across, tap the breaks to squeegee the water off the rims.

Leaves. Be careful of wet leaves. These may look pretty, but a trail covered with leaves may cause your wheels to slip out from under you. Leaves are not nearly as unpredictable and dangerous as ice, but they do warrant your attention on a rainy day.

Mud. If you must ride through mud, hit it head on and keep pedaling. You want to part the ooze with your front wheel and get across before it swallows you up. Above all, don't leave the trail to go around the mud. This just widens the path even more and leads to increased trail erosion.

Urban Obstacles

Curbs are fun to jump, but like with logs, be careful.

Curbside Drains are typically not a problem for bikes. Just be careful not to get a wheel caught in the grate.

Dogs make great pets, but seem to have it in for bicyclists. If you think you can't outrun a dog that's chasing you, stop and walk your bike out of its territory. A loud yell to Get! or Go home! often works, as does a sharp squirt from your water bottle right between the eyes.

Cars are tremendously convenient when we're in them, but dodging irate motorists in big automobiles becomes a real hazard when riding a bike. As a cyclist, you must realize most drivers aren't expecting you to be there and often wish you weren't. Stay alert and ride carefully, clearly signaling all of your intentions.

Potholes, like grates and back-road canyons, should be avoided. Just because you're on an all-terrain bicycle doesn't mean you're indestructible. Potholes regularly damage rims, pop tires, and sometimes lift unsuspecting cyclists into a spectacular swan dive over the handlebars.

LAST-MINUTE CHECKOVER

Before a ride, it's a good idea to give your bike a once-over to make sure everything is in working order. Begin by checking the air pressure in your tires before each ride to make sure they are properly inflated. Mountain bikes require about 45 to 55 pounds per square inch of air pressure. If your tires are underinflated, there is greater likelihood that the tubes may get pinched on a bump or rock, causing the tire to flat.

Looking over your bike to make sure everything is secure and in its place is the next step. Go through the following checklist before each ride.

• *Pinch the tires to feel for proper inflation.* They should give just a little on the sides, but feel very hard on the treads. If you have a pressure gauge, use that.

• *Check your brakes.* Squeeze the rear brake and roll your bike forward. The rear tire should skid. Next, squeeze the front brake and roll your bike forward. The rear wheel should lift into the air. If this doesn't happen, then your brakes are too loose. Make sure the brake levers don't touch the handlebars when squeezed with full force.

• *Check all quick releases on your bike.* Make sure they are all securely tightened.

• *Lube up.* If your chain squeaks, apply some lubricant.

• *Check your nuts and bolts.* Check the handlebars, saddle, cranks, and pedals to make sure that each is tight and securely fastened to your bike.

• *Check your wheels.* Spin each wheel to see that they spin through the frame and between brake pads freely.

• *Have you got everything?* Make sure you have your spare tube, tire irons patch kit, frame pump, tools, food, water, and guidebook.

Repair and
Mainter

Repair and
Maintenance

FIXING A FLAT

TOOLS YOU WILL NEED

- Two tire irons
- Pump (either a floor pump or a frame pump)
- No screwdrivers!!! (This can puncture the tube)

REMOVING THE WHEEL

The front wheel is easy. Simply open the quick release mechanism or undo the bolts with the proper sized wrench, then remove the wheel from the bike.

The rear wheel is a little more tricky. Before you loosen the wheel from the frame, shift the chain into the smallest gear on the freewheel (the cluster of gears in the back). Once you've done this, removing and installing the wheel, like the front, is much easier.

REMOVING THE TIRE

Step one: Insert a tire iron under the bead of the tire and pry the tire over the lip of the rim. Be careful not to pinch the tube when you do this.

Step two: Hold the first tire iron in place. With the second tire iron, repeat step one, three or four inches down the rim. Alternate tire irons, pulling the bead of the tire over the rim, section by section, until one side of the tire bead is completely off the rim.

Step three: Remove the rest of the tire and tube from the rim. This can be done by hand. It's easiest to remove the valve stem last. Once the tire is off the rim, pull the tubeout of the tire.

CLEAN AND SAFETY CHECK

Step four: Using a rag, wipe the inside of the tire to clean out any dirt, sand, glass, thorns, etc. These may cause the tube to puncture. The inside of a tire should feel smooth. Any pricks or bumps could mean that you have found the culprit responsible for your flat tire.

Step five: Wipe the rim clean, then check the rim strip, making sure it covers the spoke nipples properly on the inside of the rim. If a spoke is poking through the rim strip, it could cause a puncture.

Step six: At this point, you can do one of two things: replace the punctured tube with a new one, or patch the hole. It's easiest to just replace the tube with a new tube when you're out on the trails. Roll up the old tube and take it home to repair later that night in front of the TV. Directions on patching a tube are usually included with the patch kit itself.

INSTALLING THE TIRE AND TUBE
(This can be done entirely by hand)

Step seven: Inflate the new or repaired tube with enough air to give it shape, then tuck it back into the tire.

Step eight: To put the tire and tube back on the rim, begin by putting the valve in the valve hole. The valve must be straight. Then use your hands to push the beaded edge of the tire onto the rim all the way around so that one side of your tire is on the rim.

Step nine: Let most of the air out of the tube to allow room for the rest of the tire.

Step ten: Beginning opposite the valve, use your thumbs to push the other side of the tire onto the rim. Be careful not to pinch the tube in between the tire and the rim. The last few inches may be difficult, and you may need the tire iron to pry the tire onto the rim. If so, just be careful not to puncture the tube.

BEFORE INFLATING COMPLETELY

Step eleven: Check to make sure the tire is seated properly and that the tube is not caught between the tire and the rim. Do this by adding about 5 to 10 pounds of air, and watch closely that the tube does not bulge out of the tire.

Step twelve: Once you're sure the tire and tube are properly seated, put the wheel back on the bike, then fill the tire with air. It's easier squeezing the wheel through the brake shoes if the tire is still flat.

Step thirteen: Now fill the tire with the proper amount of air, and check constantly to make sure the tube doesn't bulge from the rim. If the tube does appear to bulge out, release all the air as quickly as possible, or you could be in for a big bang.

When installing the rear wheel, place the chain back onto the smallest cog (furthest gear on the right), and pull the derailleur out of the way. Your wheel should slide right on.

LUBRICATION PREVENTS DETERIORATION

Lubrication is crucial to maintaining your bike. Dry spots will be eliminated. Creaks, squeaks, grinding, and binding will be gone. The chain will run quietly, and the gears will shift smoothly. The brakes will grip quicker, and your bike may last longer with fewer repairs. Need I say more? Well, yes. Without knowing where to put the lubrication, what good is it?

THINGS YOU WILL NEED
- One can of bicycle lubricant, found at any bike store.
- A clean rag (to wipe excess lubricant away).

WHAT GETS LUBRICATED
- Front derailleur
- Rear derailleur
- Shift levers
- Front brake
- Rear brake

351

- Both brake levers
- Chain

WHERE TO LUBRICATE

To make it easy, simply spray a little lubricant on all the pivot points of your bike. If you're using a squeeze bottle, use just a drop or two. Put a few drops on each point wherever metal moves against metal, for instance, at the center of the brake calipers. Then let the lube sink in.

Once you have applied the lubricant to the derailleurs, shift the gears a few times, working the derailleurs back and forth. This allows the lubricant to work itself into the tiny cracks and spaces it must occupy to do its job. Work the brakes a few times as well.

LUBING THE CHAIN

Lubricating the chain should be done after the chain has been wiped clean of most road grime. Do this by spinning the pedals counterclockwise while gripping the chain with a clean rag. As you add the lubricant, be sure to get some in between each link. With an aerosol spray, just spray the chain while pedalling backwards (counterclockwise) until the chain is fully lubricated. Let the lubricant soak in for a few seconds before wiping the excess away. Chains will collect dirt much faster if they're loaded with too much lubrication.

Bicycle Clubs and Organizations

Backcountry Bicycle Trails Club

Their motto: Education, Recreation, and Advocacy on behalf of mountain bikers. Affiliated with IMBA (International Mountain Bicycling Association), the BBTC (founded in 1989) has over 400 members and is run completely by volunteers.
P.O. Box 21288
Seattle, WA 98111-3288
(206) 283–2995
bbtc@cycling.org
www.bbtc.org

B.I.K.E.S. of Everett

Established in 1979, this bicycle club promotes cycling for fun and exercise. Volunteer ride leaders sponsor rides every weekend all year; there are even regular weekday ride schedules.
P.O. Box 5242
Everett, WA 98206
(425) 339–ROLL or (206) 972–AWAY

Capital Bicycling Club

For mountain bikers and road bike riders into racing or group rides. This group has been active since 1978.
P.O. Box 642
Olympia, WA 98507
(360) 956–3321
www.newmediaarts.org/cbc/

Cascade Bicycle Club

This is the largest cycling club in the U.S. with over 5,000 members. They strongly promote safe cycling, host many road bicycling events, and are very active in cycling advocacy and education.
P.O. Box 15165
Seattle, WA 98115-0165
(206) 522–3222
www.cascade.org/

Different Spokes

Seattle's gay and lesbian bicycling club. They offer many organized rides for all levels of interest and abilities.

P.O. Box 31542
Seattle, WA 98103
Rtyrell@evansgroup.com

Emerald Tea & Cycling Society

Formerly sponsored by the Rainier Brewery, this group was formed just for fun. ("Tea" refers to the prohibition word for alcoholic beverages. The club name used to be "Team Green Death".) Meets monthly; rides for all abilities and interests.
6019 51 Ave. NE
Seattle, WA 98115-7077
(206) 522–3701

Green River Bicycle Club

This group has been around since 1982. Rides are both on and off-road in the Green River Valley and beyond.
P.O. Box 1209
Auburn, WA 98071-1209
(360) 897–8026 residence
simploe@TC-NET.com

Northwest Bicycling

Home of the Memorial Weekend Bicycling tour of Orcas Island, Washington. Food and three-day cabin stay, round-trip ferry ticket, and the works included for under 100 bucks. Since 1974. Open to mountain bikers and road bike riders.
6512 115th Pl. SE
Bellevue, WA 98006
(425) 235–7774

Northwest Mountain Bikers

Spur of the moment fun. This loosely organized mountain biking group promotes races, rides, exploration, and some advocacy.
6304 6th Ave.
Tacoma, WA 98406
(253) 565–9050

Now Bike

A non-profit advocacy group promoting "More People Bicycling More Often, Safely." They influence bicycle transportation, develop education programs for safe cycling, and encourage bicycle commuting.
Susie Stevens
P.O. Box 2904
Seattle, WA 98111
(206) 224–9252

Port Townsend Bicycle Association

Not a club, but an organization dedicated to promoting bicycling through educational, recreational, and sporting events. Host of The Roadie Tour in May, to explore and discover the rural roads of Jefferson County.
P.O. Box 681
Port Townsend, WA 98368
(360) 385–3912
jdmcc@olympus.net

Redmond Cycling Club

Road bike riders that ride together for inspiration, camaraderie, and fun. Offering rides that "cover the spectrum of cycling, from casual social jaunts to the most challenging ultramarathons to be found in the Northwest." Organizers of the Ride Around Mount Rainier in One Day (RAMROD), Don's End of the Year Century, many training rides, and the fully supported two-day ride to Mazama through the North Cascades to the Methow Valley and back; as well as others.
P.O. Box 1841
Bothell, WA 98041-1841
(425) 739–8609
info@redmondcyclingclub.org
http://www.redmondcyclingclub.org/

Single Track Mind

This club was originally formed with the thought that you never leave anyone behind. Primarily a recreational paced group, there are specific organized group rides for racers, too. They average 25 rides per month and organize five or six huge mountain biking camping trips per year in Washington and Oregon. The club began in 1994 and has 200 members, promoting cycling through stewardship and education.
6824 19th St. W #147
Tacoma, WA 98466
(253) 565–5124
www.members.aol.com/STMClub/stm-club/html

Skagit Bicycle Club

Organizers of weekly mountain biking and road biking rides for all ability levels.
1325 North 19th
Mount Vernon, WA 98273
(360) 428–9487

Spokane Bicycle Club

Ride the roads or the trails; this club has something going on all the time for everyone who wants to ride a bike and make new friends.
Gordon Savatsky
P.O. Box 62
Spokane, WA 99210
(509) 325–1171
home.att.net/~loyd.phillips/

Spokane Mountaineers

Established in 1920, there are now over 800 members to this group. Organized group mountain bike rides are held every Tuesday night and general membership meetings are held the third Thursday of every month. Other activities include backpacking, mountaineering, ski touring, hiking, and paddle sports.
P.O. Box 1013
Spokane, WA 99210-1013
(509) 838–4974
www.spokanemountaineers.org

Tacoma Wheelmen's Bicycle Club

This club has been around since 1888 and welcomes road bicycle riders of all skill levels. They promote safe bicycling for recreation, health, and alternate transportation, sponsoring two organized rides each year: the Daffodil Classic and the Peninsula Metric.
P.O. Box 112078
Tacoma, WA 98411
(253) 759–2800
www.twbc.org/

West Sound Cycling Club

Founded in 1985, this club now has about 100 members. Their main focus is promoting bicycling as a safe and healthy form of recreation and an environmental form of transportation. The club gets involved in some legislative issues and conducts several educational clinics. The two main sponsored rides each year are the Countryside Classic in July and the Tour de Kitsap in September. Weekly social rides on Saturday and Sunday for all levels, and bimonthly Welcome Rides for new members. They meet the first Wednesday of every month.
P.O. Box 1579
Silverdale, WA 98383
(360) 698–3876

Whatcom Independent Mountain Pedalers (WIMPs)

A group of mountain bikers who welcome all skill levels to wander the backroads and trails in northwestern Washington.
Craig Stephens
1410 Girard St., Suite 9
Bellingham, WA 98225
(360) 671–4107

Wheatland Wheelers Bicycle Club

Click to the website for this Walla Walla-based bike club for ride information and contact information for club officers.
www.wallawallawa.com/wheatland-wheelers.htm

Dear Reader: It's the very nature of print media that the second the presses run off the last book, all the phone numbers change. If you notice a wrong number or that a club or organization has disappeared or that a new one has put out its shingle, we'd love to know about it. And if you run a club or have a favorite one and we missed it; again, let us know. We plan on doing our part to keep this list up-to-date for future editions, but we could always use the help. You can write us, call us, e-mail us, or heck, just stop by if you're in the neighborhood.

Outside America
300 West Main Street, Suite A
Charlottesville, Virginia 22903 (804) 245–6800
editorial@outside-america.com

Further Reading

History

    Exploring Washington's Past by Ruth Kirk and Carmela Alexander

Geology

    Roadside Geology of Washington by David Alt and Donald Hyndman

    Northwest Exposures: A Geologic Story of the Northwest by David Alt and Donald Hyndman

Native Americans

    Indians of the Pacific Northwest by John A Brown and Robert H. Ruby

Special Interest

    Sasquatch/Bigfoot The Search for North America's Incredible Creature by Don Hunter and Rene Dahindenk

    Sasquatch: Wild Man of the Woods by Elaine Landau

    The San Juan Islands Afoot & Afloat by Marge and Ted Mueller

    Olympic Mountains Trail Guide by Robert L. Wood

    Guide to Trails of Tiger Mountain by William K. Longwell Jr.

    A Climber's Guide to the Olympic Mountains, published by the Mountaineers

    One Hundred Hikes in Washington's North Cascades: National Park Region by Ira Spring and Harvey Manning

Mountain Biking

    Mountain Bike Adventures in the North Cascades, by Tom Kirkendall

    Mountain Bike Adventures in the South Cascades and Puget Sound, by Tom Kirkendall

    Olympic Peninsula Off-Road, by Kathe Smith

    Mountain Bike Routes, published by the Northwest Interpretive Association and Okanogan National Forest (Ride #11 and #12)

    The Mountain Biker's Guide to the Pacific Northwest

    Gifford Pinchot National Forest collection of The "Best" Mountain Bike Trails on the Forest

    Kissing the Trail by John Zilly

    Wild Pigs by John Zilly

    Mountain Bike! Southwest Washington by John Zilly (Ride #50)

    Mountain Bike America: Oregon by Lizann Dunegan published by Globe Pequot Press

Index

Index

A

Alpine Lakes Wilderness, 72
Ape Canyon, 203–204
Ape Cave, 202
apples, 273–274
Ashford, WA, 164–168
Asotin Creek Trail (HM), 291
  Hells Canyon, 291

B

Backcountry Bicycle Trails
  Club (BBTC), 133
Bat Caves, 13
Batey/Bould Trails (HM), 289
  Oreille River, 289
Bees, 141
Belfair, WA, 34
Bellingham's Interurban Trail
  (HM), 110
  Larrabee State Park, 110
Bellingham, WA, 10–12
Beverly, WA, 308, 310
Bicycle Camping, 262
Biddle, Henry, 227
Bill Chipman Palouse Trail
  (HM), 290
Black Hills, 118
Blue Lake, 197–198
Bordeaux, WA, 123
Boylston Mountains, 306
Bremer, William, 41
Bremerton, WA, 40, 41–44
Buck Creek Trail System, 239
  *Gifford Pinchot Ntl
    Forest, 239*
  Whistling Ridge, 239
  White Salmon, 239
Buckhorn Wilderness
  Area, 28

C

Camp David Jr., 19
Capitol Forest, 118, 124
Captain Robert Gray, 267
Carlton, WA, 256
Carson Hot Springs
  Resort, 228
Carson, WA, 228, 234
Cascade Loop Highway,
  108–109
Cashmere, WA, 270, 276

Centennial Trail, 282
Chain of Lakes, 185
Chelan, WA, 259, 264
Chelatchie, WA, 218
Chewuch Inn, 250
Chuckanut Scenic Drive,
  the, 10
Clark, William, 224–227
Cle Elum Lake, 88–89, 93
Cle Elum, WA, 154, 302–303
Cliffdell, WA, 158
coastal tribes
  Chinook, 128, 142
  Nisqually, 128
  Puyallup, 128
Columbia National Wildlife
  Refuge, 310
Cooney Lake, 260
Cougar, WA, 190, 200, 230
Cowiche Canyon
  Conservancy Trails
  (HM), 236
  Cowiche Canyon, 236
  Yakima, WA, 236
Crab Creek Wildlife
  Area, 310
Cranberry Lake in Anacortes
  (HM), 110
Crystal Mountain Resort, 152

D

Dechmann, Louis, 19
Devils Gulch, 276–278
Dewey Lak, 150
Dirty Face Ridge, 28
dogs and mountain
  biking, 52–53
Down River Trail (HM), 288
Dungeness River, 28
Dungeness Spit, 25–26

E

Early Winters Spires, 106
Easton, WA, 96, 302
Echo Valley (HM), 287
Elbe, WA, 170
Elbow Creek—Walla Walla
  (HM), 292
  Harris County Park, 292
  *Tollgate Mountain
    Chalet, 292*
Ellensburg, WA, 90–91,
  304, 306

Enumclaw, WA, 146
Evangelische Lutherische
  Kirche, the, 175
Ewan, WA, 321, 324

F

Falls Creek Falls (photo), 225
Fifes Ridge, 158
Fishhook Flats, 155–156
Flora and Fauna, 2
49-Degrees North Alpine Ski
  Area (HM), 289
Francisco de Eliza, 26

G

Gibbs, George, 57
Gifford Pinchot National
  Forest, 181, 218, 224–227
Glacier Peak, 279–280
Goldbar, WA, 60
Government Mineral
  Springs, 228
Grand Coulee Dam, 267–269
Granite Falls, 71
Great Northern Railroad, 71,
  270–272
Green Mountain, 44
Greenwater, WA, 136,
  142, 148
growing bulbs, 57
Guthrie, Woodie, 221

H

Hood Canal, 34
Hotel Packwood, 179
Hubbart Peak, 69–70
Hudson's Bay Company, 220
Hurricane Ridge, 24–25

I

Ice Cave, 212–215
Ice Cave (photo), 216
Icicle, WA, 78–79
Index, WA, 66
Indian Heaven Wilderness
  Area, 209
Indian Racetrack, 209
Iron Horse Inn, 303
Issaquah Alps, 130

358

V

Vancouver, WA, 220

W

Walker Valley, 54–59
Wallace Falls, 60
Wallace Falls State Park, 60
Warden, WA, 312, 316
Washington & Idaho
    Railroad, 325–326
Washington Bulb Company,
    57–59
Washington Pass, 104–106
Weather, 1
Wenatchee Mountains, 270
Wenatchee National Forest,
    73, 154

Wenatchee, WA, 270–272
West Fork of the Teanaway
    River, 90
Western Idaho Rides, 293
    Canfield Mountain Trail
        System, 293
    Elsie Lake Trail, 294
    Farragut State Park, 294
    Fourth of July Pass, 293
    Schweitzer Basin Ski
        Resort, 295
    Silver Mountain Alpine Ski
        Area, 293
    The Coeur d'Alene River
        Trail, 293
White River, 143
Wildcat Lake, 44
Wilderness Act of 1964,
    136, 137–140
Wilderness Restrictions and
    Regulations, 3

Windy Ridge Viewpoint,
    176–178
wineries, 65
    Chateau Saint Michelle
        Winery, 65
    Columbia Winery, 65
Winthrop, WA, 102, 244,
    250
Wister, Owen, 254
Wycoff, A.B., 41

Y

Yacolt Burn (1902), 234
Yacolt Burn State Forest,
    230
Yacolt, WA, 234

Index

Meet the Authors

Amy and Mark moved to the Northwest some time ago with the sole purpose of being near the mountains. Up from the plain plains of Texas, Washington's Cascade and Olympic mountains have opened up new worlds to them beyond what their southern brows could fathom. Now living and working in the Seattle area, Amy is a freelance writer and Mark, an independent business owner and musician. And while Amy has been writing for such magazines as *Mountain Bike Magazine*, *Bicycle Retailer*, *Snow Country*, *American Bicyclist*, and *Washington CEO*, Mark has been cycling through New Mexico, Canada, Texas, North Carolina, and as far away as Scandinavia and northern Europe. Amy and Mark explore Washington's outdoors together as much as they can and, like a true husband and wife team, debate regularly over who picks the next great adventure.

Authors